WITHOUT
LOCKS and BARS

D0169272

WITHOUT LOCKS and BARS

Reforming Our Reform Schools

Grant R. Grissom and Wm. L. Dubnov

PRAEGER

New York
Westport, Connecticut
London

Library of Congress Cataloging-in-Publication Data

Grissom, Grant.
  Without locks and bars.
  Bibliography: p.
  Includes index.
  1. Glen Mills Schools. 2. Rehabilitation of
juvenile delinquents—Pennsylvania—Glen Mills—
Case studies. I. Dubnov, Wm. L. (William L.)
II. Title.
HV9105.P22G544   1989   365′.974814   88-36410
ISBN 0-275-93282-6 (alk. paper)

Library of Congress Catalog Card Number: 88-36410
ISBN 0-275-93282-6

First published in 1989

Praeger Publishers, One Madison Avenue, New York, NY 10010
A division of Greenwood Press, Inc.

Printed in the United States of America

The paper used in this book complies with the
Permanent Paper Standard issued by the National
Information Standards Organization (Z39.48-1984).
10 9 8 7 6 5 4 3 2

Copyright Acknowledgments

The following publishers have generously given permission to use material from copyrighted works:
   Adapted from *Cottage Six: The Social System of Delinquent Boys in Residential Treatment*, by Howard
Polsky, © The Russell Foundation, 1962. Used with permission of the Russell Sage Foundation.
   Claus Ottmüller, "The Glen Mills Schools: A Normative Approach to Change Delinquent
Behavior Through the Peer Group" (Ph.D. diss., University of Luneberg, West Germany, 1987).

The following persons have given permission to publish their letters: Francis X. Luther, Helene
Wheeler, Brian T. Mulhern, Robert J. McGuire, Sr., Wayne Henry, John and Carol Innis.

The Glen Mills Schools have given permission to publish all data, records, photographs, quoted
material, and any other information provided by them to the authors.

Cosimo "Sam" Ferrainola

Dedicated to Gerda and Sam Ferrainola,
without whom the new Glen Mills would never have been;
and to Gay Grissom,
without whom this book would never have been.

Contents

Exhibits   xi
Photographs   xiii
Acknowledgments   xv
Introduction   xix

1.   A New Order: Critical Events at Glen Mills, 1975–1980   1

                                              Taking the Helm   3
                     Establishing the Staff Normative Culture   13
                  Establishing the Student Normative Culture   18
                          Expanding the Student Population   24
                       Principles of Organizational Change   30

2.   Glen Mills Program in 1988   37

                                    Organizational Structure   40
                              Critical Events: 1980–1986   81

3.   The Glen Mills Experience   95

4. Program Effectiveness   105

                              Theoretical Framework   107
            The Glen Mills Student: A Statistical Profile   113
                                 Evaluation Findings   115

5. Lessons from Glen Mills: New Possibilities for
    Juvenile Corrections   170
                        Evaluating the Evaluation Literature:
                            What Makes a Program Effective? 171
                The Role of the Large Residential Institution 178
                             Security Without Locks and Bars 184
            Delinquents' Potential for Growth and Achievement 185
                                Conversations at Glen Mills 186
                    Improving Juvenile Corrections: Replication
                                of the Glen Mills Model   200
                                            Conclusion   211

Appendixes

        1. Glen Mills Norms   213
        2. Glen Mills Schools Board of Managers, 1988   218
        3. Sample Letters to Glen Mills   220

Bibliography   227

Name Index   233

Subject Index   237

Exhibits

1.1 Percent of students reporting physical confrontations, by
year of admission 23

1.2 Key elements of the Glen Mills Schools' culture 28

1.3 Glen Mills Schools: 1975 vs. 1980 35

2.1 The Glen Mills Schools molecular organization structure 42

2.2 Seven levels of confrontation 53

2.3 Polsky's diamond 67

4.1 New admissions to Glen Mills Schools residential program:
1976–1984 114

4.2 Student population profile: 1976–1983 admissions 116

4.3 Percent of admissions by county, 1976–1984 120

4.4 Percent of admissions by race, 1976–1984 121

4.5 Family composition (head of family), 1976–1984 122

4.6 Percent of admissions by offense, 1976–1984 123

4.7 Percent of admissions having history of assaultive behavior,
1976–1984 124

4.8 Follow-up sample 125

4.9 Percent of admissions by reason for discharge, 1976–1984 132

4.10 Grade level improvement in MAT math and reading
scores, by year of admission, 1976–1984 133

4.11 GED testing, 1975–1986 135

4.12 Average daily student population, 1982–1987 144

4.13   Incidents of assault on staff and students, 1982–1987   145
4.14   Incidents involving graffiti, break-ins, destruction of school
       property, 1982–1987   146
4.15   Incidents of truancy and drug/alcohol "highs," 1982–1987   147
4.16   Incidents of stealing, physical restraints, 1984–1987   148
4.17   Percent of students who went AWOL once or more,
       1976–1984   150
4.18   Percent of students who agreed that "You could get along
       Well at GMS if you were slick," 1976–1984   151
4.19   Rearrests within 27 months of discharge, by year of
       admission (1976–1984)   155
4.20   Reincarceration within 27 months of discharge, by year of
       admission (1976–1984)   156
4.21   Percent of prison releasees reincarcerated within 3 years,
       by age group   161
4.22   Philadelphia Juvenile Court Cases and Institutionalizations,
       1977–1984   168

Photographs

1   Sam and Gerda Ferrainola   92

2   Weekly Resource Team meeting of a $16 million
    organization: chaired by Mr. Ferrainola, the meeting includes
    all department heads, team leaders, and Bulls Club (student)
    executives.   92

3   Graduation Day at Glen Mills   93

4   Aerial view of Glen Mills' campus. The main quadrangle is
    bordered by six cottages and the student union building,
    with the chapel and the Administration Building at either
    end.   93

5   Bulls Club executive officers   94

Acknowledgments

This book is the product of more than a decade of research and preparation. It represents the contributions of many individuals, both inside and outside the Glen Mills community. I owe them an enormous debt, both for their individual contributions and their collective encouragement and support.

From within the Glen Mills community thanks must first be expressed to those at the core of the organization, the Schools' staff and students, for their participation in thousands of hours of individual interviews and program observation. The observation was never "announced" and not always unobtrusive.

The Schools' managers made good on their commitment to full and unrestricted access to staff, students, and records. Staff and students were cooperative in a way which is only possible for those who believe themselves engaged in an important pursuit, for whom failures are benchmarks on the path to excellence rather than occasions for embarrassment.

Glen Mills may be unique in its determination to constantly monitor and evaluate its program, and in its willingness to make its findings available to the public. A large share of the credit for this practice, which was maintained even when the findings were not favorable, must go to the Schools' Board of Managers. Since 1976 the board, through the efforts of its Research Committee chaired by Dr. Ethel Maw, has supported the development of one of the most extensive institutional data bases in the history of U.S. corrections. Without these data it would not have been possible to document the improvements in the Schools' effectiveness which followed establishment of the new program model and organizational culture.

Individual board members provided invaluable insights; their names are listed in Appendix 2. Particular thanks are due to Curtis Johnson, President, and past

Presidents Francis Plowman and Glenn Sullivan for both their encouragement and willingness to share their unique perspective on Glen Mills' recent history.

I am grateful to all who reviewed the manuscript and offered suggestions. In particular Dr. Faye Soffen—board member, mentor, teacher, and friend—provided an especially detailed and informed critique. Her eight (legal size) pages of notes contributed immensely to the improvement of the manuscript. Glen Mills' attorney, Adam Shapiro, also provided a thorough review of the material. The description of critical events in Glen Mills recent history owes much to Adam's involvement.

Data reported in this book were collected through the careful work of dozens of individuals in various roles. Four pages of data (nearly 100 items) for every new student are collected by Glen Mills' admissions staff from court records and interviews. This critical work, undertaken originally by Charlotte Beecher and more recently by Chris Havira and Terri Vicario, has been accomplished with exceptional dedication and accuracy. Special thanks are due also to Norma Parks, administrative assistant in the Group Living Department and to Dolores Thomas, executive secretary, for their help and consistently gracious manner in providing information, locating documents, arranging meetings, etc. on what must have seemed to them an infinite number of occasions.

The work has also benefitted from the efforts of many outside the Glen Mills community. No one has contributed more to documenting the Glen Mills story than my collaborator in the research program, Dr. Wm. Dubnov. Through his dedication, skill, and effectiveness over a ten-year period in seeking to locate and individually interview 3,000 students more than two years post-discharge, Dr. Dubnov has made a contribution without precedent in correctional research. For his friendship, his research and interviewing skills, and his assistance both in research design and the preparation of this book, I am deeply in his debt.

Dr. Claus Ottmüller, of the University of Luneburg, West Germany, shared very generously of his time and insights following a six month period of residency and observation at the Schools. Dr. Ottmüller alerted me to many details regarding the role, practice, and significance of the confrontation process at Glen Mills. His work is quoted extensively in the text and Appendix 1.

The work of Dr. Howard Polsky of Columbia University, particularly his book *Cottage Six*, has been central to the development of Glen Mills' program. I am grateful to Dr. Polsky for sharing his reactions to the manuscript, and specifically in his analysis of the relationships among the various organizational factors which contribute to the power of the normative culture to alter behavior.

Glen Mills' data base currently includes several thousand cases. Its usefulness depends upon the care and accuracy of data collection, handling, and analysis— the coding, data entry, verification, and statistical procedures which transform raw numbers into interpretable findings. I am pleased to acknowledge the help of a dedicated and skilled group of research associates. Coding and data verification were accomplished by Mariela Andrews and Darci Struther. Darci also collected and coded data on several hundred Glen Mills students from Philadelphia Family Court records as part of a validation study. Data entry and verification were completed with near miraculous speed and accuracy by Sister Mary Jude Adams of the Regina Mundi Priory in Devon, Pennsylvania. During the past five years Suzanne McMurphy has provided her considerable skills as a statistician, using three versions of the Statistical Package for the Social Sciences on several sometimes recalcitrant computer systems to produce all the data summaries and analyses discussed in this book. Tin-Yun (Grace) Ng, management information systems director at Integra, Inc., worked with Suzanne to overcome numerous technical problems reconfiguring the data and statistical programs so that analyses could be conducted on either a mainframe or micro-computer.

The Citizens Crime Commission of the Delaware Valley, which for more than three decades has played the leading role in the Philadelphia area in harnessing citizen and corporate support for the strengthening of the justice system, has provided staff support and encouragement. Thanks are due to Ian Lennox, president of the Commission, and to staff members Ernie Keller, Lisa Bier, Francis "X" O'Shea, Kathy Butler, and Carmela Macera.

I am very fortunate to have been able to rely on the services of Mariela Andrews for editing and preparation of the manuscript. An editorial associate at Philadelphia's University City Science Center, Mrs. Andrews helped edit the text, prepared all charts and graphs, and constructed the entire document on her word processor. I am most grateful for her dedication, careful work, and high standards; it is difficult to imagine how these vital tasks could have been more ably performed.

The writing of this book seemed to require that every spare moment for a period of over two years be devoted to "the book." This is time that would normally have been spent with family and friends. No author has ever been more thankful for the encouragement and support that he received from his family. To Erik and Merry Grissom, and especially to Gay: thank you. Thank you for helping me to make sense of what I saw at Glen Mills. Thank you for getting me through the bouts of "writer's block." Thank you for helping me to believe that I could write a book worthy of Glen Mills.

Field Marshal Bernard Montgomery said that the final test of a leader is the feeling you have when you leave his presence: do you feel upbeat and confident? In writing a book, as in building an institution, there are lots of opportunities for discouragement. Cosimo "Sam" Ferrainola provided the leadership which made both institution and book possible. Together with his wife, Gerda (who first gave up her native land, Germany, in favor of Sam and then gave up her home in Pittsburgh to "adopt" the staff and students of Glen Mills), he has moved the field of juvenile corrections a giant step forward.

Grant R. Grissom

Introduction

Driving past the fields and woods of Delaware County, Pennsylvania, and through the main entrance to the 779-acre campus, a visitor's first exposure to the Glen Mills Schools for Boys provides few clues to the Schools' primary mission. Athletic fields on both sides of Glen Mills Road are meticulously maintained. The track, baseball and football fields, equipped with spectator stands, lights for night games, and an adjoining field house would be the envy of any exclusive prep school. The sign at the entrance welcomes visitors and announces the state championship honors recently earned by Glen Mills' gymnastics, power lifting, and track and field teams. Nearby are Academic Hall and the Learning Center, which house two of the five distinct educational programs ("Schools") operated by Glen Mills.

The center of the campus is a grassy quadrangle bordered by a large stone chapel on the east, red brick Victorian-era cottages along two sides and an imposing 100-year-old Administration Building crowned with a clock tower on the west. A stone fountain in front of the Administration Building, dogwood trees along the quadrangle's perimeter, carefully tended shrubs and thick grass are reminiscent of the posh private academies on Philadelphia's Main Line, 20 miles to the northeast.

The social climate is relaxed and friendly. Most students establish eye contact and greet visitors. They are well groomed: hair is clean and trimmed, shirts are tucked in. The campus reflects the pride they feel for their school. There are no blaring radios, graffiti, or litter. Staff and students treat each other with respect.

Closer inspection confirms the initial impressions; everything at Glen Mills is first class. Cottage furniture; students' living quarters; athletic equipment; the four meals per day served to the students in a bright modern dining area;

electronic equipment in the Schools' student-operated FM radio station; computer-aided instruction in the Learning Center; vocational assessment equipment—all first rate.

And all new. Little more than a decade ago Glen Mills was near physical and programmatic collapse; its buildings deteriorated, staff demoralized, and heavily in debt. A remarkable transformation began in 1975, a transformation involving far more than the revitalization of Glen Mills' physical plant. During the past decade the Glen Mills experiment has altered the course of juvenile corrections in Pennsylvania. The Schools have provided staff training to child care workers in New Jersey, Delaware, and Maryland. Students have included young men from 20 states, Washington, D.C., and the British Commonwealth (Bermuda). Visitors from across the United States, Europe, the Middle East, and China have come to learn about its program. Glen Mills' full impact upon a field which has increasingly regarded large institutions as part of the problem of delinquency rather than part of the solution has only begun to be felt.

Glen Mills' founding and recent history both represent radical departures from the mainstream correctional philosophy of the day. The history of Glen Mills (formerly the Philadelphia House of Refuge) can be traced back to 1787, when the Society for the Alleviation of the Miseries of Public Prisons was organized in Philadelphia to improve deplorable conditions in the Walnut Street Jail. These included a failure to separate male and female prisoners, lack of clothing allowances (which meant that some male prisoners were naked), dozens of inmates sharing a single room, and an entrepreneurial jailer who was legally permitted to supplement his income through the sale of liquor to prisoners.

The prisoners included young children.

By 1826 the Society had achieved some success in alleviating all of these miseries, except for the confinement of children with hardened adult criminals. Society members pleaded the cause of the 60 Walnut Street prisoners who were under 21 years of age at a meeting of citizens in the county courthouse on February 7, 1826, over which Chief Justice William Tilghman presided. Removal of young offenders to a proposed "House of Refuge for Juvenile Offenders" was discussed. A committee was formed to make application to the Pennsylvania legislature for a charter, which was granted quickly, on March 23, 1826.

Charter or no, transformation of the House of Refuge from vision to reality would require public support. In an address "to their Fellow Citizens" the managers of the House of Refuge pointed out that "a careful inquiry has not been able to discover in the best administered prison a single instance of unequivocal youthful reform." The House of Refuge would be a place of reformation, not punishment: an asylum rather than a prison. Its directors would be friends and instructors of the inmates. The latter would be constantly occupied in labor, instruction, or supervised recreation. A series of carefully graduated honors and rewards for achievement "will afford means of cultivating a spirit of self-esteem, from which the happiest consequences must arise."

In the context of the time the address was revolutionary. The contention that reform, rather than punishment, should be the primary objective of the House of Refuge sharply challenged the prevailing philosophy of the day. It was widely accepted that wrongdoers, regardless of their age, should suffer, not enjoy honors and rewards.

Despite opposition the managers persevered and eventually received $7,104 in private contributions as well as state and county funds to establish the House. A property at the corner of Ridge and Fairmount Avenues was purchased at a cost of $5,500. The cornerstone of the main building was laid June 21, 1827. At the formal opening of the House of Refuge on November 29, 1828, a three-story main building containing 172 four-by-seven foot cells, workshops, and a library stood behind a stone wall twenty feet high and two feet thick. The total cost of the building was $38,025. On December 8, 1828, the first inmate—a 14-year-old boy committed by the mayor of Philadelphia—was admitted. The House of Refuge became the third institution for juvenile offenders in the United States. Now the Glen Mills Schools, it is the oldest still in operation.

The managers made good on their commitment to keep their charges occupied. The daily routine began at 4:45 A.M., with morning prayers and school before breakfast at 7. All inmates were in workshops from 7:30 A.M. until the noon meal. Boys worked at bookbinding, shoemaking, winding bobbins, and making brass nails, umbrellas, and furniture. Girls sewed, knit, cooked, and performed housework.

At 12:30 there was a lecture followed by shopwork from 1:00 until supper at 5:00 P.M. After the evening meal there was a brief recreation period before school classes, which were in session until 7:45. All children were locked in their rooms at 8:00 P.M., immediately after evening prayers. The House of Refuge offered few idle hands for the Devil to employ.

Twelve years after opening its doors the Philadelphia House of Refuge found itself central to one of the most far-reaching decisions in American jurisprudence. The father of Mary Ann Crouse, an inmate who had been consigned to the House on the basis of her mother's assertion that she was "incorrigible," claimed that his daughter was illegally detained because she had not been granted a trial in accordance with the Bill of Rights. Denying Mr. Crouse's appeal, the Supreme Court justices of Pennsylvania held that the Bill of Rights did not apply to minors. Their decision appropriated the English doctrine of *parens patriae*, noting that under some circumstances the common guardianship of the community could be substituted for that of a child's natural parents. Their opinion was clearly based upon the assumption that the House of Refuge had a beneficial effect in reforming its charges, explicitly differentiating it from a prison on the grounds that punishment is not its purpose (Pisciotta, 1982). *Parens patriae* was to become the legal and moral foundation of the juvenile court, surviving virtually unchallenged until the 1960s.

The House of Refuge relocated twice, moving to its present location in 1892. The move from Philadelphia to Glen Mills, Pennsylvania, symbolized the correctional thinking of the era. Adult criminals were viewed as sick individuals with character defects which made them almost subhuman. Conditions of confinement reflected the view that punishment and deprivation were their due; the habits of a lifetime were too deeply rooted to allow for any real hope of reformation. Children, however, were another matter. Due in part to the pioneering efforts of the House of Refuge, a strong movement had emerged by the turn of the century to salvage young miscreants by rescuing them from the corrupting influences of unworthy parents and deleterious social conditions.

The solution to youthful waywardness lay in reformatories, where perverse children would be saved through a demanding physical regimen and moral training in a wholesome environment. The reformatory plan

embodied the following principles: (1) Young offenders must be segregated from the corrupting influences of adult criminals. (2) "Delinquents" need to be removed from their environment and imprisoned for their own good and protection. Reformatories should be guarded sanctuaries, combining love and guidance with firmness and restraint. (3) "Delinquents" should be assigned to reformatories without trial. . . . Due process is not required because reformatories are intended to reform and not to punish. (4) Sentences should be indeterminate. . . . (5) . . . Punishment is required only insofar as it is good for the punished person and only when all other methods have been exhausted. (6) Inmates must be protected from idleness, indulgence, and luxuries through military drill, physical exercise, and constant supervision. (7) Reformatories should be built in the countryside and designed according to the "cottage plan." (8) Labor, education and religion constitute the essential program of reform. . . . Industrial and agricultural training should predominate. (9) The value of sobriety, thrift, industry, prudence, "realistic" ambition and adjustment must be taught. (Platt, 1969: 54–55)

The new site of the House of Refuge of Philadelphia, renamed the Glen Mills Schools in 1911 in keeping with its new location, embodied all these principles. The Schools' fields and orchards surrounding the main campus; the large, stone chapel near the center of the "cottage plan"; the Civil War-era cannon near the Administration Building; the network of underground tunnels allowing for carefully controlled movement between buildings: all are relics of a bygone age in juvenile corrections. Students still enjoy foodstuffs from Glen Mills' fields, but very few have any role in their harvest. The chapel is now used mainly as an auditorium. The cannon is nothing more than a decorative curiosity to most who see it, although there are still a few staff who remember the military-style drills required of Glen Mills boys a quarter century ago. The existence of the tunnels, unused for more than a decade, comes as a surprise to current students whose movement is monitored no more closely than in most high schools.

Glen Mills enjoyed a good reputation for well over half a century in its new location. Its structure and programs were typical of many institutions of the period. There was a strong emphasis upon order and discipline, enforced by cottage parents who resided in the living units. According to one description of the military-style program employed at Glen Mills during the 1940s and 1950s discipline was harsh:

Methods of sanction of the institution were mostly physical punishment. These were beating on the bare back or on the hands; standing at a wall on an angle with two fingers for support until breaking down, and standing for hours with a wooden gun raised over the head and arms stretched. A special procedure was the fight with a life-sized comic character that was painted on a brick wall. The "sinner" was forced to beat on the wall with bare fists until the officer said "stop"; after this procedure the hands often were only bloody lumps.

When children tried to escape and were caught, their head was shaved and they were forced to carry two 20-pound sacks of sand, connected with a cord, around the neck for a period of time, usually six weeks, but sometimes three months. The school paid five dollars head money for every truant caught. (Ottmüller, 1987, 62)

At Glen Mills as in other reformatories, the institutional realities were often at variance with the high-minded visions of its founders.

During the 1960s the cottage parent system and military drill gave way to the custody-clinical model then in vogue, which featured child care workers responsible for cottage life and security, teachers to provide formal classroom instruction, and social workers/counselors to help students gain self-understanding and change the behavior patterns undergirding their delinquency.

The model had wide appeal because it appeared to offer a salutary balance between the dual demands for confinement and rehabilitation. In practice, its effects were often very different than had been hoped. Ohlin (1958) was among the first to describe the dilemma, the model caused for cottage staff, who were expected to maintain order in the living unit but to avoid harsh discipline which might interfere with treatment goals set by relatively high salaried, high status professional staff. Criticisms by professional staff regarding handling of individual students were resented by cottage workers, who pointed to the isolation of the nine-to-five, central office social service workers who were nowhere to be found when disruptions occurred on grounds. Staff divisions were easily exploited. Playing one faction against the other, students were able to sabotage the program while avoiding responsibility for their own behavior.

The most common solution to the control-treatment dilemma helped make life tolerable for cottage staff, but doomed any hope of rehabilitation. Staff formed informal alliances with the natural leaders in their units. These youths received special favors and privileges in return for keeping the weaker students in line. The price is reinforcement of delinquent norms which yield rewards for those who are aggressive and manipulative, who are permitted to dominate those who are weak. In effect, the delinquent leaders have free reign of the institution.

By the early 1970s the dynamics described by Ohlin had brought Glen Mills to the point of crisis. Formally, the Schools had implemented a "team" approach involving coordinated, cooperative effort by treatment and cottage staff. Informally, blame, backbiting, and sabotage were the order of the day; do as little as possible to get through the day was the norm. The activities of delinquent thugs (cutting classes, leaving grounds, bullying other students) were virtually unchecked. In an effort to regain control, staff increasingly resorted to handcuffs, straightjackets, and locked detention cells. There was criticism of school policies and allegations that staff were repressive. More boys ran away, despite the locked doors, barred windows, and guards at the gates. Enrollment declined as judges, concerned about the deterioration of Glen Mills' program, became hesitant to commit youths to the Schools. Glen Mills, after a long history of sound financial management, deteriorated physically and programmatically under burgeoning operating losses.

Then, on December 21, 1973, a tragedy occurred which might easily have closed the Schools forever. Two boys who had misbehaved were locked in a cell of the Schools' Security Treatment Unit. One of them started a fire which resulted in a student's death. There followed a series of investigations and an ultimatum from the State Department of Public Welfare that a consultant be hired to study the Glen Mills organization and programs. The consultant, Dr. Saul Pilnick, had a distinguished background in both juvenile corrections and corporate consulting. He recommended that the Glen Mills Board offer the post of executive director to Cosimo (Sam) Ferrainola, a 44-year-old assistant professor of social work at the University of Pittsburgh whose experience spanned juvenile corrections, business development, and organizational change processes.

Sam Ferrainola was named executive director in February 1975. It was not a great honor. There were those who, familiar with the Schools' predicament, assumed that Mr. Ferrainola had to be either desperate or crazy. Glen Mills was $700,000 in debt, and its creditors were refusing to extend additional loans. The need to cover operating costs had forced the per diem rate up to $121, a rate so high that few counties were willing to commit boys to the Schools. The once-proud institution was literally and figuratively crumbling. Maintenance had been deferred for so long that the physical plant was in shambles—the 30 remaining students were living in the basements of three of the cottages which had deteriorated to the point that the upper floors had been condemned by the Pennsylvania Department of Labor and Industry as unsafe. The Schools' water system, contaminated by run-off from area septic tanks, produced a liquid that most staff and students understandably refused to drink. There were no vocational or athletic programs and few activities; the academic program was ineffective. With few exceptions, the remaining staff were those who lacked the qualifications or the initiative to find other employment. Morale was at rock bottom. In short, Glen Mills faced a crisis of enormous proportions which many thought would prove fatal.

Upon assuming his post Mr. Ferrainola began to speak of his vision for Glen Mills. The institution, he said, would be a humane, efficient, and effective institution where young men who had done bad things could find a good education, learn a trade and, most of all, develop pride in themselves and their accomplishments. A place where they would never have to be afraid that staff or other students would harm them. A school with dedicated staff and the finest programs and facilities that money could buy. A place where none, staff or student, would take away another's dignity; where basic respect would be the foundation of the social order. His goal, he said, was a Glen Mills prep school "where Rockefeller would want to send his son."

Numbered among Sam's strongest supporters today are many who, in 1975, believed he had crossed the line which separates the lunatics from those who are merely unrealistic. In the face of imminent ruin, when the Schools survived from week to week at the mercy of bankers with limited patience, Sam sounded confident, upbeat, and determined. There were some who respected his integrity and vision, but very few who really believed he could succeed. But with the Schools in crisis, there seemed no alternative: the Board of Managers gave him full administrative authority over personnel and programs.

Sam used this authority to discard the Schools' treatment philosophy and management systems, installing in their place a new organizational culture. The culture consisted of three explicit components: a set of basic *values*; *beliefs* about delinquents and their habilitation; and *norms* (not "rules") clearly defining the behavior the Glen Mills community expects of its members. Establishment of the culture, which came to be known as "the Glen Mills way," would require nearly five years.

By whatever name, the model was to prove extraordinarily fruitful. In June 1986 Glen Mills achieved its full capacity of 525 students; and it expanded in 1987 as its population topped 600. During a period when small, community-based programs were in vogue, Glen Mills' population increased from 30 to over 600 students. Since the Schools' program emphasizes small group process, it was possible to accommodate a much larger population without sacrificing program quality by increasing the number of small groups while carefully monitoring their norms.

The expansion enabled the Schools to diversify its programs, which now include 16 vocational shops operating afternoons and evenings, and 14 varsity sports. Glen Mills students operate the Schools' FM radio station, serving the surrounding community. Its baseball team conducts spring training in Florida. Gymnastics, track and field, and powerlifting teams have won state championships competing against public and private secondary schools; its football, basketball, and cross-country teams have won league championships against similar competition. Through the 1987 season, the cross-country team is undefeated in 40 consecutive dual meets. In 1981, Glen Mills' "prep" team of delinquent and nondelinquent student athletes beat Penn State's freshman squad, 18–0. (In 1982 Penn State would win the national college football championship thanks in part to the athletes who played on their 1981 freshman team.) Fifteen Glen Mills athletes have gone on to play football at major colleges. Rick Badanjek, a nondelinquent "prep" student, became an All-American at the University of Maryland and was drafted by the Washington Redskins in 1986. Marty Perkins, Glen Mills' leading student athlete, won the national high school individual shot put championship in 1987 before starting Dartmouth College in September of that year.

These athletic achievements are all the more remarkable in that new students rarely arrive with significant athletic training or experience. Very few are committed to Glen Mills for more than a year. Finally, the Schools' teams must cope with a revolving roster due to mid-season discharges.

Programs now include five levels of academic instruction. Despite long histories of academic failure, students' basic skills competencies (i.e., math and reading standardized test scores) show an average improvement of nearly two months for every month at Glen Mills. Between 1982–87, 974 Glen Mills students have earned their Educational Development Certificate (GED), more than at all other Pennsylvania juvenile correctional institutions combined. Eighty-nine former Glen Mills students went on to attend college in the six-year period.

The Schools' core values regarding the worth and dignity of its charges are communicated through the quality of its facilities, program, and staff. The results are dramatic. Where boys once survived by their wits and their fists, counting the days until discharge or escape, Glen Mills can now boast a humane environment with few equals. There have been no sustained abuse charges against Glen Mills staff for more than a decade. The proportion of students who run away has declined steadily and sharply since 1975; current students are more likely to request an extension of their commitment until they can complete an academic or vocational assignment. Former students who are unable to find employment often seek to return; there are seldom fewer than a dozen of these young men welcomed back to perform various jobs and continue their learning until they can find a better living arrangement. One particularly creative former student arrived carrying court committal papers, which he had forged. There are often 20 or more "returning students" on campus who have voluntarily returned to continue their academic or vocational program. These young men are treated exactly like the other students, although Glen Mills receives no payment for them. More than 90 percent of a random sample of 194 students interviewed two years after discharge said that they never felt afraid while they were at Glen Mills, that staff genuinely cared about them, and that they would want a close friend or relative to be sent to Glen Mills if they got into trouble.

Finally, "the Glen Mills way" has enabled the Schools to achieve its transformation while simultaneously reducing its per diem costs from $121 to $70 per student. Per diem costs at large state institutions in Pennsylvania are more than double this figure. If the 600 students at Glen Mills were to be transferred to these state facilities the additional cost to the taxpayers would be more than $40,000 per *day*.

It has been nearly two decades since there was much optimism about the rehabilitative potential of large institutions. Community corrections and the more recent call for harsh treatment of serious juvenile offenders have replaced the hopes once placed in institution-based rehabilitation. These emphases may be seriously misguided; Glen Mills has shown that large institutions can play an important role in rehabilitation. Certainly the Schools do not represent a panacea. There are delinquent young men whose placement at Glen Mills would be inappropriate. There are others who are accepted but are not helped by the program. But nine years of research data (Grissom, 1988) indicate that Glen Mills represents a humane, effective, and relatively inexpensive alternative for many delinquent youths.

An understanding of the Schools' recent history provides lessons of major importance to the field. Key issues are: How and why did Glen Mills' transformation occur?; How does it work now?; What are the results?; and What does Glen Mills' experience tell us about delinquency and its treatment?

The first chapter of this book describes how and why the transformation occurred. Its focus is the transitional years, roughly 1975 until 1980, when the custody-clinical model was replaced by a philosophy embracing very different values and embodied in a radically altered organizational normative culture. The institutional change process is a classic case study in the skillful use of administrative authority to restructure not just a treatment program and an organization chart, but an entire social system: the values, beliefs, and behaviors of students, teachers, counselors, board members, and managers; anyone having a direct impact upon the students. The transformation of Glen Mills is among the most successful and best documented examples of organizational change through the deliberate imposition of a new normative culture.

The second chapter describes the Glen Mills program of 1988. Believing that continual development and improvement are essential to effectiveness, the management team will no doubt see to it that the Glen Mills of the future will differ significantly from the current version. But the core norms and values now in place will not change as long as Glen Mills is recognizably Glen Mills. Analysis of the current program is important to understanding how this Glen Mills "culture" manifests itself in the educational, vocational, athletic, treatment, and leisure activities which constitute the life experience of Glen Mills students.

Chapter 3 describes the Glen Mills program as it is experienced by the students. The narrative, describing the experiences of a hypothetical student, represents a composite of interviews with hundreds of students during and after their stay at Glen Mills.

Chapter 4 presents findings related to Glen Mills' effectiveness; the most extensive data ever collected relating to a correctional institution, to the best of our knowledge. Staff performance, runaways, vandalism, program attendance, recidivism, student academic and vocational achievement, disciplinary incidents, staff and student norms, cleanliness of living units, assaults, and anything else deemed relevant to program effectiveness are routinely monitored by management. These data, collected over more than a decade, provide a rich source of information pertaining to the central issue of Glen Mills' effectiveness in helping young men reverse antisocial and self-destructive behavior patterns.

Chapter 5 summarizes the lessons Glen Mills' experience offers to organizational change agents and to the field of juvenile corrections. The establishment of an effective organizational culture is as crucial to the success of the United

States Army and General Motors as it is to Glen Mills; the Schools' experience is broadly relevant. With regard to juvenile corrections, Glen Mills' story makes essential a reconsideration of the significance of formal "treatment" activities and the role of the large institution. Research on the effectiveness of intervention with juvenile offenders has been hampered by its focus upon treatment modality and an understandable but misguided denigration of the role of large institutions. The Glen Mills story challenges the belief that the formal treatment program is of overriding importance, and indicates that large institutions may yet become the most effective placements for many offenders.

Those familiar with the history of juvenile corrections, organizational dynamics, and the principles of situational leadership will find few surprises in this text. Certainly Glen Mills is not the first institution to value human dignity and growth, to refuse to see its charges as "bad." Striving for excellence is a theme familiar to the business community long before Peters and Waterman's (1982) In Search of Excellence became required reading for corporate managers. Organizational principles essential to the program, (e.g., the need to recognize the powerful influence of the informal organization and insure, through constant attention to the normative culture, that its effect is to promote the goals of the formal organization) have been recognized for decades. In the 30 years since Guided Group Interaction (GGI) was pioneered with delinquents at Highfields (Weeks, 1958), there have been no shortage of adaptations of the technique in combination with athletic, vocational, and academic programs.

In short, many of Glen Mills' program elements have been "borrowed" and adjusted. To use Sam Ferrainola's favorite analogy, Glen Mills has fostered not great inventors but great bakers. The main ingredients for the Glen Mills "cake" are the Schools' core values, organizational structure, normative culture, diversity of programs, and sociological theories of delinquency. Add the findings of key researchers such as Howard Polsky, whose Cottage Six is read by Glen Mills' staff during their training. Pour in high expectations and large doses of recognition of students' achievements. Bake and eat. Honestly assess its taste. Then repeat, varying ingredients that hold promise for improving the product. If the cake does not meet your hopes learn what you can from the experience and move on. Never fail to acknowledge the contributions of any who did their best to produce a better cake. Never say "this cake is good enough."

The basic ingredients include no wonder drugs, no elixir with the power to transform juvenile offenders or the programs which serve them. But after a decade of development the Schools' normative culture has produced results which compel a reexamination of some of the most basic issues in juvenile corrections: the key elements in program effectiveness, the role of the large institution, the expectations which society may realistically hold for its correctional programs, and even the fundamental nature of the juvenile offender.

This book was written in the hope that Glen Mills' recipe will be of value to the policymakers, administrators, and staff into whose hands our society has committed the lives of its delinquent youth and its hopes for a safer society.

WITHOUT
LOCKS and BARS

1

A New Order:

Critical Events at

Glen Mills,

1975–1980

There is nothing more difficult to carry out, nor more doubtful of success,
nor more dangerous to handle, than to initiate a new order of things.

Machiavelli

The five-year period beginning with Sam Ferrainola's arrival at Glen Mills in 1975 brought sweeping changes to the Schools. By 1980 only the Schools' name remained unchanged. All else—physical plant, treatment philosophy, programs, staff, organizational structure, fiscal operating principles—had been sharply altered; a new order established.

Organizational theorists believe that institutions, like individuals, mature through a series of predictable developmental stages characterized by periods of substantial turbulence or crisis sandwiched between relatively calm periods of development (Greiner, 1972). As in individual development, where stage theorists since Erik Erikson have described the interrelationships between adjacent stages, each organizational phase is seen as an outgrowth of its predecessor and containing the seeds of its successor. But in the case of Glen Mills, the period 1975–80 represents a time of such radical change and discontinuity that it is more accurately understood as a rebirth than as a developmental phase. In 1975 the Schools faced a fiscal, programmatic, and organizational crisis of such proportions that an orderly, continuous change process addressing areas of weakness while building upon strengths was unthinkable.

Within five years' time a new foundation for Glen Mills would be laid. Fiscally, the Schools' operating practices and philosophy would come to resemble that of a for-profit business. While the language of management by objectives, marketing strategy, product diversification, return on investment, capitalizationplanning, and financial monitoring and control systems was rarely employed, economic ruin was averted by a sophisticated business development process which encompassed all these elements. The new operating philosophy contrasted sharply with the "government-will-provide" mentality to which administrators of social service agencies are especially vulnerable, particularly those whose formative years in their professions spanned periods of strong government funding for social service programs.

Programmatically, the custody-clinical treatment model was supplanted by its antithesis: in the new Glen Mills any student who wishes to leave is permitted to do so, and boys admitted to the Schools are considered normal young men whose misbehavior primarily reflects their needs for acceptance and status among their peers. "Treatment" (the term is almost never used at Glen Mills) involves establishing and maintaining a milieu where students experience peer recognition and status through prosocial behavior; where the street norms of status-seeking through conning, intimidation, and disrespect for authority figures are snuffed out so that untapped academic, vocational, and athletic potential can be realized. The term "student" is used very deliberately, since the Schools' charges are engaged in a normal learning process. They are not in "treatment" to overcome "personality disorders"; they are not "bad" children whose character defects require corrective action in the form of deprivation or punishment. Glen Mills does not seek to *rehabilitate* moral and psychological invalids. It seeks to *habilitate* young men whose life circumstances have left unrealized a potential which far exceeds what is commonly associated with the label "delinquent." It is impossible to overemphasize the importance of this point. The belief that Glen Mills students are no less deserving of dignity and respect and suffer from no more serious psychological problems than their noninstitutionalized peers, and have enormous potential for growth, has far-reaching implications for program development and the norms governing staff-student interactions. It is the sine qua non of Glen Mills' culture, a guiding principle of overriding power and significance.

Organizationally, Glen Mills in 1975 was typical of a common institutional model characterized by a hierarchical structure, with all formal decision-making power vested in degreed professional staff, operating through directors (e.g., clinical, cottage life, academic, etc.) whose primary responsibility was the administration of their own program area. Having experienced firsthand the weaknesses of this model and familiar with the work of researchers (e.g., Ohlin, 1958; Polsky, 1962) who had documented its deleterious effects, Sam Ferrainola was committed to abolishing it.

Within five years he had guided the development of an organizational structure unique in the field and differing from its predecessor in all significant respects. Designed to facilitate teamwork, eliminate structural causes of staff conflict, and support the establishment of strong campus norms, Glen Mills' trainers refer to the model as a "molecular " system. It features staff allegiances and responsibilities differing markedly from those in hierarchical organizations. Decision making is invariably participative and usually achieved through open discussions involving a team and its supervisor. Department heads' primary responsibilities are to the management team and only secondarily to the administration of their own departments. The new structure and role descriptions are carefully designed to reinforce a norm of shared responsibility where each department is responsible for helping other departments to achieve their goals. There is no faster route to unemployment for a Glen Mills manager than to adopt a "That's his problem, not mine" attitude.

The story of Glen Mills' rebirth is important to an understanding of Glen Mills as it exists today. The Schools' philosophy and normative culture, in place by 1980, represent the foundation upon which all later programs have been erected. The story involves three important change processes which ebbed and flowed in concert to produce a new treatment modality, power structure, and organizational culture. It is told here through the recounting of a series of critical incidents which shaped the schools and continue to do so by embodying its ideals and giving expression to the central values of the new Glen Mills.

TAKING THE HELM

Sam Ferrainola moved into the large director's residence adjacent to Glen Mills' campus in February 1975. With him were his wife Gerda, and three of their five children, Rose (17), Rita (16), and Tresa (4).

Sam had been recruited by the Board of Managers' trusted consultant, Dr. Saul Pilnick. The institution was in such crisis that the board's options were limited. Very few experienced administrators were interested in presiding over a dying facility. The board decided to act upon Dr. Pilnick's recommendations, but not without misgivings. Sam had never served as a top administrator of a residential facility. Moreover, he was clearly cut from a different mold than his predecessor and the majority of the board members. The board was dominated by older, reserved, meticulously dressed and groomed gentlemen with backgrounds in business and the professions. Sam had the large frame (250 pounds) of a former athlete; an outgoing personality and some of the mannerisms of his working class Sicilian background. He was as likely to attend board meetings in a Glen Mills shirt than wear the tie and jacket de rigueur for male members of the board.

Sam brought no blueprint for change. He arrived at Glen Mills with a conviction that delinquent behavior is intolerable but delinquents are not; and a determination to build an institution whose purpose would be the habilitation of young men with enormous potential, rather than the rehabilitation of bad kids. His bag of tricks consisted of an understanding of normative systems change and training skills. His belief was that if he worked hard, relied on his instincts, and tried to make Glen Mills a little better each week, good things would happen.

On February 7, 1975, the day after his arrival at Glen Mills, Sam addressed the 30 boys then in residence. Staff were shocked and disbelieving when he announced that, as his first act as executive director, he would order all locks and bars removed from the dormitory areas. There would no longer be a gate or guards controlling access at the Schools' entrance; no more security aimed at preventing escapes.

The boldness of this move by a man who had taken the reins less than 24 hours earlier was stunning to the Glen Mills staff. The decisions announced in the speech must have sounded impulsive and dangerously naive. They were neither. More than a decade of experience in juvenile corrections had persuaded Sam that deprivation, punishment, and coercion were incompatible with habilitation. He had accepted the position at Glen Mills to prove that an open system approach could work with serious offenders. His speech served notice that a new man was in charge, that fundamental changes would occur.

Speaking with conviction of his vision of a new Glen Mills which students would be proud to claim as their own, Sam underlined his sincerity with a closing offer: anyone wishing to leave need only ask. Like the decision to remove all locks and bars, this offer had been well thought out. The intent was to underscore Sam's intention to make Glen Mills a place where students would want to live. But the offer also reflected the reality that, in a truly open system, there would be no way to prevent escapes. Since Glen Mills' campus is in a semi-rural area with no transportation, a runaway student might well decide to steal a car from a nearby home or burglarize an area residence to get money. Either event, coming early in his administration and following the controversial decision to adopt an open campus approach, would be a serious setback creating strong community and board opposition to Sam's plans. The offer to provide transportation to anyone wanting to leave minimized the risk.

Two boys asked to leave and were sent back to court the following morning. If necessary, Sam was ready to send them all back and start from scratch. As they came to know him better, staff would learn that Sam Ferrainola does not make an offer he does not intend to honor or a threat he is not prepared to carry out.

It was necessary to establish early and forcefully the core values of the new order. Most fundamentally, Sam insisted that the boys at Glen Mills were to be treated as students in an exclusive prep school. Staff training would emphasize this theme: If you were to send your son to a fancy prep school, wouldn't you want him to be given good food? Decent living quarters? A good education? Wouldn't you want him to be treated with respect and feel safe? No doubt Rockefeller expects this for his children—are Glen Mills' students less human or less deserving?

The new director's actions spoke even more forcefully than his words. One of his first decisions was to substantially upgrade both the quality and quantity of food served to the students. Directing that students be given as much food as they wanted as long as it was not wasted, Sam ordered his director of food services to purchase nutritious high quality foods and increased the number of meals by adding a late evening "snack" which usually consisted of hamburgers, hot dogs, hoagies, steak sandwiches, milk shakes, or other popular foods. The monies to implement the new policy would come from reduced personnel costs: Glen Mills was overstaffed with nonessential professional personnel whose salaries could be put to better use. By providing top quality food and a pleasant dining atmosphere, Glen Mills would bolster students' pride and self-respect while underlining its program philosophy of nondeprivation. The policy would also reduce late evening acting out: adolescent boys, like lions, are less restless and aggressive when they are well fed.

The decision to accept staff reductions as the price of establishing a new program philosophy further alienated staff who were already suspicious of the new director and resistant to his ideas. Veteran staff groused among themselves and assured each other that this too would pass; that Sam could not last long. Passive resistance to Sam's leadership became the order of the day. Unsure of his own strength (it was Saul Pilnick, not he, who had the confidence of the board) and hoping that the power of his dreams for the Schools and the positive results of the new philosophy would eventually bring staff around, Sam did not take strong action against the foot-dragging.

That changed when staff behavior threatened the students' security. Knowing that intimidation by stronger boys is the chief cause of fear and abuse in institutions for delinquents, the new director had made it clear that staff were to intervene whenever they became aware of threats, harassment, or any form of physical or verbal abuse. They were never, under any circumstances, to stand idly by while someone "took a student's dignity." This proved a difficult order. As in many institutions, Glen Mills' staff had found an effective device for keeping order and control. They had established informal alliances with the more aggressive students: in return for not causing trouble the toughs would be permitted to bully and dominate the weaker students, within limits, without fear of staff intervention. Unable now to rely upon locks, handcuffs, and other restraints to enforce discipline, staff were hesitant to surrender this last tool of control. The new policy was largely ignored until an incident in the dining hall pushed the director past the limits of his patience.

While eating his lunch in the dining room Sam noticed a long-time employee, one of the leaders in the staff's informal passive resistance campaign, eating at a nearby table with a new student. They were joined by two other boys who soon began to mock the new student. The staff did nothing. Frightened, the new boy was about to leave when one of the older boys "accidentally" knocked a glass of milk into his lap. The staff person continued to eat his lunch as though nothing had happened, until Sam arrived at the table and fired him on the spot.

Those who were unwilling to accept the new director could not rely on passive resistance to thwart him. They would bide their time until the moment was right for a more direct approach.

During the first six months of Sam's tenure Glen Mills was in chaos. The foundations of the old system were destroyed, but the new philosophy was not working. The financial crisis led Glen Mills to accept for admission virtually any male delinquent, including those with very serious offense histories whom other institutions would not accept. Tom Beecher, now director of group living and an employee for more than 30 years, was a cottage staff worker in 1975. He recalls the difficulties of those first months:

It was exhausting just trying to keep some control. Every night kids would go off grounds and head over to Sleighton (a nearby institution for delinquent girls). Some of us would be out each night until one A.M. trying to round them up. Another favorite pastime was to push the Schools' bus over the top of a hill. I finally got so tired that I'd let the air out of the tires so I could get some sleep without worrying about it.

By late spring of 1975 many of Glen Mills' staff expected that the new director would soon be relieved or at least forced to reinstate the security policies of prior administrations. There was increasing pressure to install at least one security unit where students could be locked in their rooms. Staff were quick to recommend that difficult students be returned to court, expecting that the financially strapped board would find this option unpalatable and hasten the restoration of locks and bars. Those who were struggling to keep the lid on were beginning to feel hopeless in the face of continuing turmoil.

The new director spent all of his days and most nights and weekends on campus, working along with his staff. Whenever there was a problem he was quickly on the scene. Whatever their other misgivings, staff began to respect his directness and willingness to get involved. Sam could be counted on to be there when the going got tough. This style contrasted sharply with that of his predecessor. Sam was very approachable (Tom Beecher remembers thinking of him as "an Italian grandfather standing on the corner, talking to anyone who happened by"), hard-working, and committed, but by the summer of 1975 even those who wished him well harbored large and growing doubts that his approach could be made workable.

The director was determined to resist the pressures to restore locked units. He believed that the ineffectiveness of his approach had been due to staff resistance, and was unwilling to reward it by returning to a coercive program. Glen Mills should be in the business of changing, not controlling, behavior. Locks and bars are instruments of control. Sam had come to the Schools convinced that they were obstacles to the change process. He was not ready to abandon that position.

Outwardly, Sam continued to project a positive, upbeat confidence about the program. But privately, he began to wonder whether he could succeed. After six months of his leadership there were glaring weaknesses in the program, a student body out of control, and staff disaffection at all levels. With a student population that fluctuated between 30 and 40, Glen Mills lacked the revenues required to upgrade its programs. The academic program serviced only one-third of the students. There were no intramural or vocational programs, no weekend program, and only very limited evening activities. Students lived in poorly furnished open dormitories. Bullying, fighting, and stealing were daily occurrences. More students cut classes than attended them. They routinely left campus without permission, failed to comply with the 9:30 curfew, and did not return on time from home visits. There were numerous break-ins at the kitchen and the student union. Disruptions were the norm in the dining room and classrooms.

Line staff commitment to the program was weak. Few were either confronting negative behavior or modeling positive behavior. Many were uncooperative and resistant to the open campus concept. Rather than work with troublesome students staff wanted to expel them. None felt pride in their work or the Schools.

Line staff attitudes reflected those of their team leaders and top management team. When problems arose, these individuals blamed rather than supported one another. There was little accountability. Teamwork was nonexistent. Managers were openly disrespectful to each other and the director. Even top managers—the directors of group living, education, and the business manager—had little confidence in the open system or felt responsible to make it work.

A key problem was the weakness of Sam's position as director. Saul Pilnick held the real authority at Glen Mills. The board respected him. Their contract with Saul was nearly triple Sam's $24,000 annual salary. Dr. Pilnick's leading role in the recruitment and training of senior staff meant that few felt any personal commitment to Sam. The entire top management team had been put in place by Dr. Pilnick, with Sam's acquiescence. Unable to command their loyalty, the director felt increasingly impotent and isolated in his struggle to stem the disorder.

In September 1975, with his dream for Glen Mills unraveling daily, Sam's discouragement deepened and turned to despair when his youngest daughter, Tresa, was hit and nearly killed by an automobile in front of their home. In sore need of time away from the Schools, the Ferrainolas took a short vacation during Tresa's recovery. Sam, a football player in his college days and an avid sports fan, purchased Michener's *Sports in America* only to find that it begins with an account of physical abuse at Glen Mills.

By December 1975, faced with the failure of his program and the stress spilling over onto his wife and children, Sam had decided to leave Glen Mills. Failure would be a bitter pill for this proud man, but he could no longer justify subjecting his family or himself to the constant strain.

In the nick of time the first in a series of events occurred which ultimately preserved the Schools and enabled the open program concept to succeed. Ironically, the viciousness of several Glen Mills staff intent on driving Sam away and destroying his program would instead preserve it.

Before Sam could inform board members of his decision to resign, they had received a very different communication. An unsigned letter, sent to board members and court officials in Delaware County, accused Sam of "outright thievery and corruption"; a wide range of misconduct including the replacement of dedicated staff by "Sam's unqualified stooges," diversion of the Schools' property and funds for his personal use, failure to honor commitments, irrational and arbitrary behavior toward staff, and failure to support his team leaders. Various accusations against Sam's children were included.

Had the authors delayed a few more days there would have been no need to write the letter, and Glen Mills' open campus would have become one more discredited treatment model. The letter was quite possibly the only thing in the world that could have persuaded Sam to remain at Glen Mills. Sam could accept failure, but never dishonor. To resign would be to lend credence to the outrageous accusations in the letter. Furthermore, he had some suspicions regarding its source. He would avenge this insult to his family and his honor.

Sam did not know how the board, still very uncertain about his leadership, might react to the letter. The board had met to discuss it and then asked Sam to come into the meeting room. When Sam entered the room Francis Plowman, one of the most respected board members, tore up the letter saying "This is what I think of it." For the present, at least, his position was secure.

Eager to remove those who had insulted him and sabotaged his program, Sam rejected suggestions that he "forget the whole thing." He told the board that in sending the letter to court officials, those responsible had injured Glen Mills and would have to be discharged. The board agreed and appointed two of its members to assist Sam in an investigation. The director was ready to abandon efforts to woo those who undermined his efforts. He would purge the staff retaining only those who were committed to the open program concept or, at a minimum, those who were not aligned with his enemies and who were doing their job well. All others would go, and the first order of business was to remove those responsible for the letter.

The leaders of the staff resistance proved to be long time, high status employees, some with close ties to several board members. They felt protected, realizing that Sam would be unable to prove that they were responsible for sending the letter. They reasoned that Sam, lacking strong support from the board, would be unwilling to risk accusing veteran staff who had curried the board's favor.

They did not understand that their adversary was past caring about his own future at the Schools. Having satisfied himself that he knew who was responsible, Sam called an attorney who assured him that since Glen Mills was a private facility with no union, staff contracts, or personnel manual he had the authority as executive director to fire anyone he pleased as long as the reasons did not involve discrimination on the basis of race, age, or sex. He hung up the phone and called each individual into his office one at a time, to fire them. Given the choice between upholding the firings or removing Sam as director, the board supported Sam.

The director's leadership skills were developing rapidly. The past twelve months had taught him that he would have to claim his authority as executive director. He had learned that his coveted "win-win" approach may not always be viable, that leadership sometimes requires hard decisions where some people "lose." He had learned that a leader cannot hold his job too dear: he had been able to take decisive action only after reaching the point where his own survival as the Schools' director was no longer uppermost in his mind.

With the opposition leaders gone, Sam became determined to take control of his program. For a full year he had tried to work with resistant staff. The time had come to clean house, to replace staff who were unwilling or unable to work within the new system. In addition to those already terminated, Sam marked 20 percent of the remaining staff for discharge. Unfortunately, his own position was not yet strong enough to expect that the board would support this new round of terminations, which included some of the top managers Dr. Pilnick had recruited, merely because Sam felt the individuals had not "bought in" to the new treatment philosophy and his leadership. The board would, however, accept staff cuts as a response to fiscal crisis, and there was one on the horizon.

The juvenile court officials who had received the letter accusing Sam of mismanagement were reluctant to send boys to Glen Mills. The Schools would first have to provide an explanation and assurance that the program was sound. A proactive campaign was clearly required to restore confidence. Sam was certain that he could reassure the judges, but decided against taking immediate action. By delaying, he could create a (reversible) decline in admissions sufficient to justify the cuts he felt necessary.

The strategy worked. By early spring the staff had been purged and Sam had filled key management slots with staff loyal to him. Two in particular—Tom Beecher as director of group living and Garrison Ipock ("Garry") as director of admissions—would play major roles in building the new Glen Mills. Furthermore, the decline in admissions had been reversed as Sam and Garry devised a strategy to "market" Glen Mills to the juvenile courts.

There remained a single top manager, the director of education, who had been selected by Dr. Pilnick and felt neither loyal to Sam nor committed to the new program philosophy. By April 1976, the director of education had alienated both Dr. Pilnick and the board, who instructed Sam to dismiss him. A golden opportunity, but one which Sam decided to decline. Control over hiring and firing is an important prerogative for a strong executive director. Sam waited until July, then "permitted" the manager to resign.

The nucleus of an effective and loyal top management team had been assembled. The director's own authority remained clouded by Saul Pilnick's involvement. Sam respected Dr. Pilnick and regarded him as a mentor. Much of the new Glen Mills program philosophy was developed by Dr. Pilnick. His ideas became incorporated in the Schools' normative culture and GGI program. He was a superb theoretician and organizational analyst. But the consultant's involvement in operations—especially in staff selection and training—tended to undercut the position of the Executive Director.

With growing misgivings about the scope of Dr. Pilnick's involvement and its effect upon his own authority, Sam worked to maintain a cooperative relationship with Dr. Pilnick and his firm, Human Systems Institute (HSI) through the spring of 1976. With his own staff increasingly capable of conducting staff training, Sam expected that a reduced and less conflicting role for HSI could be negotiated upon the June 30 expiration of its current contract.

In early May Sam learned that the president of Glen Mills' Board of Managers had agreed to support the renewal of a $70,000 annual contract to HSI. Sam met twice with Saul to voice his strong opposition to the agreement. Glen Mills' annual budget was only $1,300,000; the Schools were struggling financially; money was badly needed for restoration of the physical plant and program development; payment of $70,000 to a consultant was unconscionable. With his managers feeling more confident of their own abilities, the full range of HSI services were no longer required. Sam asked Dr. Pilnick to "back off," reduce the scope of his involvement, and allow the director to run the Schools. Would he accept $25,000?

Definitely not. The original HSI contract had cost $70,000. It had been renewed once at this level. The Schools were in far better shape financially now than in either of the two previous years. The HSI intervention had been cost-effective for Glen Mills. The board president had already agreed to the second renewal. Why should he even consider Sam's preposterous proposal? The second meeting ended with Dr. Pilnick's refusal to renegotiate his agreement with the board president. He also suggested that job stress had taken its toll on Mr. Ferrainola's judgment and ability to manage the Schools.

With this impasse, the director abandoned all hope for a working relationship based upon mutual respect. Sam now believed that there were only three options available to him: resign; remain on board as director by title but Dr. Pilnick's assistant by function; or work to rid Glen Mills of his former mentor.

For months Sam had urged his staff to cooperate fully with HSI trainers despite staff concerns about their competence and methods. As Saul Pilnick walked to his car, Sam telephoned Tom Beecher and told him that Glen Mills staff need no longer cooperate. Their new objective would be to remove Dr. Pilnick and HSI.

The board president, who was persuaded of Dr. Pilnick's competence and not at all certain that Sam Ferrainola could get the job done without him, was very concerned when he learned of the conflict between the two men. He ordered the principals of HSI and Glen Mills to meet to resolve the problems. Dr. Pilnick and his assistant were to meet with Sam, Tom Beecher, and Garry Ipock in a conference room at a nearby hotel.

The Glen Mills managers, who had so often worked long hours to solve difficult problems, entered the room having already agreed upon an unusual goal: to make certain that no problems were resolved.

Dr. Pilnick opened the meeting with the suggestion that they discuss their concerns regarding the relationship between HSI and Glen Mills. There was no response. For the next hour and a half, no word was spoken. As the alotted two hours elapsed, Dr. Pilnick suggested having coffee. The gesture succeeded in breaking the silence but not the deadlock; the meeting ended with no progress.

Though the initial stonewalling had succeeded, the director felt that it would be difficult to maintain the impasse for the remaining six weeks of HSI's contract without seriously alienating his board president. Feeling that he could not continue to be present but unresponsive, Sam took his wife on a five week trip to Europe. He left Tom Beecher in charge with explicit instructions: Should the president ask you to meet with Dr. Pilnick, tell him that the earlier meeting had been fruitless and that further meetings would serve no purpose unless the director were present; if he insists, go to the meeting but get up and leave after ten minutes. Sam left no phone number or address where he could be reached.

Shortly after Sam's departure the board president contacted Mr. Beecher, who persuaded him that it would be pointless to meet prior to Sam's return.

Frustrated by the administration's stonewalling, Dr. Pilnick addressed the board at its May meeting and made a series of allegations against the director. Claiming that Mr. Ferrainola had lost the confidence of his own top administrators, Dr. Pilnick concluded that Sam was unfit to serve as executive director and proposed that the board immediately give him executive powers, including authority over the director.

Faced with yet another crisis in an unrelenting stream of problems, the board established an ad hoc committee to investigate Dr. Pilnick's allegations. The committee was chaired by Dr. Faye Soffen, a respected professor at Bryn Mawr College who had recently been elected to Glen Mills' board and had close ties to neither Saul nor Sam.

The committee conducted its investigation by interviewing senior staff. Three of the four top managers—Tom Beecher, Garry Ipock, and Mr. Sam Costanzo (training director)—had been appointed by the director and respected him. The Achilles' heel was the Schools' business manager, Mr. Joseph Braun, who had been recruited by Dr. Pilnick and felt little loyalty to Sam. When the three men learned they would be contacted by the board's committee they went to see Mr. Braun and told him, in effect, that he would have to choose sides.

On June 30 the committee reported that Dr. Pilnick's charges appeared groundless; that all senior staff had said they respected Sam and had confidence in his leadership. The board accepted its committee's report, informed Sam of their findings, and gave him complete authority in regard to the HSI contract. Sam immediately terminated Glen Mills' relationship with HSI.

On July 1, 1976, seventeen months after receiving the title, Sam Ferrainola became executive director in fact.

Now firmly in charge, the director set out to establish a positive normative culture at Glen Mills. The new top management team had now to demonstrate its own competence and authority in restoring order to the campus. Their priorities were:

1. Curb student disorder without resorting to locks and bars;
2. Increase the rate of admissions of new students;
3. Recruit and train new personnel;

4. Implement a fiscal system based upon sound business practices;
5. Redirect funds to the remodeling of classrooms and dormitories;
6. Expand the dining facilities to accommodate a larger student population.

These fundamentals of institutional development would have to take precedence over the long-term goal of building strong academic, vocational, recreational, and athletic programs.

The new management team and philosophy would not be credible until they had demonstrated their ability to alter negative student and staff norms. Two of the most troublesome were targeted: students' disregard of the 9:30 P.M. curfew, and staff tendency to press for expulsion of misbehaving students. The former was symptomatic of a general lack of control, the latter contributed to the Schools' fiscal problems by making it difficult to build a larger student enrollment.

A plan was devised to attack both norms simultaneously. In August the director announced several new policies. First, if the Glen Mills student population were to fall below 56 students there would be a 20 percent staff reduction in all departments. Second, any student not in his cottage by 9:30 P.M. would be brought before a disciplinary committee at 8:30 A.M. the following day and, if he did not have a legitimate excuse, he would be expelled. Finally, any cottage whose population falls below 15 students would be closed and the staff laid off. These pronouncements were posted next to a chart showing daily changes in student population.

The policies provided staff with a powerful incentive to work together in an effort to save, not expel, problem students, and to work harder to enforce the curfew. Simultaneously, Sam demonstrated his willingness to use his most potent sanction (expulsion) to establish an orderly and disciplined student body.

The strategy was risky. Juvenile court judges, whose favor Sam had worked hard to cultivate, would be angered if Glen Mills were to expel students for tardiness. They would have difficulty understanding the importance of normative change and why it required expelling a young man convicted of assault simply because of a curfew violation.

Sam was prepared to carry out his threat. On the night of his announcement, six boys failed to return to their cottages by 9:30. The next morning, all six were expelled. The following night two boys were tardy; both were expelled. The third night one boy was late and he was sent back to court the next morning. From then on, all students were present and accounted for at 9:30 P.M. sharp.

August 1976 proved to be a turning point for Glen Mills. A well established and important norm had been identified and altered. The new administrative team had shown strong, cohesive leadership.

With order restored, subversive staff dismissed, the student population stabilized, and leadership clearly established, staff stress declined steadily through the autumn of 1976. A sense of excitement began to build about the Schools' future. If the threat of expulsion from a struggling program was effective in changing behavior, how much more powerful might this sanction be if Glen Mills were a "good prep school"? For the first time, there was a reason to believe that the behavior of serious delinquent offenders could be changed without locks and bars.

The past ten years had seen a steady erosion of control and hope at Glen Mills. However satisfying and significant in retrospect, the events of the summer were only a small first step toward reversing the long decline. So much had yet to be done: rebuilding the deteriorated physical plant; developing strong programs; establishing a sound board-administration working relationship; building an effective and cohesive staff; restoring financial stability; and replacing the students' "street" norms with a culture which would engender learning, responsibility for self and others, pride, respect for others, and self-respect. By all appearances, very little had changed. The difference was that Glen Mills was now led by a management team with clear authority, respect for one another, and enthusiasm for their role—individuals who were willing to row hard and pull their oars in the same direction.

ESTABLISHING THE STAFF NORMATIVE CULTURE

Where to start? Realizing that a strong staff is basic to all the other tasks that lay before them, the administration devoted its energies to reassignment of existing staff, and the recruiting and training of new staff.

By far the most important consideration in assignment of existing staff was loyalty. Key roles would be filled by individuals loyal to the new management team. Individuals with skill deficiencies could be reassigned to more appropriate roles as performance standards were raised, but the transition period required, above all else, leadership which worked together as a team.

The administrative team wrestled with the issue of recruiting cottage staff for the new Glen Mills. What sort of person to hire? Relevant qualities included personal values, personality, and skills. The qualifications were unusual. Prior experience did not matter, since the "Glen Mills way" would be very different from other programs. More likely than not, prior work in institutions would engender negative attitudes toward the students, cynicism about prospects for success, and a long list of poor work habits which the candidate would have to unlearn.

Strong academic credentials were suspect, because exceptional scholastic ability might suggest a preoccupation with intellectual rather than relational values. A C or low B average indicated a healthier balance. Academic achievement is valued—Glen Mills reimburses its staff who pursue advanced degrees—but only when other more important qualities are also evident.

Those with backgrounds in the helping professions need not apply, since they too often treated delinquents as psychologically deformed victims of their life circumstances rather than well socialized (i.e., in relation to their peer group) young men with enormous academic and social potential. Habilitation at Glen

Mills would not come primarily through individual, staff-student "helping relationships," but through carefully managed peer group pressures.

The ideal staff candidate would be a physically strong, athletic young man or woman comfortable in the company of teenagers, to whom Glen Mills' students could relate as a role model. Someone who had succeeded, despite obstacles, in achieving a championship ring or a college diploma. Someone willing to learn and not easily intimidated; secure enough to have no need to throw his or her weight around but willing and able to do so when the situation required. Someone with a bent toward constructive action who would take initiative in solving problems rather than griping about them. From a strong family. With a sense of humor. Above all, a team player who knew the meaning of hard work and loyalty.

Glen Mills was able to find a pool of qualified applicants in college and university athletic departments. Careful hiring would need to be followed by strong training. The director made only minor changes to Saul Pilnick's training design. One of the most extensive institution-based training programs in juvenile corrections, Dr. Pilnick's program is still used to train new employees at Glen Mills. Addressing both theoretical and performance issues, the training covers Guided Group Interaction (GGI), norms, leadership, and the Schools' Performance Evaluation System (PES).

The module on norms is of particular importance, since the systematic manipulation of norms is fundamental to both institutional management and treatment at Glen Mills. The Schools' trainers define "norm" as a behavior which a group expects of its members. The power of norms in determining the behavior of group members derives from the members' needs for acceptance and status within the group. These needs are common to all of us but especially to adolescents, including the vast majority of delinquents. Individuals gain status when they conform to group norms and lose status when they transgress them.

A norm is very different from a rule. In the institutional context, a rule is a directive for conduct imposed by the institution and enforced by the staff through a system of penalties. While both norms and rules deal with standards of conduct, the former are products of the informal system, enforced by group pressures. Rules are tools of the formal system, enforced by authoritarian sanctions. Rules describe behavior desired by authorities. Norms describe behavior expected by groups. For example, on American turnpikes the rule is that traffic speed should not exceed 55 miles per hour, while the norm is to drive between 55 and 65 miles per hour.

A second important difference relates to the consequences of nonconformity. Among delinquents it is not unusual to gain peer group status by violating a rule. The act demonstrates bravado, or at least a refusal to obey the edict of an established authority. In contrast, violation of a group norm leads to loss of status within the group. The seriousness of the consequences depend upon the cohesiveness of the group, the importance of the norm, and the stature (within the group) of the violator.

Reliance upon rules to maintain control in institutions for delinquents suffers from several weaknesses. First, the delinquent has been socialized in a subculture which places high value on the ability to manipulate or "con" others, especially authority figures. Since many have little respect for authority and a strong incentive (i.e., peer group status) to disobey them, the imposition of rules confirms the delinquents' view of authority as oppressive and provides them with an opportunity to earn their stripes by "getting over on" (subverting) those in authority. Rules are rarely presented (never convincingly) as in the best interests of the boy. They are seen as instruments of control established by and for the convenience of institutional authorities; staff spend an inordinate amount of time enforcing them. They represent a challenge which the boys readily accept as part of a game that the institution finds difficult to win without abandoning all pretense of rehabilitation. In short, rules often create a "we-they" polarization of staff and students antithetical to a cooperative living environment.

Second, violation of rules must carry consequences, usually in the form of sanctions imposed by staff. If the sanctions vary from case to case, the staff are seen as unfair and "playing favorites." If the sanction is the same for all offenders, the results can be damaging in cases where the penalty is inappropriate. For example, loss of a home visit is a common sanction which can—for some boys (e.g., where interaction with family members is important to treatment goals)—be precisely the wrong course of action. Isolation is another common sanction which can have disastrous consequences for some boys. All the available options—consistent penalties, varying penalties or (perhaps most common of all) inconsistent enforcement of rules—are unsatisfactory for an institution which must provide both control and treatment.

Finally, reliance upon rules denies students participation in structuring their own living environment. Rules are imposed and enforced by staff, students have no role in the process beyond, perhaps, a token representative on a disciplinary committee. It is difficult to learn to live responsibly when the only decision you are ever asked to make is whether or not you will abide by someone else's code of conduct. There is no room in such a system for the notion of responsibility for *others'* behavior, which is essential to individual maturity and a core tenet of successful communal living arrangements.

Glen Mills has no rules.

Lack of rules does not suggest that Glen Mills is indifferent to student behavior. There are few institutions on earth which devote as much time and energy as Glen Mills to altering the behavior of its residents. But behavioral change is not achieved through administrative rules but through painstaking, systematic manipulation of peer group pressures. Rather than issue rules, Glen Mills' staff induce student leaders, and through them the peer group, to adopt and reinforce the desired behavior.

Like all institutions Glen Mills has norms, behaviors that residents, staff, and administrators expect of one another. The difference is that Glen Mills has shaped these norms, made them explicit and monitored them to insure that they are consistent with the goals of the institution. During his or her training, a new staff member learns the art and science of engineering group norms and social systems, what "the Glen Mills way" is, how to identify norms, why they are powerful in affecting behavior, and how to change them. One learns that, "around here," all staff and students

—treat each other with respect

—show pride in our own achievements and achievements of others

—take good care of property

—confront negative behavior.

These and dozens of other norms become evident as the trainee performs his or her role, talks with staff and students, observes others' behavior, experiences confrontation personally after transgressing a norm, and undergoes formal training.

Most importantly, the trainee learns how to confront. At Glen Mills confrontation is not a negative, destructive process; it is never intended to demean or humiliate. The Schools "normative systems" approach cannot succeed without constant attention to behavior, even behaviors that are seemingly inconsequential. Strong norms are established by rewarding positive behavior and confronting violators appropriately. It is essential that confrontations be respectful and not conducted out of arrogance or ego needs to exert authority. Staff work constantly to develop an appropriate confrontation style.

Equally important, staff learn to support confrontations by others when the subject of the confrontation is resisting ("blowing off") the confrontation. Positive norms cannot be maintained without confrontation, and confrontation will not occur unless the person doing the confronting feels secure in the knowledge that, if necessary, others will come to his support. Of all the norms at the Schools, none are more critical than these three: *treat others with respect; confront negative behavior; support confrontations.* All three are applicable to both staff and students. Without any one of them, Glen Mills' program would quickly disintegrate.

By the time training was completed the new staff members understood the Schools' philosophy and values. They understood the normative culture approach and the reasons Glen Mills had adopted it. Performance expectations were clear; they would feel no need to disguise any uncertainties since the "help" norm insured that they could count upon their supervisor and co-workers for guidance.

The campaign to establish positive staff norms would have to go beyond hiring and training. It would be necessary to shield new staff from negative influence by elements of the "old guard" who did not welcome the new regime.

Establishment of Glen Mills' normative culture would require staff who were physically and psychologically able to challenge delinquent norms. Men who were not intimidated by students' posturing or aggression. "Street smart" individuals who could not be conned. This profile contrasts sharply with that of the "helping profession" staff who had enjoyed high status under the prior regime. Resistance to the new staff role was nearly inevitable.

Tensions between veteran staff and the recent products of Mr. Ferrainola's training program surfaced on numerous occasions. In one instance two recent staff recruits came upon a student who was threatening his peers and staff with a section of lead pipe. A large group of students had assembled and were listening to several "old guard" staff attempt to persuade the boy to hand over the pipe. At the first opportunity, the two new staff wrestled the boy to the ground and took the pipe out of his hand. No one was injured.

The veteran staff were outraged. They expressed their disapproval of the two "street fighters" to both the administration and board members.

To no avail. The director praised the actions of his young staff. Imposition of a normative culture which insured staff and student safety required immediate and uncompromising response to any violence or threats. Some "street fighting" would be necessary to establish staff control of the institution and ensure that students could not achieve status through manipulation and violence. The primary issue at Glen Mills was appropriate student behavior. Students would not feel secure unless they could depend upon intervention against any who would intimidate them. Staff intervention to prevent aggressive behavior must be immediate; feelings could be dealt with later.

Some veteran staff were unconvinced, and they represented a significant threat to the new program model. The management team, experienced in the social dynamics of institutions, realized that the finest staff with the strongest possible training would be unable to maintain their effectiveness if placed in a cottage where their co-workers' norms were negative. The new staff worker would not long retain a positive attitude where the norms were to complain, to scapegoat, subvert, and avoid responsibility. Although most of the negative staff had been fired or laid off during the purge earlier in the year, a few cottage staff still lamented the loss of lock-ups and continued to grumble about the new leadership and treatment approach.

Needing a tool to develop an appropriate strategy, the director introduced his managers to the Lewinian method of force field analysis. The technique required the team leaders in each living unit to evaluate each staff members' role in maintaining the normative climate of the cottage. Who had high status? How much influence did they have with co-workers? Did they take initiative and accept responsibility? Were they good team players? Did they treat others, including students, with respect? Did they understand and support the program philosophy? How effectively did they confront negative behavior? Were they supportive of other staff? Did they play a positive, neutral, or negative role with regard to maintaining positive staff norms? Hundreds of hours of management time were used to analyze each cottage's "force field"—the constellation of positive and negative pressures a new staff member would experience if assigned to the unit.

The goal was to place new staff in the most positive force field possible. At that time (1976) there were three open cottages; it was decided to transfer all negative staff to one of them. No new staff were assigned to that unit. This was the final element in the strategy to create a positive "culture" or staff working environment. Applicants were carefully screened for the values and personal qualities (*not* prior experience) appropriate to their role. Then they were simultaneously immersed in a work setting from which negative influences had been systematically removed, and thoroughly trained in both the undergirding theory and the day to day performance requirements of the "Glen Mills way." Finally, the all-important team leader (cottage supervisor) slots were filled with individuals whose performance as counselors demonstrated their leadership ability, loyalty, and commitment to the program philosophy.

By the summer of 1977 a positive staff climate had been established. Staff in the "negative" cottage had succumbed to the now positive campus force field and had reformed, resigned, or been fired. In all, three-fourths of the 1974 staff complement had resigned or been forced out and replaced by young recruits attuned to the new system. The house was clean. The management team could now turn its full attention to the students.

ESTABLISHING THE STUDENT NORMATIVE CULTURE

It is not possible to overemphasize the importance of student norms, because positive peer group norms are an essential ingredient to individual growth. It is a rare adolescent who values the respect of adults above that of his peers. Consequently, the most skilled counselors will have little impact where the peer group norm is to bully, cheat, deny personal responsibility, and con authority figures; particularly in an institution where one or two hours per week is spent with the counselor and the remainder of the 168 hours with the peer group. When tardiness, disrespect for instructors, poor preparation, and denigration of education are valued by one's peers, even the best-stocked libraries and committed faculty will be ineffective. Modern equipment and training by experienced tradesmen will not produce skilled trainees where norms around care of tools, acceptance of supervision, and individual effort are weak. In a few cases instructors or counselors succeed in establishing ties with individual students strong enough to withstand negative peer pressures, but the price is rejection by one's peers. The adolescent's natural, healthy need for peer group acceptance usually overwhelms the efforts of even the most skilled staff in the absence of positive peer group norms.

Positive norms alone do not insure a strong program. Additional requirements include skilled instructors, adequate equipment, and techniques for evaluating performance. The norms represent a foundation; where they are weak the efforts of the finest instructors prove fruitless.

The major steps to the establishment of a positive student normative culture were clear. Glen Mills' leadership would first identify the norms to be established. Next, a mechanism would be developed to familiarize all new staff and students with the norms. The last and most difficult step would be to manipulate peer pressures to insure that high status in the student peer group was closely associated with conformity to positive prosocial norms.

The desired culture would be based upon the values of individual responsibility, support and respect for others, and achievement in academic, athletic, and vocational training. At Glen Mills, individuals would show respect for one another and never take another's dignity. Students would help each other and show pride in their peers' achievements. They would accept responsibility for their own behavior and confront negative behavior by others. Property would be respected. Students would demonstrate self-respect through cleanliness, a neat appearance, and an orderly living area. Participation and achievement in academic, vocational, athletic, and social programs would be acknowledged and supported by one's peers. When confronted about his behavior, a student would listen and accept the confrontation without argument. If he felt the confrontation was inappropriate, he would have the responsibility to raise the issue in a GGI session or cottage meeting.

Several dozen norms would be adequate to lay the foundation of the culture. In addition, however, Glen Mills' effectiveness was felt to require a clear differentiation of its normative culture from "street" norms. The personal values of the Schools' leadership were explicitly and unashamedly middle class. Glen Mills' students would be far better equipped to succeed in life if they were accustomed to living and working environments where middle-class values were dominant. Consequently, Glen Mills' experiment in social engineering would extend to the minutia of student behavior. For example, dress norms would be established to place one's foot inside sneakers (as opposed to the "street" style of tucking the back of the sneaker under one's heel); use only one's own soap; dry hair completely before going to the dining room; talk in a quiet, conversational tone of voice in the dining room; shave all facial hair; carry towels in hand when walking to the pool (as opposed to the "street" style of wearing them around the neck) etc. At the outset, it would only be necessary to identify a preliminary list of norms to be established. Having achieved success in establishing and changing norms, Glen Mills' management knew that the culture could be modified as the need arose.

Staff were familiarized with the student norms during their training. New students were oriented by their peers. During a cottage meeting on the boy's first night at the Schools, he is introduced to his cottage mates. Each in turn states his name and recites a norm: "I am Greg Williams and around here we eat all the food we take"; "I am Warren Smith and around here we keep eye to eye contact when spoken to"; "I am Larry Barnes and around here we don't yell on campus." The new student is assigned a "big brother," chosen for his positive behavior and high peer group status, who is responsible for the student's initial adjustment to the Schools. Finally, staff are especially attentive to his behavior and supportive of the big brother during the initial adjustment period.

A particularly vital staff role during the transition period was that of the "norm stabilizer." Norm stabilizers are physically powerful and unintimidatable staff whose primary responsibility is to ensure that campus norms are strong. Essential qualities include a positive attitude toward students, readiness to confront negative behavior, and a secure personality which does not seek to gain respect through intimidating others. Typically large, strong, streetwise, and easy going, norm stabilizers are both respected and liked by most students. They are able to literally and figuratively "speak the language" of the students.

The norm stabilizer function was key to the establishment of a safe and orderly campus where students need not fear intimidation, and where staff "technicians" (e.g., teachers, vocational instructors, coaches) could devote their time, expertise, and energies to instruction rather than the struggle to maintain order. The norm stabilizers radically altered the ground rules for achieving peer group status. Where disrespect, bullying, and "getting over" were once sure tickets to peer group status, they now invited relentless confrontation.

As staff confrontations increased, the incidence of bullying by students declined. However, the central goal in the normative culture approach—active student involvement in reinforcing normative behavior—had yet to be achieved.

By far the most difficult task in establishing the student norms is insuring that the students themselves reward and confront behaviors appropriately. GGI, with its emphasis upon use of peer pressures to mold behavior, is an important tool. But the key to success is the "turning" of natural student leaders from negative to positive role models. As long as the strong, high status students persist in "street" behavior no contending normative system can take hold.

The establishment of a positive student culture was a gradual process requiring many thousands of confrontations. In 1978 and 1979, two events were critical: the "turning" of Troy Upland (pseudonym) and the establishment of the Bulls Club.

Troy Upland was a street-smart Philadelphia gang leader committed to Glen Mills for armed robbery, and gang rape. He quickly became a strong but negative leader at the Schools. Operating through several henchmen, he intimidated other students and took anything he wanted from them. New students were introduced to Troy through his insistence that they buy a "bag of grass" from him for five dollars. Troy would take the money, bend over and tear up a handful of grass, put it in a bag, and give it to the boy. Most did not protest, the others were quickly and painfully put in their place by Troy and his henchmen.

Troy's influence was so powerful and so negative that there seemed little alternative to expulsion. But when his case was discussed with the director, he saw an opportunity to both help Troy and strengthen Glen Mills. Sam Ferrainola saw great potential in Troy and liked him. Troy was a natural leader, and very smart. If he could be "turned" positive, his leadership skills might be instrumental in establishing a constructive student culture.

Glen Mills had an unusual and important leverage with Troy. Both the director and Troy knew that the committing judge had kept charges open against Troy and mandated monthly review of his progress at Glen Mills. He had warned Troy that if he failed at Glen Mills he would be certified for trial as an adult and sent to prison. Sam Ferrainola reasoned that Troy was smart enough to realize what prison would mean for him and want to avoid it at all costs.

The director summoned Troy to his office and confronted him: "We can't both run this School. You want to do it the 'street' way through bullying, cheating, and stealing. That's not the Glen Mills way, and I won't let you do it. If you continue your way one of us will have to leave, and I am not ready. From now on, there will be no more conning and pushing around other students. You will set a good example, because if I even *suspect* that you're involved in misbehavior I'll send you back to court the same day. And I don't have to *know* you're involved. Staff will be watching your lieutenants, and the second any of them steps out of line we're coming after *you*. Now get out of my office. What you do will determine what I do."

Sam and Troy understood each other. Sam would do all he could to induce Troy to use his considerable leadership talents toward positive ends, but Troy had no doubt that Sam would make good on his threat. Suddenly there was a strong incentive not only to clean up his own act, but (and this is the crucial point) also to exert a positive influence upon his followers. Troy Upland was to become Glen Mills' first powerful, high status student committed to upholding positive norms. Initially, he did not internalize Glen Mills' values, but his role was pivotal in eliciting behavioral conformity—an important step in the establishment of a positive peer culture at Glen Mills.

The modeling of positive behavior by a high status group member has a powerful impact on group behavior even when the leader conforms for the "wrong" reasons. Often, a change in attitudes follows behavioral change. In Troy's case, he and his lieutenants developed real pride in Glen Mills, leading the Schools' football team to a 7–2 season and a stunning upset of the league champion in the final game. Troy returned to Glen Mills after his discharge to work as a staff aide.

Troy would not be at Glen Mills forever. The maintenance of a positive normative culture would require systematic change, not reliance upon individual students' influence. It would require a mechanism to ensure that strong, high status student leaders modeled and supported appropriate behavior. The vehicle chosen was an elite club for high status, positive student leaders. The club would have its own lounge and officers, operating with the guidance of a staff advisor. Membership, which would bring special privileges and important responsibilities, would be earned through positive behavior, academic achievement, and documented diligence in supporting campus norms. The Bulls Club would be, in effect, a well-organized and highly cohesive "gang" whose members were dedicated to upholding the Schools' values and norms. With the power of the club behind them, individual Bulls could successfully confront even the strongest negative students. Once established, the club would become a potent force insuring that street norms could never again gain a foothold at Glen Mills.

During the period 1977–80 four attempts were made to establish the Bulls Club, with the first three ending in failure. The major problem was that the club could not be started by the weaker students, nor permitted to operate under the leadership of high status negative students. A club without high status students would be powerless, a club dominated by negative leaders would be dangerous. A successful club required leadership from high status students who wielded real influence in their peer groups and had demonstrated commitment to the Schools' norms. The "natural leaders," however, had earned their reputations on the streets, achieving high status through delinquent behavior. They were the least likely to embrace the *via positiva*.

Success finally came through a combination of factors. Jay Halverson, a team leader in the Group Living Department, established a strong personal relationship with several high status students and began to meet with them regularly as a group. Recognition as a "club" brought with it specific privileges (e.g., use of a lounge with a pool table) and responsibilities. The latter were, initially, attacks upon specific but relatively minor norms such as shaking the game machines in the student union. Bulls were trained in how to confront other students in a way the students could accept, without demeaning them or causing them to lose face. When they failed to confront negative behavior or support a confrontation, staff would reprimand them. Gradually, Bulls were given authority commensurate with their responsibilities. For instance, Bulls were expected to monitor norms in the student union and had the authority to evict offenders. Finally, Bulls were given special incentives (e.g., home passes) to perform their jobs well.

By 1980 the student force field had tilted toward prosocial behavior, thanks to the role of the Bulls Club. Campus norms are monitored constantly by unit counselors and reported by their team leaders at a Monday morning meeting chaired by the director and attended by all senior staff. The Bulls Club officers are also present and participate in both the discussion of problems and development of strategies—the club works openly and directly with the Glen Mills administration to maintain "the Glen Mills way."

Exhibit 1.1 illustrates the dramatic effect of positive peer group norms and involvement of student leaders in maintaining the culture. Staff increasingly challenged negative student behavior during 1977–1980, and incidents of physical confrontations (i.e., those involving restraint or hitting) between staff and students rose sharply. As staff took control of the campus away from aggressive students, bullying declined equally sharply. After 1980, with high status students actively supporting the Schools' norms, the incidence of physical confrontations involving staff dropped by 75 percent, reflecting the diminished necessity for harsh confrontations as students and staff joined forces in support of a positive normative culture.

A core issue in building positive norms is the response to strong, negative

Exhibit 1.1
Percent of Students Reporting Physical Confrontations, by Year of Admission

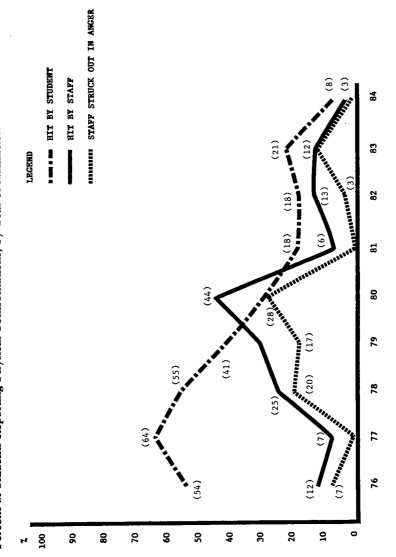

students who challenge the system. Prior to 1976, Glen Mills' staff was quick to press for expulsion of these students and the administration usually obliged. When Mr. Ferrainola asked his staff to work harder with these boys, he established a Review Board of department heads and unit team leaders to deal with disciplinary matters. The goal was to avoid expulsion and the process was harsh verbal confrontation of the misbehaving student by the board. The Review Board helped to stabilize the campus, contributed to staff cohesiveness, and helped enhance the status of the team leaders. But it too often traumatized the student who was the subject of the hearing. As the Bulls Club developed, it became an effective instrument for salvaging disruptive students, enabling Glen Mills to disband the Review Board in 1984.

EXPANDING THE STUDENT POPULATION

In addition to the establishment of an able and cohesive management team, recruitment and training of staff, and the establishment of a positive student culture, the expansion of the student population was essential to building the new Glen Mills.

Where peer norms were positive, the full development of students' intellectual, vocational, and athletic potential would be possible. A strong athletic program would bring physical fitness and an experience valuable to psychological development—achievement through teamwork and individual effort—while contributing to students' pride in their school. The director believed that his students' failure in the public schools stemmed more from a combination of the school system weaknesses and the boys' troublesome behavior and negative attitudes toward education than from a lack of intelligence. In the right social-psychological environment (i.e., peer group normative culture), with instructors skilled in group dynamics and supported by cottage staff, with first-rate libraries, laboratories, computers, and other instructional materials, a high school diploma and even a college education would be a realistic goal for many Glen Mills students.

For those interested in vocational training it would be necessary to provide an assessment center and a range of training options, with each requiring work space, shop equipment, and an instructor skilled in both his trade and Glen Mills' system. Finally, optimal learning and personal development would require attractive and comfortable surroundings: it is difficult to feel motivated and proud when one lives in squalid surroundings. Students' living space would have to be remodeled for comfort and privacy; furniture replaced; a new dining hall built; athletic fields and training rooms provided; landscaping upgraded, and a long list of other renovations to the physical plant completed.

Development of the finest program in the nation, Glen Mills' goal, would require more than just money. There were those who felt that delinquents do not *deserve* to be treated "like Rockefeller's kids." Indeed, Glen Mills' insistence on a top quality program ran directly counter to a prevailing sentiment as old as penology: the living conditions of criminals should not be more pleasant than those of even the poorest law abiding citizens. Why should society reward or cater to the needs of bad people? Even the strongest advocates of rehabilitation usually draw the line when it comes to serving choice cuts of steak and shrimp to inmates, or outfitting the track team with professional quality running shoes at $100 per pair.

Whatever the merits of this view as it applies to adult criminals, Mr. Ferrainola felt strongly that it was both morally wrong and, from a pragmatic perspective, foolish when applied to juveniles. The doubters would be won over as the students' pride, behavior, and achievement improved along with the quality of the program. Everyone's goal was to provide a humane and cost-effective program to help troubled youths become proud and productive citizens. The director was certain that deprivation for deprivation's sake was an impediment to the habilitation process. Glen Mills' achievement of the goal would prove this to even the most skeptical open-minded observer.

The philosophical/theoretical issues, though important, were long-range concerns. In 1977 the immediate need was to stem operating losses and bring in the revenue required for the transformation of Glen Mills. There were two keys to success. The first would be to minimize staffing costs. Overstaffing is both expensive and ineffective. It tends to reduce individual initiative and, permitting unmotivated staff to hide in the bloated bureaucracy, can be disastrous for maintaining a strong and positive staff normative culture.

The second need was to increase the student population. The Admissions Department would have to be restructured. Historically, Glen Mills' admissions policy had been reactive: Admissions staff would await calls from juvenile court workers seeking to have students admitted. The director introduced a new role for Admissions: it would become the Schools' marketing and sales department. Staff would become proactive and skilled in "selling" Glen Mills to the various counties.

The director found a willing and capable admissions director in Garry Ipock, whom he appointed to the position in early 1976. Both men worked hard to promote Glen Mills, with the director focusing upon Pennsylvania's two largest counties and Mr. Ipock marketing Glen Mills to the other counties in the eastern and central regions of the state. As recently as 1975 half of Glen Mills' admissions were from a single "client" county, Philadelphia. Were this to continue, the Schools would be vulnerable to pressures from Philadelphia officials. The marketing goals were to diversify, and to familiarize the various county juvenile courts with the new Glen Mills program and philosophy. Court personnel would henceforth be treated like valued customers.

The marketing strategy was highly effective. Most counties knew nothing of the new administration or the Schools' admission policy which, back in 1976, had been to accept any breathing male delinquent. Court officials, who were unaccustomed to personal attention and professional courtesies from institutional directors, were pleased at Glen Mills' eagerness to identify and accommodate their needs (e.g., in relation to timely and complete reports, etc.). They were gratified by the invitation to visit the Schools and discuss its program personally with staff and students. Ipock and Ferrainola conveyed a sense of purpose and excitement about Glen Mills. Most institutions received visitors with the same enthusiasm as dental work: a necessary evil, but nothing to look forward to. There was something different about an institution which welcomed them with an openness and pride they had seldom experienced ("Come any time you'd like. Choose any student, and that student will show you our School. Spend as much time as you want discussing what it's like here. Afterward, we hope you'll have time to join the director for lunch or dinner. Students and staff eat together here, so you'll have a good meal and an opportunity to observe and ask questions.")

During his years in the Pittsburgh area Mr. Ferrainola had earned the respect of officials at the Allegheny County juvenile court. Drawing upon these contacts, he was able to achieve some early success for his new marketing program. As usual, Glen Mills would make every effort to service the county. In this case Glen Mills purchased a bus to provide for cost-effective, regular home visits for Pittsburgh area students, who would need to be transported more than 300 miles each way.

Glen Mills' marketing strategy has been extremely successful. Since 1976 the Schools' student population has steadily increased and the "client" base diversified with reduced dependence upon Philadelphia and Pittsburgh. By the end of 1978 Glen Mills was out of debt and achieved an operating surplus.

While courtesy and attention to the county officials has been a cornerstone of the admissions policy, the more fundamental key to success has been the quality of the program itself. As admissions expanded to 32 of the 67 Pennsylvania counties and several other states, the basic marketing message was always the same: Evaluate our program for yourself; if you can obtain better or more cost-effective services for your young men someplace else, go there. But if not, give us a try.

While the director and Garry Ipock played the most visible roles in building the student population, success was ultimately due in equal measure to the ability of the Group Living Department under Tom Beecher to maintain the campus normative culture during periods of rapid growth. Staff were continually asked to stretch a little further to accommodate more students, until the opening of an additional cottage and hiring of new staff could be justified. Student norms were continually challenged as successful, positive boys were discharged and a larger number of new students, fresh from the streets, took their place. The impact of 20 new students is easily absorbed when there are 300 students upholding positive norms. But the acceptance of the same 20 students presents a threat to the normative culture of 50 students, especially when the 10 most mature and positive students have recently been discharged. If the new group includes a strong negative leader, the campus force field could be in real danger.

The general strategy of the Group Living Department was to (1) carefully monitor new students, (2) attempt to "turn" strong negative leaders and, if this failed, to (3) discharge those who posed a threat to peer group norms. Every student at Glen Mills was evaluated weekly by the cottage team within the framework of Polsky's "diamond" (Polsky, 1962); results of the evaluation were posted on the cottage bulletin board; leaders and their lieutenants were iden-tified. All staff on campus were made aware of new students with the potential to influence campus norms. Their behavior and GGI participation was carefully observed; any negative behaviors quickly drew staff attention in the form of confrontations and individual counseling. Discharge was a last resort but pref-erable to endangering the all-important normative culture.

By the end of 1980, with the student census at 292 and rising, the population had grown large enough to support strong program development and diversifi-cation. The foundation of the new Glen Mills, its culture, was in place.

The Schools' distinctive normative culture is the indispensable core of Glen Mills' treatment model (see Exhibit 1.2). All else—the nature of Glen Mills' traditions, relationships with external systems, even the daily routine and the physical plant—are designed to strengthen the basic fabric of the culture. No employee is hired or promoted, no program is developed, without considering the impact upon the culture.

Every organization has a culture. Glen Mills' culture is unusual in three respects. First, the culture is explicit. In most organizations culture is not directly discussed and its power to influence organizational effectiveness is only vaguely perceived, if at all. At Glen Mills, norms, values, and even the concept of the normative culture are central elements in the orientation of all staff and students. Second, Glen Mills' culture is consciously, deliberately designed to promote the Schools' objectives, the habilitation of "socialized" male delinquents. The Schools' culture does not evolve by chance, but is carefully engineered to serve its intended purpose. Finally, the culture is continually monitored, both directly (using a norms measurement tool developed at the Schools) and indirectly (via charting the incidence of various student behaviors). Evidence of the weakening of the culture in any living unit or program provokes an immediate, coordinated response by the entire management team.

At Glen Mills, the culture is more than an important ingredient in treatment. The culture is considered the sine qua non for program effectiveness. The primary responsibility of Glen Mills staff is not to help individual students, but to maintain a strong and positive institutional culture.

Students' social behavior and their progress in academic, vocational, and athletic programs are more strongly determined by the normative culture than by the dedication and competence of staff. When the culture is strong and positive, conditions are optimal for the full flowering of individual potential. If the culture is weak, or encourages delinquent values and behaviors, even highly capable students with the most technically skilled teachers and counselors will frequently fail to show positive change, since to do so is to risk ostracism (or worse) from one's peer group.

Exhibit 1.2
Key Elements of the Glen Mills Schools' Culture

CULTURE

The totality of socially transmitted behavior patterns, arts, beliefs, institutions, and all other products of human work and thought characteristic of a community. (American Heritage Dictionary)

Listed below are the core beliefs, values, behavior patterns (norms) and taboos of Glen Mills' culture.

BELIEFS

Glen Mills students are not "bad" people. They are as deserving of respect and dignity as our own children or any other adolescents.

Glen Mills students are as psychologically sound as any other group of adolescents.

The primary causes of most delinquency are individuals' needs for survival, belonging and status coupled with the inability to satisfy these needs through prosocial behavior within one's community.

Staff and students alike have enormous potential for growth which can be realized if the social environment is both supportive and challenging.

Habilitation is achieved most effectively and most economically when programs, facilities and equipment are of top quality.

Innovation in pursuit of an important objective can never fail. Either it will succeed, or enable us to proceed toward the desired results with a better understanding.

VALUES

Respect for self and others	Academic and Vocational Achievement
Persistence in working toward goals	Cleanliness
Teamwork	Pride in self and Glen Mills
Self-discipline	Loyalty
Enthusiasm	Involvement

STUDENT NORMS

There is no formal list of Glen Mills' norms, but there are well over one hundred relating to interpersonal behavior, dress, hygiene and work habits; as well as conduct on and off campus, in cottages, classrooms and the dining room, and at athletic events. Some examples:

At Glen Mills, we...

    Treat all others with respect
    Confront all negative behavior
    Accept confrontation
    Support confrontation
    Do not touch others in an unwelcomed way
    Do not "con" or "get over" on others
    Never intimidate others or give them a "hard look"
    Bathe daily
    Maintain a clean and neat appearance
    Keep shirt tucked in
    Lace sneakers all the way up
    Always wear socks
    Complete assignments on time
    Set personal goals for academic growth and strive to achieve them

Exhibit 1.2 (continued)

```
Wash our own laundry
"Own up" during cottage meetings and apologize for any negative behavior
Keep beds made and living area neat and clean
Show pride in our own and others' achievements
Take good care of all property and equipment
Behave like gentlemen
Establish eye contact and greet visitors
Pay attention in class
Support our athletic teams
Do not "table hop" in the dining room
Show courtesy to students and athletes of other schools at athletic events
Speak in conversational tones in the dining room
```

A list of norms prepared by Dr. Claus Ottmüller (1987) is included in Appendix 1.

STAFF NORMS

At Glen Mills, staff...

```
Treat all others with respect
Confront all negative behavior
Support confrontation
Accept confrontation
Discuss any concerns with their supervisor
Provide all possible encouragement and support to students
Volunteer for assignments beyond their job responsibilities
Give and accept honest feedback regarding job performance
Support projects and programs of other staff
Show pride in Glen Mills
Model appropriate behavior
Demonstrate loyalty to other staff; work as a team
Never undercut other staff
Initiate creative projects
Perform job responsibilities to the best of their ability
Take good care of property and equipment
Strive to make Glen Mills a little better each week
```

TABOOS

```
Treating anyone disrespectfully
Failure to get involved
Withholding requested support
Avoiding responsibility
Competitiveness in lieu of cooperativeness
```

The values and beliefs listed in Exhibit 1.2 define and are essential to Glen Mills' normative culture, as are the student and staff norms directly related to maintenance of the culture (e.g., those dealing with confrontation) or to its core values (e.g., "At Glen Mills, we treat all others with respect"). Less crucial, though still important, are the dozens of norms (e.g., "At Glen Mills, we lace our sneakers all the way up") established to differentiate Glen Mills from the street culture. The objective of the latter is to encourage students to disassociate from delinquent reference groups and adopt the prosocial values and behaviors promoted by Glen Mills.

Glen Mills' culture is radically different from that of most large correctional institutions. The belief that students are "neither bad nor mad" sets the Schools apart from punitive and therapeutically oriented institutions, respectively. Glen

Mills considers itself a fine prep school, *not* an institution for bad boys. It labels its students "normal."

Visitors are invariably struck by the quality of the Schools' physical environment. Institutions rarely provide their residents with top quality facilities. It is felt that delinquents do not deserve or would not take care of fine furnishings, equipment, clothing, etc., and that funds are better used to expand staff or improve salaries.

Residents of institutions are usually considered to be unpromising material, with little potential for positive change. This view, in effect, blames the students, rather than the program for lack of growth. At Glen Mills, the failure of students to make strong progress is considered evidence that the program, not the student has failed.

Glen Mills' emphasis upon innovation is unusual in large institutions, which are highly vulnerable to bureaucratization and tend to pay lip service to innovation in principle while discouraging it in practice.

Finally, the consistent emphasis upon respect and the absolute right of every person to be treated with dignity differentiates Glen Mills from many confrontation-based or behavioristic programs. Establishment of a powerful normative culture requires a mechanism for shaping behavior. Glen Mills relies heavily upon confrontation but confrontation can only be effective if it is deeply rooted in respect and caring. It would not be too wide of the mark to describe Glen Mills' approach as behavior modification with a heart.

Establishment of the new culture had required five years and the termination, voluntary or otherwise, of most of the staff who had served under the previous administration. The transition had been difficult. But Sam Ferrainola and his management team, having led the Schools safely through a period of crisis, had earned the confidence of both the Board and staff. All things were ready for the next stage of Glen Mills' transformation.

PRINCIPLES OF ORGANIZATIONAL CHANGE

The events at Glen Mills from 1975 to 1980 illustrate several principles of institutional change which are applicable in other juvenile correctional settings, and perhaps to organizations in general. They are presented here in the belief that administrators will find them useful and thought provoking.

The first principle is that in organizational development, as in individual development, *crises present opportunities* for fundamental change which must be recognized and seized if similar crises (or worse) are to be avoided in the future. The Chinese word for "crisis" consists of two characters, one representing "danger" and the other "opportunity." Crises are painful periods of stress and turmoil, times when something has "gone wrong" and the usual methods of coping are ineffective. If the response is to relieve the pain without addressing the basic causes, the crisis is sure to recur unless the patient (individual or organizational) dies. The problem is that fundamental changes are acutely anxiety-provoking.

In organizational terms they produce maximum uncertainty about the future and frequently involve a reallocation of roles and authority which threatens the positions of influential staff. Furthermore, no one can guarantee that the changes will prove any more salutary than the status quo. For every one of history's crazy ideas that turned out to be a brilliant solution to a theretofore insoluble problem, there are hundreds of crazy ideas that turned out to be crazy ideas. For these reasons, those advocating fundamental changes find few allies but many strong opponents.

The scope of the crisis at Glen Mills in 1975 was frightening, the Schools' future very much in doubt. Ironically, a lesser crisis may well have proved fatal, since it may have made possible successful resistance to sorely needed changes. The changes introduced by Mr. Ferrainola were radical, particularly the dismantling of the custodial-clinical treatment model in favor of the normative culture coupled with the absurd notion that delinquents should be treated like rich people's kids. So deep and sweeping a change would have been unthinkable in the absense of a major, life-threatening crisis. By 1975 most staff feared that Glen Mills' campus would soon become yet another suburban housing development. The director's strength was in his ability to use crises to build support for change, and to project the optimism and commitment necessary to induce others to support his unusual vision for Glen Mills' future.

A second principle is that *organizational change requires simultaneous attention to political, cultural, and, technical systems.* How and by whom are decisions made, resources allocated, and policies implemented? What are the values and norms of the desired culture? What are the tools and processes through which the organization's work is carried out? Historically, organizational change theorists have focused upon one or another of these questions in isolation from the other two. Glen Mills' experience supports the view of Noel Tichy (1983), whose contributions to the field include the principle that the change process requires simultaneous attention to all three systems, since they are interdependent.

In Glen Mills' case, for example, the "molecular" organization (political systems issue) is congruent with the (cultural) values of teamwork and shared responsibility, while a hierarchical model is not. Had Glen Mills restricted its attention to the cultural arena and attempted to graft a new normative culture onto the existing hierarchical organization, the likelihood of success would have been greatly reduced. A second example involves the cultural and technical systems. The (cultural) norms relating to respect for teachers, and the values placed upon academic and vocational effort are essential to the success of the "technical". educational programs. In fact, the most important component of the technical system (i.e., the process through which "treatment" occurs) is the culture itself! There is no chance that an upgraded treatment program, however great the resources committed to it, would have been effective unless it was accompanied by significant cultural changes. Finally, by establishing a (technical) training system that "fit" the Schools' culture, Glen Mills avoided a problem well known to corrections officials. Training of corrections staff is often ineffective because the policies and values implicit in the training are antithetical to those of the staff culture (Duffee, 1974). At Glen Mills, the primary focus of training *is* the culture.

Because the political, cultural, and technical systems are so strongly interdependent, the change process requires a vision of how all three will be effected. Criteria for staff selection and the specification of roles, both of which impact the political system, depend in part upon a definition of the treatment ("technical" system) process. The treatment process, if it is to be effective, must be consistent with the institution's culture; therefore the development of programs must take cultural factors into account. Staff and student norms must in turn be supportive of treatment objectives.

The three ring circus quality of this process suggests a third principle, that *the change process is heuristic, requiring careful monitoring of effects.* During and subsequent to Glen Mills' transition period there was a "let's try it and see if it works" orientation to program development which strongly encouraged experimentation with different educational and treatment approaches, constrained only by the requirement that they be consistent with the Schools' values. These various experiments were evaluated through careful monitoring of their costs and effects upon campus norms and student achievement. A similar approach was used for personnel assignments, and role definitions. Here again, the process illustrates both an experimental approach to institutional management and the interrelationships of political and cultural issues. When an individual was promoted to a new position but, despite genuine effort, did not perform satisfactorily, he was reassigned without stigma to a role where he could better serve Glen Mills. For staff who are committed to the Schools there is no such thing as a demotion, only a change in responsibilities.

Glen Mills' creativity, openness to new ideas, and willingness to risk failure and learn from mistakes are among its greatest strengths. These appear to be characteristic of effective correctional programs in general as suggested by a Rand Corporation study of treatment programs for serious juvenile offenders:

The best programs we encountered seemed to be using their failures as a guide to new initiatives and eventual success. They were conscious of their own performance and took a frankly problem-solving, trial-and-error attitude toward their work. Given what is known—and especially what is not known—about intervening with serious juvenile offenders, such an heuristic management strategy is emphatically indicated. (Mann, 1976: 80)

Ingredients of the Schools' culture which nourish creativity include a belief that the "state of the art" in corrections is primitive and that there is a great deal of room for improvement. Perseverance, innovation, and the desire to improve one's own performance and that of the Schools' are highly valued. The management process is highly participatory; everyone's ideas are heard. There are strong norms requiring honest and direct discussion and feedback. Unequivocal interpersonal and interdepartmental support is expected of all staff. Perhaps most importantly, it is safe to voice unconventional opinions or suggest novel approaches because of the very strong taboo against "put downs," whether expressed directly or disguised as constructive criticism.

Finally, several additional change principles are suggested by *Modern Management and Machiavelli*, Richard Buskirk's (1974) application of Niccolo Machiavelli's maxims for governing a state to the problems of managing organizations. Noting that Machiavelli's reputation for unscrupulous cunning and dishonesty is largely undeserved and has served to obscure the value of his insights for managers, Buskirk presents several pertinent pieces of advice gleaned from Machiavelli's writings:

An army should have but one chief: a greater number is detrimental. . . . It is better to confide any expedition to a single man of ordinary ability, rather than to two even though they are men of the highest merit. (pp. 189–90)

Both Sam Ferrainola and Saul Pilnick were highly qualified and experienced professionals. Both wanted to do a good job. But there was no "chief": Mr. Ferrainola had the title but Dr. Pilnick had both the board's confidence and the leading role in the crucial areas of senior staff recruitment and training. With two leaders of the highest merit, little positive change occurred.

A prince must not mind incurring the charge of cruelty for the purpose of keeping his subjects united and faithful. . . . He will be more merciful than those who, from excess of tenderness, allow disorders to arise, from whence spring bloodshed and rapine; for these as a rule injure the whole community, while the executions carried out by the prince injure only individuals. And of all princes, it is impossible for a new prince to escape the reputation of cruelty, new states being always full of dangers. (Buskirk, 1974: 53)

Many staff at Glen Mills were resistant to the radical changes introduced by the new director. Some disagreed with the new program philosophy and/or its implementation. Others felt they would lose status or influence under the new system. Still others engaged in scapegoating to avoid accepting responsibility for the prevailing chaos, thereby setting themselves at odds with the most basic element of the new director's management approach, his insistence on teamwork. The director spent an entire year in the attempt to win over these individuals; in many cases he did not succeed. Perhaps a different but still "kind" approach would have been successful; perhaps the objective was impossible to achieve. What is clear is that the continuing staff fractiousness was harmful to staff and students alike and severely damaging to the "whole community." The healing and growth process did not begin until the staff purges of December 1975 and early 1976.

Machiavelli's thesis about the precedence of the needs of the community over individual needs is nowhere more evident than at Glen Mills. Basic to Glen Mills' philosophy is the belief that individual student's needs for safety, security, belonging, education, etc., are best secured when group norms are strong. The Schools' goal is to maintain an environment which benefits all students. For example, Glen Mills' administration believes that all students have the right to a good education, and that this requires classroom norms restricting individual's rights to distract others by unnecessary movement, talking out of turn, etc. The Schools encourage individuality, but never at the expense of group rights, including the right to learn in a safe and orderly environment. Tolerance for negative acts which interfere with these rights, defended by some programs as an acceptance of individuality or an accommodation to students' limitations, is regarded by Glen Mills as a serious offense against the community which ultimately victimizes the actor as well.

Whoever becomes prince . . . , especially if the foundation of his power is feeble (should) organize the government entirely anew. (Buskirk, 1974: 98)

In late 1975 and early 1976 the foundation of the director's power was feeble indeed, but it was during this period that Mr. Ferrainola appointed Tom Beecher and Garry Ipock to key management positions and began to replace key staff recruited by Saul Pilnick with individuals loyal to himself who shared his vision for Glen Mills. His tenure would have been brief had he relied for the implementation of his policies upon senior staff who felt neither indebted toward him nor committed to his goals.

There can be no worse example in a republic than to make a law and not observe it. (Buskirk, 1974: 109)

Top management modeling of behavior is essential in any system that relies upon the power of a normative culture to regulate behavior. Establishment of the Glen Mills' norms required that the entire community (staff and students) treat one another with respect, confront negative behavior, and support confrontations. Conformity to these and less critical norms by top management was essential and expected. Staff are themselves subject to confrontation, as the director learned upon lighting his cigar in the dining room when he (mistakenly) believed that all the students had left the area. Mr. Ferrainola was confronted politely by a student, put out his cigar, apologized, and then commended the student.

Contempt and insults engender hatred toward those who indulge in them, without being of any advantage to them. (Buskirk, 1974: 136)

The Glen Mills program is anchored in the bedrock of basic respect for human dignity. Confrontations can be harsh and sometimes angry when individuals lose control of their emotions. But the demeaning of another person is a rare event, and one that does not go unconfronted regardless of the status of the speaker.

Exhibit 1.3
Glen Mills Schools: 1975 vs. 1980

	1 9 7 5	1 9 8 0
Operant view of causes of delinquency	Social/Familial deprivations lead to character disorder	Social/Familial deprivations lead to delinquent behavior
Program goals	Custody and rehabilitation	Custody and habilitation
Program methods	Locks, bars and individualized treatment	Normative culture
Organizational structure	Hierarchical	Molecular
Physical plant	Deteriorated/Condemned	Restored
Fiscal operating principles	Social service agency	Business
Financial status	Near bancruptcy after successive annual operating losses	Operating surplus
Programs	Social casework; limited academic and recreational	GGI, academic, athletic, recreational, limited vocational
Student population	35	270
Per diem charges	$121	$70

With regard to the importance of basic respect during Glen Mills' transition, it should be noted that the director had numerous opponents during his first 15 months while his supporters were few and lukewarm. Had he lashed out contemptuously he would have driven those who were open-minded into his opponents' camp.

Finally, it was the violation of Machiavelli's dictum by Mr. Ferrainola's opponents that led to their undoing. The viciousness of the letter sent to Glen Mills' Board in December of 1975 resulted in the discharge of its authors.

To summarize, by the end of 1980 strong and capable staff had been recruited and trained (see Exhibit 1.3). An expanded population provided cash flow required to restore and expand the physical plant and strengthen the fledgling academic, vocational, athletic, and recreational programs. A performance evaluation system had been developed to clarify staff responsibilities and provide for accountability and staff development. The admissions process had been greatly strengthened and a strategy designed to reduce Glen Mills' dependence upon Philadelphia and Allegheny (Pittsburgh) counties. Most important, the values and norms of the Glen Mills culture were firmly in place and there was a sense of excitement about the Schools' future at all levels.

The Schools had begun the metamorphosis from institution to community.

Relationships among administrators, staff, and students were increasingly governed by an emotional identification with Glen Mills and a feeling of belonging. The notion was beginning to take hold that, by working together, everyone in the community could benefit more than by putting their own interests first.

Programmatically, much remained to be done and the director frequently reminded his managers that "We're not a good school yet." But the viability of Glen Mills' program was no longer an issue. It remained to be seen how good the Schools could become.

2

Glen Mills

Program in 1988

I must study war and politics so that my children shall be free to study
commerce, agriculture and other practicalities, so that their children can
study painting, poetry and other fine things.

John Adams

The early years of Mr. Ferrainola's administration were dominated by the study
of "war and politics"—the need to establish his authority as executive director,
build a capable and loyal staff, and restore an orderly atmosphere on campus.
By 1980, with these objectives achieved and Glen Mills' philosophy and culture
firmly established, a shift in priorities signaled a new phase in the Schools'
development. Glen Mills managers turned their attention to the development
of a broad range of academic, vocational, and athletic programs. These would
provide students with the practicalities of knowledge, skills, and teamwork to
prepare them for life in their communities.

Glen Mills would seek to develop the finest programs available in the nation.
Funding for equipment, facilities, and staff would have to come from operating
revenues, which in turn would require an expanded enrollment. Accordingly,
program development and increased enrollment became the primary objectives
from 1980 through 1986. The objectives proved mutually reinforcing: revenues
from larger enrollments enabled the Schools to expand and diversify its programs.
Conversely, the availability of a broad range of programs contributed to the
success of Glen Mills' proactive admissions (marketing) department in recruiting
new students.

The program development plan involved recruiting instructors and coaches
from the ranks of the cottage workers, for two reasons. First, cottage staff have

the skills necessary to work within the Glen Mills system. It is considered essential that all programs reflect the Schools' philosophy and operate within the framework of the campus normative culture. For example, students in a vocational shop are never "punished" for violating shop "rules"; they are confronted for transgressing shop norms. Since order is a prerequisite of effective instruction, it is important that teachers be skilled in Glen Mills' approach to the management of peer group pressures and confrontation. The cottage is the arena where these skills are sharpened. Second, prior working relationships with cottage staff facilitate performance as an instructor or coach. Cottage treatment activities (e.g., GGI) and program participation are all part of an integrated treatment process requiring a very high level of staff cooperation and teamwork. The latter are core values of the Glen Mills culture. Staff who are unwilling to go the extra mile to support peers in their own and other departments are soon weeded out. The assignment of instructors with prior experience as cottage staff facilitates teamwork.

The major steps in the program development process were, first, to be sensitive to applicants' special skills or hobbies when interviewing prospective cottage counselors. An individual who had experience as a tutor, or enjoyed photography, or had played on his college soccer team could be a future teacher, vocational trainer or coach. Second: provide strong support for staff who take initiative in developing a program area. For example, a cottage counselor who wishes to form a new athletic team will be helped to assess student interest, schedule practices, recruit assistants, obtain top quality equipment and uniforms, etc. Significantly, he will not receive extra salary or be relieved of his cottage responsibilities: the motivation must be to take advantage of Glen Mills' support to develop a program of which he and the Schools will be proud. Third, develop specific, measurable objectives for both staff and students in each program area and monitor performance. Fourth, hold staff accountable for achieving results.

In a field which frequently blames students for their failure, the latter principle deserves special emphasis. Glen Mills' managers believe that the Schools' students arrive with enormous potential. Their academic potential, for example, is unrealized because they have not experienced an educational system featuring both cooperative efforts of skilled teachers and a peer culture supportive of scholastic achievement. Since Glen Mills provides the peer culture, good facilities and equipment, and supportive ancillary programs and staff, the rest is up to the individual instructors.

It is considered axiomatic that a normal adolescent will succeed if teachers are competent and instruction is provided in an environment where academic programs are appropriate to his level; where peers and staff alike encourage academic effort; where effort brings meaningful rewards and recognition; where role models include many young men who succeeded despite deficits similar to his own. It is the staff's responsibility to provide both the instruction and the environment. Therefore, at Glen Mills *only the faculty or system can fail, never students.*

The fifth program development principle is: honor those who work hard to make a program succeed. Ultimately, the success of a project is of less concern than a willingness to extend oneself in service to the Schools. There is no shame in doing one's best in a losing cause. Glen Mills' managers believe that the state of the art in juvenile corrections is primitive; that pioneers are needed to blaze new trails and that pioneers can be expected to make a wrong turn occasionally. The most effective staff may have the most failures to their "credit," not because they are less competent but because they are willing to risk and extend themselves where others fear to leave the well-marked paths. Glen Mills' goal is to nurture staff who are willing to break new ground, who have the determination to push through obstacles and the ego strength to risk failure in order to achieve their goals.

It is worth stressing that the valuing of creativity at Glen Mills extends well beyond a willingness to accept wrong turns as the price of progress. Rather, it involves the core belief that an attempted new approach consistent with the objectives of the organization *cannot fail.* It will either succeed, or open new avenues to achieve the desired result. In the words of Henry Ford, whose credentials as a pioneer are quite good: "Failure is the opportunity to begin again more intelligently."

The program development and "marketing" strategies were highly successful. During 1986 the student population reached 525, the Schools' capacity. The academic program included five levels of instruction. A rigorous vocational assessment process and 18 job training courses were offered. The athletic department fielded 13 varsity teams; all students participated in an innovative intramural program. A full schedule of day, evening, and weekend programs was run by 333 full- and part-time staff. By 1988 expansion had enabled the Schools to enroll more than 625 students, with 372 full-time and 16 part-time staff (.62 staff per student).

Programs in all Glen Mills' departments and the organizational structure itself continue to evolve. Cultural supports for innovation and continual progress serve as a protection against stagnation. Frequent and honest feedback, objective evaluation, and management by objectives guard against wasting resources on "crazy ideas."

Innovation is strongly encouraged at all levels: individual, departmental, and organizational. For example, at the individual level academic instructors have immediate access to as much as $500 which can be spent without prior approval to promote educational objectives. One instructor, faced with several students who found the statement "One-eighth is less than one-fourth" to be counterintuitive, asked his charges whether they would prefer an eighth or a quarter of a pizza. He then ordered several pizzas and distributed the different sized slices accordingly, providing a lesson of impact to those who had opted for the "eighth"!

Innovations at the departmental level have improved programs while containing costs. The Group Living Department, for example, provides a $400 monthly allowance to each cottage for the purchase of cleaning and maintenance materials; any unspent funds are credited to a cottage entertainment fund each month. The result has been that students have assumed the responsibility to clean and care for their living units to maximize the monies available for parties, purchase of TVs, trips, etc. Since standards are high and performance of chores carefully monitored, the cottages are spotless. The Group Living program was strengthened and its cost reduced through a policy that provided an incentive to student responsibility for their living units. Academic Hall and Tradesman Hall, honors units where living unit staff also serve as teachers and vocational instructors, are further examples of innovations which were both programmatically and fiscally sound.

At the organizational level, the molecular structure and the normative culture itself are the most important innovations at Glen Mills. Other examples include programs that cut across departmental boundaries. The most ambitious of these was the "Prep" program, which provided financial support for 20 talented athletes to work, train, and study at Glen Mills, enabling them to qualify for admission to major universities.

Typically, "Prep" students were athletically skilled and motivated minority high school graduates who failed to receive athletic scholarships solely due to poor scholastic records. These young men were offered student jobs and courses designed to upgrade their academic skills, enabling them to qualify for admission to college. Their presence at Glen Mills provided positive academic and behavioral role models for the other students, strengthened the Schools' athletic program, augmented the ranks of the cottage staff, and led to the development of the College Prep program, which subsequently became a core program of the Academic Education Department.

The Prep program exemplifies the Schools' win-win philosophy: programs and policies will be successful to the extent that all stakeholders derive significant benefits from them. In this case, the "Prep" athletes, the Glen Mills students, and the Schools' Group Living, Academic, and Athletics programs were all "winners." In addition, the Schools' business manager was able to add 20 staff at minimal cost, making productive use of "excess capacity" in the form of unfilled beds. The Admissions Department welcomed the considerable favorable publicity generated by the program.

The "Prep" program for athletes was discontinued in 1982, but the college prep course of study which it spawned is still available to Glen Mills' students.

The Schools' emphasis upon continual growth ensures that any description of its organizational structure is soon outdated. The following sections provide a "snapshot" of Glen Mills' structure in 1988 and the critical events that helped to shape it.

ORGANIZATIONAL STRUCTURE

Many factors contributed to the Schools' success. A dedicated Board of Managers maintained its resolve despite recurring crises. A strong and determined executive director earned the loyalty of his top managers and molded them into a cohesive, effective team. The carefully constructed Glen Mills "culture"—the beliefs, values, and behavioral norms of staff and students—was fertile soil for the development of strong programs, run by carefully selected and trained staff who took as much pride in the Schools' and students' accomplishments as in their own. If there is a single "secret" to the Schools' success, it is management's recognition of the interdependencies among all these factors; the ability to exploit each in support of the others, recognizing that the whole is indeed far greater than the sum of the parts. Glen Mills is managed as a system of highly interrelated functions, not as a collection of quasi-independent departments. This is achieved through an organizational structure unique in the field.

The role and importance of Glen Mills' "molecular structure" have been poorly understood by most visitors to the Schools. The structure is designed to promote teamwork and mutual support among departments, a goal reflected in the designation of staff allegiances and responsibilities (see Exhibit 2.1).

The molecular structure sharply reduces the interdepartmental "turf" battles that plague large organizations. The structure is unique in that senior staff are primarily concerned with campuswide issues rather than the operation of their departments. Team leaders, the senior Group Living Department staff responsible for the management of the cottage teams, have the maintenance of campuswide norms (not the effectiveness of their individual cottages) as their primary responsibility. Likewise, Glen Mills' top managers owe their primary allegiance to each other rather than to their individual departments. In combination with strong norms of staff participation in decision making and unqualified support for team decisions, the structure insures that managements' approach to campuswide issues will be uniform, coordinated, and supported by all departments.

The molecular structure is a good "fit" to the Schools' culture. Key elements of that culture are values and beliefs relating to groups and individuals. At the student level, the needs of the group are valued over the needs of individuals. It is believed that individual growth comes from the harnessing of peer group pressures. Individuals are encouraged to help others and share responsibility for their peers' welfare. The molecular model operationalizes identical values at the organizational level: the needs of the institution are given precedence over those of individual departments. Individual departments benefit from the coordinated support of all department heads; top managers are primarily responsible to help each other through "a cohesive team approach," and only secondarily for departmental advocacy. All staff are responsible to support the cottage units.

By stressing the norm of shared responsibility the molecular structure facilitates systems solutions to problems requiring interdepartmental coordination. A typical instance involved the underutilization of the afternoon vocational training programs, a concern raised by the department's director during a meeting of the executive director and his "resource team" of department heads. Discussion indicated that the crux of the problem was the reluctance of cottage counselor-teachers to release their charges from individualized basic skills instruction.

Exhibit 2.1
The Glen Mills Schools Molecular Organization Structure

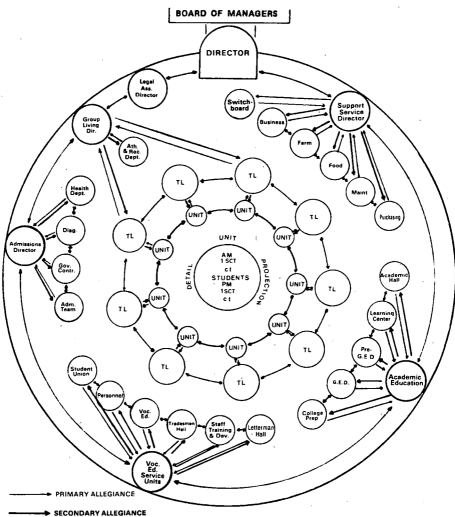

— PRIMARY ALLEGIANCE

━━ SECONDARY ALLEGIANCE

	RESPONSIBILITIES		ALLEGIANCES	
	PRIMARY	**SECONDARY**	**PRIMARY**	**SECONDARY**
Counselor Teachers (CT)	Cottage Norms Acad.Voc.& Life Skills Development	Cottage Norms	Senior Counselor	Teaching Team
Senior Counselor (SCT) Teachers	Cottage Norms	Management of A.M. or P.M. Staff	Team Leader	Senior Counselor and Shift Team
Team Leaders (TL)	Campus Norms	Management of Cottage Team	Other Team Leaders and Group Living Director	Assigned Unit Team
Vocational Education Service Units	Maintenance and Development of their area of responsibility	Resource for the needs of cottage units	Department Head	Individual Teams
Administrative Team	To maintain a cohesive team approach to all areas direct or indirectly affecting the organization	Supervision and management of the assigned departments.	Other Administrative Team Members	Line Supervisors
Executive Director	To safe guard the philosophy of the school and to make priority decisions for school growth.	Supervision of administrative team	Administrative Team	Board of Managers

• All staff and students have Responsibility to confront negative individual behavior and negative norms.

Intermediate level instruction (fourth to eighth grade levels) is provided in the student's cottage. The teachers are expected to achieve at least 1.5 months' growth in basic skills for every month of instruction; they want to have as much time with the students as possible. (A novel experience for delinquents: many teachers can't wait to get rid of them.)

The academic director noted that, while teachers should not feel pressured to release students for whom the afternoon instruction was vital, there were doubtless some students who could progress satisfactorily without it. This would include boys the teacher wished to retain because they exerted a positive influence on the group, or those whose test performance was expected to be good (helping the teacher to achieve his or her performance goals) but no longer required individualized instruction. The group living director offered to ask each of his team leaders to prepare a list of students from each cottage whom their instructors would be willing to release. Instructors would be informed about the reasons for the request but under no pressure to contribute to the list. The vocational training director agreed to redouble his efforts to inform students about the opportunities available through the afternoon programs. He would discuss with his staff how new students could be recruited through current participants who were positive toward the program.

The remarkable aspect of the meeting was not the solution itself but the process: there was no defensiveness or attempt to allocate blame. Every manager focused full attention on the discussion. The underlying assumption was that everyone in the room, not just the vocational training director, shared the responsibility to solve the problem and do what they could to help make the vocational program as effective as possible.

The power of the molecular structure to promote teamwork becomes most evident when it is contrasted with the more conventional hierarchical model. In a typical hierarchical structure, responsibilities and allegiances are arranged vertically between levels; primary allegiances are to one's superior and never to one's peers. Cottage staff report to a team leader whose primary responsibility is the functioning of the cottage. Team leaders report to a group living director who advocates strictly on behalf of his department to the executive director. Similar arrangements of authority and responsibility in other departments insure that the executive director is the only individual whose primary concern extends to the whole institution. All others are rewarded on the basis of their *department's* performance. The result is that senior managers, far from treating one another as allies with a common goal, regard their fellow managers as competitors for resources (staff, equipment, budgets) which are never adequate to meet the needs of all departments. Those who aspire to climb higher on the organization chart have an incentive, which is in no way checked by the hierarchical system of allegiances, to subtly sabotage their peers. The organization can resemble a loose confederation of warring divisions with the executive director as referee.

The contrast between the molecular and hierarchical models is most sharply defined when organizational resources must be allocated among departments. In the molecular model allocation decisions are made by the top management team based upon the criteria of maximum benefit to the organization as a whole. While each manager is expected to make certain that the needs of his own department are recognized, none has an incentive to act selfishly since rewards flow to those who work "to maintain a cohesive team approach" to decision making. Status and respect are earned through support of other departments. The norm is, never miss an opportunity to make your colleague look good when he has done his job well.

The strength of the molecular structure lies in the coincidence of organizational interests and individuals' self-interests.

In contrast, the hierarchical structure provides a strong incentive for top managers to advocate primarily on behalf of their own departments even where what is best for the department may not be in the best interest of the broader organization. At best, this means that the broader organizational goals do not coincide with those of the most influential staff. At worst, where key managers are competing for promotions infighting can weaken the management process to the point where there is little relationship between individuals' motivations and organizational needs. When problems arise, department heads are as likely to blame one another as to work cooperatively toward a solution. Forceful and politically savvy managers build strong departments while their less persuasive (or less well-connected) colleagues build resentments. While a variety of factors (e.g., a powerful and astute CEO) may mitigate the more destructive forms of competitiveness, the model itself invites it by placing cooperation and self-interest at odds.

The staff allocation process is one example illustrating the dissimilarity between the two models. When Glen Mills adopted a proactive, "marketing" strategy to increase enrollment, management was faced with important staffing decisions. Since the role would require "selling" Glen Mills' unusual program to court officials, candidates would have to be knowledgeable about the Schools' treatment approach, articulate, and enthusiastic, with good interpersonal skills. Those who best fit this profile turned out to be staff who were also very effective cottage counselors. This posed a clear conflict between departmental and institutional needs. In a hierarchical organization, the team leaders and group living director would resist the reassignment of their key staff to a new department. The resolution of the dilemma would likely depend upon the political acumen of the admissions director versus that of the group living director. At Glen Mills the conflict did not arise, since there was little incentive to "protect" departmental staff. Status comes not through building the strongest department but through contributing to the achievement of institutional goals. The group living director and team leaders made it clear that they were able to reassign any individuals required for so vital a role. Their willingness to make this important sacrifice earned them respect and reinforced the Glen Mills "help others" norm, payoffs far more important to the Group Living Department than the assignment of any individual staff.

To summarize, the hierarchical and molecular models embody very different organizational cultures. The hierarchical model is consistent with cultures that reward individual performance in the belief that success comes most surely through the efforts of talented individuals spurred on by competitive instincts and individual gain. The ubiquitousness of the model is due, perhaps, to the dominance of individual over communal values within the American culture.

Glen Mills' culture, on the other hand, values teamwork and holds that the habilitation of delinquents is best achieved by a cohesive staff spurred on by their commitment to the institution and its goals, plus mutual respect, support, and loyalty. While individual effort is recognized and applauded to a far greater extent that in most organizations, rewards are based upon *team* accomplishment and are seldom individualized. The molecular structure both models and realizes Glen Mills' culture.

The center of Glen Mills' "molecule" is the student body, symbolizing the commitment of all Glen Mills staff to support the students and their living units, and the ultimate responsibility of the cottage counselors for the academic, vocational, and behavioral growth of their students. The day to day operation of Glen Mills' program is carried on through the activities of the executive director, his secretary, and 386 staff assigned to six departments represented in the outer orbit of the structure: Group Living, Athletics, Admissions, Vocational Training, Academic, and Support Services. The Battling Bulls Club, though it appears on no organization charts, could be considered a seventh "department" by virtue of its strong impact upon Glen Mills' culture. Ultimate responsibility rests with the Schools' Board of Managers.

Group Living Department

With 160 staff and responsibility for operating nine cottages, Group Living is Glen Mills' largest department. Its most important functions are to safeguard the Schools' normative culture, conduct Guided Group Interaction (GGI) sessions, provide individualized intermediate academic instruction, and ensure that the students' cottages are safe, clean, and orderly.

Each cottage houses 40 to 50 students, subdivided into four living areas of 10 to 15 students each, which determine GGI group membership. The cottage is staffed by a senior counselor, two counselor-teachers and one counselor-specialist during both the morning (7 A.M.–3 P.M.) and afternoon (3 P.M.–11 P.M.) shifts.

Counselor-teachers are primarily responsible for providing academic and life skills instruction to students functioning on an intermediate (i.e., fourth to eighth grade) level academically. Classes are small, typically 10 to 16 students, with an emphasis upon individualized instruction. Each of these students receives four hours of academic instruction daily; classes are conducted in the cottage.

The primary responsibility of the counselor-specialist is to maintain cottage norms. This "norm stabilizer" function is necessary to the success of all programs at Glen Mills. Just as a surgeon cannot work successfully in an operating environment that has not been sterilized, neither can a teacher be effective in an institution where tardiness, inattentiveness, disorder, and disrespect are the norms. By ensuring that the normative culture is conducive to learning, the counselor-specialist creates the social conditions necessary for student growth.

Norm stabilizers tend to be physically big and strong, with good self-control and self-confidence. They are the type of individual you like to have on your side. They are neither mean nor demeaning. The Schools' screening process excludes the type of individual who likes to intimidate others, or is too quick to respond aggressively when his authority is challenged. The ideal candidate is a caring and secure individual who is not easily manipulated or intimidated, understands that in an institutional context "helping students" requires both frequent support *and* frequent confrontation, and has the skills and commitment to do both.

Unlike the traditional counselor, the norms stabilizer is not primarily concerned with establishing helping relationships with individual students. His primary responsibility is to maintain positive group norms, not to foster the growth of individual students. This minimizes the possibility of staff manipulation by students, which plagues many traditional programs.

Norm stabilizers work closely with counselor-teachers and other program staff to ensure that serious misbehavior is confronted at several levels. As in many other institutions, a Glen Mills student who has misbehaved in class will be confronted by his instructor and by his counselor. But thanks to the efforts of the counselor-specialist in shaping cottage norms, the student will also be confronted by his peers for disgracing their unit. This comes as a surprise to the newer students, who expect their peers to encourage or at least accept acting out behavior. Where the norms are strong there are few repeat offenders.

Cottages have a senior counselor in charge during each of the two daytime shifts. Like the counselor-specialists, the primary responsibility of the senior counselor is to safeguard the all-important cottage norms. Their secondary responsibility is to supervise the other counselors assigned to their shift.

Both senior counselors report to the cottage's team leader, the highest ranking staff person associated with the unit. It is at the team leader level that Glen Mills' organizational structure is markedly different from conventional institutional arrangements. The team leaders' primary alliances are *not* with their cottage teams but with each other; their primary responsibility is *not* the management of their units but the maintenance of campuswide norms. This arrangement necessitates teamwork and effectively short-circuits the inter-cottage antagonisms that plague many institutions. Team leaders' advocacy on behalf of their individual units is secondary to their responsibility for the campus as a whole. The result is that the team leaders assign the most effective staff and the most positive students to the cottages where they are most needed, rather than hoard them in their own units.

In further support of the norms favoring teamwork the Schools' salary administration policy provides for all team leaders to receive the same salary increase, based upon the performance of the weakest individual. Self-interest dictates doing everything possible to support a peer who is struggling; indeed the entire

Glen Mills system is designed to make self-interest and the Schools' interest coincide whenever possible.

Team leaders report to the top official in the Group Living Department, its director. As a member of the top administrative team, the director is only secondarily concerned with the operation of his department while primarily responsible for maintaining a team approach in resolving any issues facing the institution.

The extreme emphasis upon teamwork at Glen Mills is nowhere more evident than in the Group Living Department. The director of group living considers that his most important job in the department is to ensure that the team leaders always present a united front on campus. Meetings can be long and invariably highly participative, not to say boisterous. The length is due to a norm that genuine consensus be reached. "I disagree, but I'll support it" won't do. No one leaves the room until each individual has expressed his opinion, and the group has formulated a strategy which *all* agree to be the best possible.

The effectiveness of Glen Mills' Group Living Department reflects the design of the roles, responsibilities, and allegiances represented in the molecular model. It is also a tribute to the leadership of Tom Beecher. With 34 years service, Mr. Beecher is the Schools' longest term employee. Since his appointment as the department's director in 1976, Mr. Beecher has guided the development of one of the most unusual and effective departments in residential corrections with skill and dedication.

The best designed programs are sterile without sound implementation. Mr. Beecher is cut from the same cloth as most of Glen Mills' leadership: beyond the obligatory team orientation, key strengths include the ability to inspire loyalty and self-confidence among staff; a goal-oriented penchant for action; a direct and unpretentious personal style that evokes trust and belies a depth of understanding of group dynamics and individual behavior which would be the envy of even the most widely published academician.

All but two (i.e., Mr. Beecher and his administrative assistant) of the Group Living Department's staff have maintenance of the normative culture as either their primary or secondary responsibility. The major tools to accomplish this task are GGI, individual counseling, and confrontation of negative behavior.

Guided Group Interaction. GGI is the most formal component of the Schools' attempt to harness peer group pressures to promote prosocial behavior. Glen Mills has adapted the GGI technique first employed in a juvenile setting by Lloyd McCorkle (McCorkle, Elias, and Bixby, 1958) a quarter century earlier. Implementations of GGI vary widely, but the distinguishing characteristics of the method (Allen et al., 1971; Haskell and Yablonski, 1970; MacIver, 1966) include:

1. A group process involving five to twelve group members and a trained adult group leader. Attendance is mandatory.

2. The objective is the alteration of delinquent behavior. This is to be achieved by channeling group pressures toward prosocial goals. Behaviors and values are considered to reflect adaptations to the peer social group rather than immutable personality characteristics.

3. The peer group wields genuine power in the treatment process. It may set its own agenda, place one of its members on the "hot seat" (i.e., subject his behavior to extensive scrutiny by the group) or prescribe negative sanctions (e.g., work detail, withdrawal of privileges) in order to alter a member's deviant behavior. Glen Mills' implementation differs from some in that only the Schools' staff have authority to impose sanctions, though the GGI group may recommend them.

4. Formal process. Each member is required to explain how he got into trouble. On the basis of his response and the ensuing discussion, he is assigned problems or "road-blocks" which he must overcome. Acceptance by the group comes with evidence of the member's efforts to overcome these group-assigned problems. Status is accorded for assisting others and for efforts to understand the "why" of one's own and other's behavior. The acceptance of responsibility for one's own behavior and the exposing of manipulation or "conning" on the part of other group members are especially highly valued.

5. Role of the leader. The most important function of the leader is to channel group pressures and mold norms so that prosocial behavior and the expression of prosocial attitudes are reinforced and delinquent norms or attitudes are challenged. He must manage the formal process by seeing to it that every boy "tells his story" and that the boy's problems are labeled by the group. He should remind the group, when necessary, that negative sanctions must be applied constructively and must not be strictly punitive.

Glen Mills' implementation shares these characteristics. Both staff and students are trained in the social constructs and processes (e.g., roles, norms, group dynamics) which underlie the GGI method.

Staff training includes a four-day experiential design dealing with the "art and science" of GGI. From the outset, the training process is grounded in the Schools' values and beliefs:

Our first step in understanding the science of GGI is to ask "What is delinquency?" Delinquency is a social fact—nothing more and nothing less. It is a social fact just as poverty and divorce are social facts. Delinquency is not a psychosis or neurosis or character disorder . . . it is not a psychiatric syndrome. . . . [If a delinquent is emotionally disturbed] the problem is not his delinquency—the problem is his psychiatric disorder. . . . This disturbed person needs placement in a mental health facility. By eliminating the disturbed individual . . . we are left with socialized delinquents, not disturbed. This is the type of youth at Glen Mills. (Glen Mills Schools' Trainers' Manual)

The training continues with a definition of GGI as a "form of group process that utilizes peer group pressure to change behavior" and proceeds to focus upon group dynamics, the importance of peer group pressures in relation to delinquency, methods for observing behavior and changing it through the channeling of peer pressures. Staff are taught that their effectiveness as group leaders will require learning the underlying science and moving on to master the art of GGI, developing their own individual style of leadership. Guidelines include:

- Be clear about the nonnegotiable ground rules of GGI groups at Glen Mills: mandatory attendance; need for unanimous decisions subject only to the group leaders' veto power; all·interaction must be intended to strengthen the group process, help others or get help for yourself.
- Practice methods (several are suggested) for eliciting group members "stories," i.e., their modus operandi or delinquent pattern of behavior.
- Always confront delinquent norms/behaviors. Every failure to do so reinforces the behavior or norm and makes it more difficult to change.
- Do not become "one of the group" or hesitate when necessary to make decisions that group members won't like.
- Make certain that group members accept responsibility for their behavior. Do not permit projection of blame upon other members, yourself, or persons outside the group.
- Do not be concerned about the language used by group members, since this can inhibit free expression. But always confront any effort to take the dignity of another group member.
- Begin each session by following up on any commitments made by members during the previous session, to ensure accountability. Then ask if any group members have issues for discussion. If not, you may raise an issue for the group to deal with.
- Give precedence to process over task. Do not hesitate to interrupt an issue to focus attention on the group process.

One of the chief skills developed in GGI is the ability to "read" group dynamics and individual behavior. Awareness of interpersonal cues is highly developed among staff. Among the most significant differences between the team leader role at Glen Mills and that of traditional institutions is in their use of time. Where paperwork accounts for one-third or more of team leaders' time in many facilities, Glen Mills team leaders have almost none. Communication takes place face-to-face. There are no memos. Staff spend much of their time monitoring ("reading") student behavior. "What's your read on . . . ?" is a common question among staff. There are few more effective early-warning systems.

GGI at Glen Mills is expressly designed to fit the Schools' culture. The model is heavily confrontational, but always within the strict limits of respect for others: no one need fear humiliation disguised as "help." Its effectiveness derives from the channeling of peer pressures, which Glen Mills holds to be the dominant factor in most delinquency. The GGI process encourages "owning" (accepting responsibility for) one's behavior and helping others, dual pillars of Glen Mills' culture. The goal of GGI (behavior change) is strongly consonant with Glen Mills' belief that its students are psychologically sound, and do not require a therapeutic approach aimed at personality change.

There is little evidence for the effectiveness of GGI as an independent treatment method. It is likely that the effectiveness of GGI (or, for that matter, any other treatment modality) is largely a function of its goodness of fit with the institutional culture. This point is made very clearly in Glen Mills' training manual: "GGI is not a panacea for anything. GGI is only one tool that can be successful *if it has an environment that can support it*" (emphasis added).

Analyses of program evaluation (Greenwood and Zimring, 1985) indicate that an institution's treatment modality, when considered as independent of the broader institutional environment, is not a primary determinant of institutional effectiveness. Managers at Glen Mills feel GGI is a valuable tool: it helps students learn to confront and accept confrontation, give and receive feedback, read non-verbal signals, recognize subgroupings and leadership struggles, expose and confront hidden agendas, develop trusting and supportive peer relationships, and to give and receive help with specific problems. But in terms of its contribution to the Schools' effectiveness, its importance lies less in its usefulness as an independent treatment tool than in its role in helping to maintain the wider Glen Mills culture, which is the true habilitative agent.

Individual Counseling. Each counselor-teacher and counselor-specialist carries a case load of six or seven students in his unit. The counselor is expected to meet individually with each counselee for at least two half-hour sessions each week. Counselors relate to students as young adults, never as children.

The counselor's role differs from that of therapists in traditional clinical-custody programs in three key respects. First, the primary goal of the process is not therapeutic change but to help the counselee derive maximum benefit from Glen Mills by setting social, educational, vocational, and athletic goals; ensuring that the counselees' medical, dental, and clothing needs are met; arranging for home passes; maintaining contact with the counselee's parents; familiarizing himself with the counselee's background and communicating any special needs or concerns to the cottage team; and preparing reports describing the student's progress at Glen Mills.

Unlike the custody-clinical model, there is no expectation that the counselor-student relationship per se will be a key ingredient in the boy's progress. Trust will develop as the student observes that his counselor is direct and dependable. Emotional closeness is not a goal. Staff discussions of individual students are invariably objective. Sympathy regarding the student's life circumstances, or any messages suggesting that the student is a victim of his past experiences, are rarely expressed.

Second, while the counselors may help their students on a confidential basis to deal with personal issues, the dominant emphasis is upon "here and now" behavior and program participation. The past is explored only to the extent necessary to identify the student's modus operandi, or characteristic patterns of behavior, never to uncover the developmental roots of psychopathology. The counselor encourages a student to deal with his problems in the GGI setting rather than confine his sharing to the one-on-one setting.

Third, the counselor has ultimate responsibility for the student's growth and development at Glen Mills. Accountable for academic growth, the counselor must ensure that the student is evaluated, an educational plan developed, an appropriate program placement made, and his progress monitored. Accountable for vocational development, the counselor must arrange for the student to be assessed and exposed to the range of vocational options; he must assist him in choosing among them and make certain that his attendance and effort are satisfactory. Accountable for his social development, the counselor must monitor the student's participation in GGI and his behavior on campus, encouraging him to model Glen Mills' norms and strive for membership in the Bulls Club.

To say that personality change is not a primary goal of Glen Mills' program is not to imply that the Schools have little impact upon students' self-concept and self-esteem. In these areas Glen Mills' goals are similar to those of traditional counseling programs, but the approach is radically different. Through careful control of the normative culture, Glen Mills enables its students to achieve dramatic behavioral change. As a student accomplishes academic and vocational goals and functions as a mature, responsible member of the community, his self-definition changes as well.

Program models that rely upon individual counseling as the primary change agent are vulnerable to a wide range of weaknesses. First, to the extent that counselors view their charges as emotionally disturbed (often an implicit assumption of the "medical model"), their interventions will be inappropriate in many instances. Second, in their endeavor to establish trusting and accepting relationships with students, counselors can fall prey to manipulation by their counselees, and tend to discredit the judgments of cottage staff who raise the issue. This exacerbates the divisions between the professional therapists and the paraprofessional child care workers. Counselors concerned with the progress of their individual counselees, and child care workers focused upon the needs of the entire cottage unit, easily find themselves in opposition to one another. A typical instance might involve the question of a home pass for Johnny, when his counselor believes the home pass to be a therapeutic necessity despite the staff's unwillingness to reward his poor behavior in the cottage with a home visit. Third, when therapists focus upon past history and deprivations in helping the counselee to understand his current feelings and behavior, they risk disempowering their client by reinforcing the rationalizations he uses to escape responsibility for his acts. To the extent that he experiences acceptance and "caring" (sometimes the counselor's own need to be liked masked as caring for the client, who is victimized a second time in this supposedly therapeutic interaction) in his posture as a victim, he will feel little incentive toward more acceptable behavior.

It is true that skilled therapists are unlikely to fall into these traps. However, most skilled therapists prefer to work with clients who acknowledge their need to change and freely seek treatment. Neither of these conditions, which are minimal requirements of effective therapy, pertain to most institutionalized delinquents. Consequently, though there are numerous exceptions, therapists in institutions tend to be relatively inexperienced or unskilled.

Even the most competent counseling intervention is very likely to fail in the face of delinquent peer pressures when the counselee leaves the therapist's office. It is naive in the extreme to suppose that an hour or two with a therapist will significantly affect the behavior of a student who must live the remainder of the week with peers who have very different expectations for his behavior, and whose acceptance is far more important to him psychologically. For all these reasons, Glen Mills' model relies upon the normative culture to produce behavioral change and a more positive self-concept and enhanced self-esteem. Individual therapy plays no role.

The above concerns notwithstanding, the role of individual therapy within the normative culture program model remains controversial, even among some at Glen Mills. It is further discussed in the final chapter.

Confrontation. Glen Mills relies upon confrontations—thousands each day— to sustain its normative culture. The Schools' locks and bars were replaced by three tools of behavioral change and control (confrontation, peer pressure, expulsion); confrontation is the most direct and impacting of the three. All staff and students are expected to confront negative behavior, that is, behavior inconsistent with the Schools' values. Any failure to do so conveys the message that the behavior is acceptable, weakening the Schools' normative culture.

The overriding purpose of confrontation is to maintain the normative culture. The effect upon the individual student is of secondary importance. It does, however, help the student to master two important life skills. He learns to accept and act upon constructive criticism without feeling a loss of face, an ability important to success in many life situations but particularly in the workplace. Second, in his role as confronter, he becomes skilled at standing up for his own rights, beliefs, and opinions while showing respect for others. Glen Mills' alumni frequently credit the Schools with teaching them how to confront and resolve differences without resorting to their fists.

Staff and students alike are trained in Glen Mills' confrontation process, which involves seven levels or gradations of forcefulness ranging from a "friendly non-verbal" to physical restraint (see Exhibit 2.2) The confrontation process is designed to alter behavior without "taking the dignity" of (disrespecting) the individual being confronted. Nowhere is the interrelationship between the Schools' culture and its treatment approach more evident than in this area: the "respect" norm and the "help others" norm are absolutely essential to the success of any program which relies upon confrontation to change behavior. A young man who is confronted in a degrading or abusive way experiences the confrontation as a challenge and must resist it in order to save face. Confrontation can only be effective as a change agent, as opposed to a method of control, when the confronter is genuinely seeking to help the person confronted. Only then can the student accept the confrontation without losing status.

Glen Mills' confrontation methods would be ineffective (or worse) if transplanted to an institution whose culture did not include the relevant norms of respect and support. A sign in the office of the director of group living puts it

Exhibit 2.2
Seven Levels of Confrontation

I.   Friendly Non-Verbal

When an individual observes a student violating a norm he will give this student a friendly non-verbal gesture, typically with his eyes, hands, or head. These gestures are intended to change the behavior of this student at the immediate time of the problem.

II. Concerned Non-Verbal

The concerned non-verbal involves stern and forceful facial gestures, finger pointing, hand gestures or other non-verbal signals.

III. The Helpful Verbal

The confronter verbally communicates in a cordial manner his concern with the behavior of the student involved in the incident.

IV. Concerned Verbal

The concerned verbal informs the student that his actions are fast becoming a major concern. The confronter accomplishes this by using different voice levels, facial expressions, or other gestures not involving physical contact with the student.

V.   Request for Staff and/or Student Support

Verbal support is requested of other staff members or students when the concerned verbal is ignored by the student. This is used to alert the student that his actions have reached a high level of concern and to enlist peer group pressure to help alleviate the situation.

VI. Touch for Attention (Staff only)

A staff member touches the student below the neck and above the waist for attention. If at this point, the student has not accepted any of the non-verbal or verbal confrontations, the staff member might then place his hand on the student to show that he is extremely concerned about his present behavior and would like him to cease his negative action. This is the last level where the student has an opportunity to desist and not lose face or peer group status.

VII. Physical Restraint (Staff only)

After other levels of confrontation have failed, it is the responsibility of staff to hold the young man until he appears to settle down. If the student during any of the levels of confrontation attempts to walk away, turn around, etc. the staff responsibility is to hold him and keep him under control. The confronting staff will use the least amount of physical restraint possible until the student is no longer out of control or a threat to himself, others, or property. At this time, staff will talk to the student and use the incident to help the student mature and grow.

well: When a climate of trust is created by genuine support, the relationship can endure challenge. Confrontation without support is disastrous, support without confrontation is anemic.

There are several guidelines for confrontation. First, the *lowest* level of confrontation appropriate to the situation is to be tried *first*. An intervention to prevent a fight may require a level IV (concerned verbal), while a friendly nonverbal of often sufficient to remind a student to tuck in his shirt. The large majority of confrontations at Glen Mills involve no negative effect. Ironically tension, hostility, and fear are very rare at Glen Mills—not "despite," but rather, *because* of the thousands of confrontations which occur every day.

Second, confrontation must always be accepted. If a student believes he is being confronted unjustly or inappropriately, he must listen respectfully, comply with the confrontation, and raise the issue later in GGI or the daily cottage meeting. Resisting ("blowing off") a confrontation is a serious transgression of an important norm.

Third, every student and staff is responsible not only to *confront* negative behavior, but also to *support* confrontations when necessary. Just as all confrontations must be accepted, all must be supported regardless of individual's beliefs about whether the original confronter acted appropriately. The certainty of support accounts for the readiness of staff or students to confront even the most aggressive individuals, since resistance touches off an immediate response from all staff and students in the area in support of the confronter.

Fourth, an individual who requests support during a confrontation (level V) should *withdraw* and permit the confrontation to be carried on by others who were not involved in the original interaction. The confronter must be in control of himself. When a confrontation is resisted the confronter may feel challenged and overreact in an attempt to save face, resulting in increased resistance and a dangerous deterioration of the situation. This can be prevented if the confronter disengages and allows others to carry through the confrontation.

Fifth, never "*drop*" a confrontation or permit an individual to resist it. Failure to initiate and pursue a confrontation until it is successful, however long it takes, reinforces negative behavior and makes it more resistant to change.

Finally, students do not confront at level VI or level VII since both involve physical contact, in violation of an important student norm. A confrontation which goes beyond level V attracts enough staff attention that physical support by students is unnecessary.

Like "treatment," the term "confrontation" is used by different programs to describe vastly different processes. It is instructive to compare and contrast Glen Mills' process with that employed by other programs. In one program,

confrontations are directed by the senior staff and generally occur when the staff feels that the youth is continuously behaving inappropriately or is failing to deal with some unresolved issue. Confrontation generally begins with three or more staff surrounding a youth, one of them assuming a nose-to-nose/eye-to-eye stance squarely in front of the youth. The verbal style is loud and challenging. If the youth tries to turn or back away, he is held in position to maintain eye contact. . . . A confrontation may continue for up to 30 minutes or until the staff feels the issue has been resolved. During this period, the youth might go through a sequence of arguing, struggling, crying, being still, and finally engaging in quiet conversation. The restraining holds of the staff change to affectionate hugs near the end of the process. (Greenwood and Turner, 1987: 17)

In short, the confrontation is conducted by staff, initiated after behavior has been continuously unacceptable for some period of time, and carried out in a prolonged "loud and challenging" style. The experience is highly stressful to the student. There is no attempt to avoid physical restraints during the confrontation itself, which is designed primarily to impact upon the student and only secondarily upon the larger group. The interaction is highly personal in both verbal and physical dimensions.

"Confrontation" at Glen Mills differs from that described above in nearly every significant respect. The goals, participants, and the nature of the process itself are all markedly different. At Glen Mills, the goals are to maintain the normative culture by changing individuals' behavior through a process involving minimum stress to the student. Students and staff alike are trained in the process, confrontation by students is nearly as common as by staff. The graduated nature of Glen Mills process is intended to minimize the frequency of "loud and challenging" interactions. Confrontations are initiated immediately in response to any misbehavior, however minor. They are focused squarely upon the student's behavior; any personal component is kept to a minimum. The vast majority are completed in a matter of seconds. The Glen Mills process is designed to *avoid* the need for physical restraints and their occurrence is rare, accounting for much less than 1 percent of all confrontations.

Athletics Department

Glen Mills boasts one of the nation's most extensive and successful institutional athletic programs. Since 1983 when the Schools were accepted into the Pennsylvania Interscholastic Athletic Association, Glen Mills has competed successfully against large urban and suburban public high schools in the Delaware Valley League and District 1 (southeastern Pennsylvania).

Athletic programs and facilities are managed by Director Peter Forjohn and eight staff. This number does not include team coaches, who are drawn from the staff of other departments.

Mr. Ferrainola's efforts to develop a first-class athletics program met initially with strong staff resistance. The infamous letter condemning Sam to Glen Mills' Board in December of 1975 read in part: "Our football team cost $10,000 to outfit, the locker room cost $7,000 with its wall-to-wall carpeting. An additional $3,000 was spent to have a football game in Pittsburgh. . . . That's $20,000 for six games, for a school as pinched for pennies as we are, this is simply outrageous!"

The letter exaggerated the expenditures. However, the "outrageous" $20,000 would later seem like pocket change. By 1987 Glen Mills had invested well over a million dollars in athletic fields, a new field house, stadium lights, uniforms, and professional-quality equipment for its athletes.

Glen Mills fields varsity teams in football, soccer, cross-country, golf, hockey, powerlifting, baseball, tennis, and lacrosse. The Schools also compete at the junior varsity level in each of these sports. Its record of successes (see Chapter 4) is impressive by any standard; among correctional institutions it may well be unequaled in the nation.

The Schools' athletic achievements demonstrate the commitment and talents of Glen Mills' staff and the vast, untapped potential of those society regards as "losers." Every team is coached by staff members, mostly cottage counselors whose primary responsibilities lie elsewhere and who receive no additional pay for coaching. With few exceptions the Schools' athletes arrive with very limited experience in organized athletics. Most play only one season; Glen Mills does not have the public school's luxury of a four-year period to develop its athletes. Each squad must cope with the mid-season loss of players when they are discharged from the Schools. Most coaches would regard these obstacles as insurmountable.

Astoundingly, Glen Mills' students master the necessary skills and teamwork to compete successfully in a strong interscholastic arena. The dedication and hard work required would be impressive from any healthy, achievement-oriented adolescent. At a minimum, Glen Mills experience indicates the need to re-examine the labels—"lazy," "dumb," "quitters"—often attached to delinquents.

Glen Mills' Board and administration are absolutely persuaded of the value of athletics to the Schools and to its students. Coaches are honored and their programs supported "to the hilt," which at least partially explains why non-salaried coaching positions involving hundreds of hours of extra work rarely go unfilled:

If you ever had any doubt that Glen Mills takes pride in its athletics program, look no farther than a classified ad the school recently placed in a local newspaper. It began: "Coaching positions are available in 13 varsity sports." The ad was not meant to imply that the school had coaching vacancies, but that prospective applicants [for cottage staff positions] could aspire to a coaching position. (*Philadelphia Inquirer*, Jan. 21, 1988)

However impressive the Schools' trophy cabinet, the effectiveness of athletics at Glen Mills is measured less in terms of win-loss records than its contribution to Glen Mills' culture and the players' psychosocial development. Athletics are a valuable tool for helping student leaders to get involved in the program and seek status from positive achievements, to take pride in their Schools. It contributes to the normalization of the correctional experience, by promoting habilitation through activities which are a part of normal adolescent development rather than through "treatment."

Many students have considerable undeveloped potential. Acquisition of skills is relatively easy. More difficult is nourishing the determination to practice hard today to prepare for a contest that may be a week or more away. Students must learn to bounce back after losses; to play hard but fair; to treat opponents with respect even when the respect is not mutual. In short, the primary goal of athletics at Glen Mills is development of life skills. A "perfect" season is one in which a team wins all of its games except one—an undefeated team never learns how to overcome disappointments; to accept a loss without making excuses; to learn from a setback and become even stronger. Vince Lombardi could not have earned a coaching job at Glen Mills, where winning is neither the most important nor the "only" thing. It is not the outcome of a contest, but the student's response to the outcome which determines whether he will be a "winner" or a "loser" in life. Glen Mills' students' lives contain more than their share of adversity. These lessons are more important than a championship ring.

The athletics program is designed to fit the Schools' culture. Coaches confront, prod, and motivate individual students when necessary, but the primary method for building strong teams is the channeling of peer pressure. On one occasion three of the football teams's starting players arrived late for practice before an important game. At most schools, the coaches would have confronted the three boys. The Glen Mills coaches confronted the rest of the team because they (the team) had not done the confronting. At Glen Mills it is the team, as well as the coaches, who are expected to insist upon responsible behavior from their peers.

Glen Mills culture requires that individuals be responsible to and for the community. Similarly, Glen Mills' athletes are encouraged to do more than develop superior skills. They must strive to become the type of player who helps their teammates play their best. On the field and in the cottage, Glen Mills experience suggests the intriguing possibility that individuals flourish where the primary focus is on the group and its norms.

Winning is as important to Glen Mills as to any other school. But winning must never come at the expense of the Schools' values. One of the most successful coaches in Glen Mills' history was confronted by the director when he needlessly pushed a player whose performance had been disappointing. The coach was replaced after a similar incident later in the season. He had forgotten that the primary objective of athletics at Glen Mills is not to win games but to make students winners.

The athletic program touches the entire student body. All students are expected to support Glen Mills teams. Some home games are attended by all students. Prior to the contests staff discuss appropriate behavior: show respect for opponents; act like gentlemen around coeds from competing schools; cheer for our team; etc.

Particularly important is the distinction between supporting your own team versus showing disrespect for the opposing team. When several Glen Mills students watching a soccer match laughed at an inept play by an opponent, a staff member stood up and, in a voice that could be heard throughout the stands, said "that young man (the opponent) is playing his heart out to help his team. Which of you think that's funny?" There was no more laughing. The Glen Mills students applauded both their own team *and* the opponents as they left the field.

In addition to the varsity teams, the Schools provide an extensive intramural program in which all students participate weekly, year round.

Athletics are a cornerstone of Glen Mills' program. The sports activities put adolescents' energies to productive use; all institutions understand the value of activity and involvement. But beyond draining excess energies, athletics help build school pride and, most important of all, help students to see themselves differently. Something very important happens to society's failures when they find they can compete successfully against teams from the best suburban schools; when they earn a place on the team and are provided a uniform and equipment acceptable to a professional athlete; when they see the effort their coaches invest for no pay; when they read about their team and see their own names honored in the newspapers; when their long hours of practice are rewarded with an important victory or the respect of an able opponent; when in response to their inevitable mistakes and misplays they hear from their peers in the stands: not derision, but the Battling Bulls Club leading a chant "That's all right! That's OK! We're gonna beat'em anyway!"

The athletics program creates favorable publicity. Newspaper coverage helps build respect and pride. As adults from the surrounding communities come to Glen Mills to attend an event they soon find that the Schools are very different from what they had imagined. Improved community relations is a significant, if secondary, by-product for Glen Mills.

Primarily, Glen Mills' management values the athletic program because it powerfully reinforces and communicates the Schools' culture in a way that is credible to adolescent boys. Consider the new student sitting in the stands as he spots some of his old friends from the neighborhood gang playing for Glen Mills. They cared little for school before, and seldom put much energy into anything adults would applaud. They seem now to be playing with real intensity, and acting like models of sportsmanship. He wonders whether they're "fronting," or whether Glen Mills is a very different kind of school.

Athletics at Glen Mills help students to understand that effort and teamwork can lead to success even when the odds are against you; to discard the image of "quitter" and "loser"; to internalize the critical distinction between "defeat" and "failure" which is essential to coping positively with life's inevitable setbacks. It achieves these ends through activities which students embrace as a normal part of male adolescent development. As a component of Glen Mills' habilitation program, athletics are no less important than GGI or other explicitly "therapeutic" interactions.

Admissions Department

The Admissions Department, directed by Bernard Krieg, represents one of the most dramatic differences between Glen Mills and its more conventional institutional counterparts. The admissions function in most institutions tends to be routine and passive. In contrast, Glen Mills' department operates like an aggressive marketing division of a private sector business. Admissions workers are no less important to Glen Mills than are marketing and sales representatives to IBM.

The 39 department staff are responsible for public relations, attracting new students, evaluating them, and serving as a liaison with the family and court systems of students accepted for admission. Emphasis is upon consumer service and responsiveness.

All admissions workers have experience as cottage staff. They understand and can explain, without defensive non-verbals, how Glen Mills' system works to court officials who are skeptical and sometimes challenging.

Each admissions coordinator is assigned to one or more jurisdictions. An important objective is to educate court personnel as to the type of student who is most appropriate for Glen Mills. Coordinators contact direct referral agents (probation officers, social services workers, or judges) in each jurisdiction, meet with them to describe Glen Mills' program, and arrange a visit to the Schools. Once a jurisdiction begins committing students, the coordinator serves as Glen Mills' field representative insuring that all necessary reports are submitted on time; court personnel are notified about home passes or truancies; questions regarding the student's progress are answered; student travel arrangements made; discharge planning coordinated with the committing county.

Performance standards for coordinators reflect activity goals rather than new student quotas. Staff are evaluated on the number of presentations made, number of visits to the counties in their district, number of visitors sent to the Schools, etc. Activity goals avoid the risks posed by a quota system, which could hurt Glen Mills by providing an incentive for coordinators to relax admissions criteria.

Four staff are assigned to service Philadelphia's Family Court, Glen Mills' biggest client. Twelve staff (admissions coordinators) are assigned to other county court systems in Pennsylvania and across the United States. Through their efforts, Glen Mills has admitted students from half of Pennsylvania's 67 counties, from 20 states, the District of Columbia, the federal government, and Bermuda.

The Schools' policy of placing admissions coordinators in the field to service remote jurisdictions has helped Glen Mills achieve its goals for expansion. The practice has proven cost-effective. A key innovation was conferring upon admissions staff the authority to make an on-the-spot decision during an adjudication hearing to accept or reject a prospective student. The availability of a representative authorized to admit a student and arrange for his immediate transfer to the Schools is sometimes decisive to the commitment decision. Each commitment represents approximately $20,000 in revenue.

Admissions Criteria. Glen Mills' program is designed for socialized, male adjudicated delinquents. Admissions criteria are rigid only in excluding boys who have severe physical handicaps, require individual supervision (e.g., those with a history of fire-setting or suicidal tendencies) or those for whom GGI is contraindicated. The latter group includes boys exhibiting severe emotional problems or overt homosexuality. Offense history (except where it evidences psychopathology) is considered irrelevant to the admissions decision. The ideal candidate is the older socialized delinquent: an extroverted gang member who is at least 16 years of age.

The preference for "socialized" delinquents—those whose misbehavior primarily reflects material deprivation coupled with social/peer pressures rather than psychopathology—reflects the Schools' belief that these youths are most likely to benefit from Glen Mills' culture. Where negative role models, antisocial peer pressures, and a deprived environment are key factors in the etiology of delinquency, positive models and prosocial peer pressures in an enriched environment are the "treatment" of choice. Furthermore, the socialized delinquent is most likely to have internalized values (loyalty, concern for others) which will serve him well at Glen Mills.

The preference for older delinquents reflects both the Schools' goals of preparing students for independent living and their suitability for GGI participation. There is no attempt to provide treatment to a student's family or involve it in the Glen Mills program. Furthermore, Glen Mills has no impact upon any delinquent norms which may prevail in its students' home communities. Many students return to dysfunctional environments after discharge. Accordingly, the Schools seek to help older students to develop the ability to recognize and resist antisocial pressures or, where this proves impossible, to relocate and live independently. Second, as adolescents become older they increasingly rely upon their peers rather than their families for affirmation and acceptance, making them more likely to respond favorably to GGI and Glen Mills' positive peer culture.

The final factor bearing upon the admission decision distinguishes Glen Mills' "marketing" approach from the traditional admissions function. Businesses that depend upon a single client do so at risk of their own autonomy, since the client will necessarily wield considerable influence over the business's practices. Similarly, institutions that depend upon a few jurisdictions for commitments find themselves in a difficult situation when county officials attempt to influence institutional programs or policies. With nearly three-fourths of its students coming from Philadelphia and Pittsburgh in 1980, Glen Mills became concerned and asked its admissions group to recruit students from new counties and states. Since achieving a larger "client base" is considered an appropriate and important objective, geography can be a significant consideration in borderline cases. A Michigan judge who wishes to commit a 14-year-old loner to Glen Mills is more likely to succeed than his counterpart in Philadelphia, since there are relatively few Glen Mills students from Michigan. The boy would almost certainly be admitted if he were from Wyoming.

Admissions Process. Unlike many institutions which require administrative and treatment staff review of candidates for admission, Glen Mills authorizes its coordinators to make the admissions decision at the time of adjudication, without further review. This avoids delays of days or even weeks in case processing, delays costly to the court and anxiety-producing for the boy. Since all coordinators are trained in the Glen Mills approach and most have experience as cottage staff, their judgments regarding the student's prospects for success are well grounded.

A student may be admitted to the residential program or to the Diagnostic and Evaluation (DE) unit of the Admissions Department. The DE students are housed in living units with boys in the residential program. The difference is that DE students are admitted on a provisional basis and undergo extensive evaluation by a psychologist and cottage staff during their first month at the Schools. Younger students and students from unfamiliar jurisdictions are frequently admitted initially to the DE unit. For DE students the cottage is a social laboratory where staff observe their method of relating to others. Housing the DE students in the stable, positive environment of the residential program is less stressful to the boys than isolating them in a separate unit, and provides for a more accurate assessment of their ability to succeed in the regular program. When the evaluation is complete, DE and group living staff, rather than the admissions coordinator, decide whether to admit the student to the residential program. Approximately 30 percent of residential students are admitted first as DE students; 90 percent of DE students continue into the residential program.

Vocational Education and Career Development Department

Glen Mills' Vocational Training Department employs 59 staff. They provide vocational assessment and employment skills training, operate a dormitory (Tradesman Hall) for advanced vocational students, conduct training in 16 shops, assist students in finding employment or more advanced training after discharge, and provide a variety of services (e.g., staff recruitment and training, switchboard, students' union supervision, housekeeping) to the Schools.

Programs. Glen Mills provides programs in welding, photography, journalism, woodwork, optics, radio broadcasting, printing, small engine repair, residential carpentry, architectural drafting, auto repair, electronics, masonry, plumbing, retail management, and arts and crafts. During a student's first two weeks at the Schools he visits each of the shops and is evaluated at Glen Mills' Vocational Assessment Center. The evaluation includes five components. The first is an interview regarding the student's vocational interests and background. The student is asked about prior training and work experiences. The interviewer then briefs the student on the testing process and its importance. The second assessment component is a series of paper and pencil tests of general learning and reasoning, ability to understand words and ideas, and arithmetic skills. Third are tests of motor coordination measuring finger dexterity, eye-hand-foot coordination, color discrimination, spatial and form perception, upper extremity and whole body range of motion. The fourth step is review of an audio visual inventory relating to 12 potential vocational interest areas. Finally, the student discusses his interests and test scores with a counselor and selects three shops. The Assessment Center staff assign him to one of the three programs based upon the assessment results, the student's preference, and space availability. All assessment information is provided to staff in the student's living unit.

Before enrolling in any vocational program the student must complete course work at the Vocational Learning Center, which provides him with classroom instruction relating to his assigned shop. Individualized lesson plans to upgrade reading and math skills are developed from standardized diagnostic tests and the requirements of the student's specific shop assignment. The lesson plan incorporates assignments in vocational textbooks and use of audiovisual devices allowing for self-paced instruction in shop safety, shop math, and work habits.

Students typically complete the course of instruction in the Learning Center in two to four weeks, and then enroll in beginner's classes in their assigned shops. These classes are conducted by an instructor and one to three student aides. Most shops are open between 6 P.M. and 9 P.M. Monday through Thursday. Class sizes range from 15 to 24.

Students who do not succeed in their assigned shops may request a transfer to another shop or drop out of the vocational program in favor of academic or athletic training. Those who demonstrate interest and aptitude qualify for placement in their shop's advanced program. Advanced classes are smaller (usually 10 students or so) and meet each weekday from 1 P.M. to 3 P.M. The emphasis is upon preparation for entry level employment or enrollment in a trade school after discharge.

In keeping with the Schools' norms relating to pride and service to others, the emphasis upon fiscal responsibility and operating economies, and the instructional benefits of useful projects, Glen Mills shops provide numerous services and products for the Schools' use. The photography program provides photos of Glen Mills sporting events and assists in the development of public relations materials, the Schools' yearbook and annual report, etc. Journalism students provide articles for the *Battling Bulletin*, the Schools' monthly newspaper, produced by students in the print shop. Any student needing glasses takes his prescription to the optical lab, where fellow students show him a wide choice of frames; produce, test, and insert the lens; and make any necessary final adjustments. Glen Mills and the surrounding communities enjoy the broadcasting of the student-operated FM radio station, WZZE. The auto shop helps the Schools maintain its fleet of vehicles in top condition. Students in the retail management program help operate the Student Union. Major construction projects and the Schools' routine maintenance have involved dozens of advanced welding, carpentry, masonry, electrical, small engine, and plumbing students.

Students who are positive role models in their cottages and also do well in advanced vocational classes qualify for Tradesman Hall, the residential unit for vocational honors students. Tradesman Hall was established in 1981 at the suggestion of Sam's son, Joseph Ferrainola, director of vocational education and career development. By establishing an honors unit for outstanding vocational students and utilizing vocational instructors as unit counselors, the Schools were able to strengthen the vocational program while expanding dormitory space to accommodate students. This resulted in additional annual revenues of 1 million dollars, with only a negligible increase in staff costs. Since all vocational instructors have experience as cottage counselors, they were well prepared to operate the new unit.

Upon completing eight months at Glen Mills students in advanced vocational courses are enrolled in a career placement program. Designed to help students find employment or gain admission to a trade school, the program helps students prepare a resume, complete job applications, and develop interviewing skills. Students critique videotaped interviews with staff in the role of potential employers. They think through how they might respond to tough questions ("What kind of school is Glen Mills?"). They prepare portfolios containing photos of their work, and records of achievement in the program. Shop instructors help students to "network" their way to a job and encourage them to keep in touch. The successes of former students are announced to help motivate those still in the program.

When a student and his counselor agree that he would benefit from employment off-campus, a job search is initiated. To encourage area employers to hire its students, Glen Mills offers to pay the student's full salary during a two-week trial period.

With many components established within the past five years, the vocational program is in a relatively early stage of development. Through 1987, 1,244 students received certificates indicating successful completion of training. Ninety-one were placed in "co-op" jobs enabling them to earn money while enrolled at Glen Mills. Upon discharge, 51 were accepted in trade schools, and 14 were placed in jobs.

Role of the Vocational Instructor. The instructor is expected to develop curricula, order supplies, maintain equipment, and provide instruction. He is required to prepare tests and materials relating to his shop for use by the Vocational Learning Center. In addition to shop-specific responsibilities, the instructor serves as a counselor for several Tradesman Hall students. This requires two hours per week with each counselee in one-to-one sessions and contact with each boy's parents before and after every homepass, as well as bimonthly progress reports. Finally, he is expected to provide a wide range of services to the campus which may include coverage in the cafeteria, support of the intramural program, assistance with maintenance, transportation of students, attendance at varsity sporting events or helping to coach an athletic team.

Vocational instructors work closely with counselors in the Group Living Department. Like all Glen Mills staff, instructors have a responsibility to confront negative behavior and support confrontation at all times. In doing so they assist group living staff, who carry the primary responsibility for campus norms. Conversely, instructors depend upon cottage counselors to encourage student participation and reward vocational achievement. Staff whose concern with their own role causes them to lose sight of their primary objective—to make Glen Mills the best institution possible through teamwork—do so at their peril. Six vocational instructors were once fired in one day because they had developed a "we-they" attitude with respect to group living staff.

Personnel Recruiting and Training. The Vocational Department is responsible for recruiting and training the Schools' staff. Recruiting focuses almost exclusively upon cottage line staff because Glen Mills fills virtually all other positions by promotion or transfer from within. Exceptions are specialized support personnel (e.g., maintenance, kitchen workers) who are hired directly through the Support Services Department. Work in the cottages is to Glen Mills what basic training is to the military: an experience indoctrinating the newcomer into the organization's culture and shaping his attitudes and work habits.

The ideal candidate sought by Glen Mills has had no experience in other institutions and is therefore more open to accepting Glen Mills' approach. He is a team player who is less motivated by individual recognition than the satisfaction of contributing to a successful team effort. It is the personality of the offensive lineman, not the superstar quarterback, that is wanted. A scholastic grade point average around 2.5 reflects respectable academic effort balanced by social, vocational, and athletic involvements. Athletic experience is particularly desirable. He must have a desire to work with young men and not feel intimidated by them, show self-confidence but not arrogance. Close family ties are a plus, since he will be expected to treat staff and students with the respect, loyalty, and support due kinfolk. The recruiter looks for evidence of overcoming obstacles to achieve personal goals; staff are expected to take their work seriously and show persistence in the face of difficulties. Since cottage staff are behavioral models, a neat (but not overdressed) appearance and good personal hygiene are important. A high energy level and enthusiasm are necessary to involve students in Glen Mills' program: it is quite certain that, if staff don't show enthusiasm about the program, students won't either. Friendliness and a sense of humor are highly valued. "Felicitators" who have an instinct for recognizing and celebrating others' achievements are particularly welcome. Arrogance, rudeness, laziness, timidity, apathy, rigidity, and conceit are fatal weaknesses.

Candidates for employment come from referrals by current staff, former students, newspaper advertisements, and college recruiting. The hiring process includes interviews by the senior counselors and the team leader of the unit to which the new counselor will be assigned. In addition to the qualities listed above, the candidate is evaluated as to how well he meets the cottage's special needs. Does the unit require a norm stabilizer (see Group Living Department, this chapter) primarily or a "technician" with teaching or recreational skills? The next step is an interview with a group of team leaders. The group then discusses the applicant and gives feedback to the team leader who proposed the candidate. Since the team leader's primary responsibility is for campus norms it is important that the whole group accept responsibility for all staffing decisions. If team leader approval is unanimous, the candidate and his future supervisor are interviewed together by the group living director. The final step is a meeting with the director who welcomes the new counselor to the Schools.

The new employee in 1988 received a base salary of $15,500 plus fringe benefits which include subsidized housing; free meals on campus; medical, dental, and optical benefits; life insurance; tuition reimbursement; 12 vacation days, 10 paid holidays, and 12 sick days; and a generous 401 (K) retirement plan. Annual salary increases are based upon performance and average $800 per year.

The new staff member begins work immediately in his assigned unit. Thrown into the cauldron without any formal training in Glen Mills' system, he must rely upon his fellow staff members for guidance. As he senses that Glen Mills is very different from other organizations he has known, looks to others to determine the Schools' expectations and make sense of its strange culture, witnesses and undergoes confrontation for unacceptable behavior, and feels affirmation and support when he turns to his peers for help, the new employee experiences firsthand the power of norms, peer pressures, and peer group support. He learns that his inevitable mistakes and failures do not count heavily against him; that the cardinal sins at Glen Mills are a failure to get involved, accept responsibility, support others, and request help when needed. He soon discovers that he has learned not only how to do his job, but also what it is like to be a new student at the Schools.

Following a four-week probationary period the cottage team meets to discuss the candidate's performance. Based upon this peer evaluation, the team leader decides whether to make the individual's status permanent.

Having been subjected for a month or more to the forces that fuel Glen Mills' program, the not-so-new recruit begins the formal training with an experience base and awareness that make clear the relevance of the course work. Training includes norms, GGI, and the Schools' Performance Evaluation System (PES).

Two full days are devoted to norms. Training objectives are to understand norms and their impact upon organizational effectiveness; learn the normative history of the Schools, recognize and measure norms, and develop strategies for normative change. Work group norms have a powerful impact upon the behavior of individual employees; it is therefore essential that work group norms be consistent with the Schools' values and objectives. This can not be assured unless key norms are identified and monitored. Glen Mills devotes as much effort to monitoring staff (and student) norms as it does to evaluating individual performance.

During training, staff draw upon their observations at Glen Mills to develop lists of positive and negative norms relating to each of ten areas critical to the success of the Schools: organizational pride, performance excellence, service delivery, teamwork, planning, supervision, training, student relations, honesty, and employee initiative. Having learned to identify norms, staff are next introduced to the instrument (GERI—Groups Expected Responses of the Individual, a questionnaire developed at the Schools) and process developed by Glen Mills to monitor staff norms in the ten areas. Finally, trainees examine elements of a normative change process: specifying the norms to be established, obtaining management commitment, modeling the desired behavior, communicating the objective throughout the organization, obtaining unanimous staff commitment, confronting transgressions, rewarding those who exhibit the desired behavior, monitoring conformity, recruiting staff who conform to the norms and orienting them to the desired behavior.

The GGI training is both experiential and cognitive. The experiential component is based upon the T-Group model (Bradford et al., 1964) developed at the National Training Laboratory. In all, the module occupies four days during which trainees learn the history and theory underlying the technique, gain an understanding of group dynamics, and learn the mechanics of leading a GGI group. An important goal is to master three tools useful in observing and understanding group behavior: factors governing interpersonal behavior in groups; Polsky's "delinquent diamond" (Polsky, 1962); and Lewinian force-field analysis (Lewin, 1951).

Trainees study eight factors affecting group behavior. The first is norms: the Schools' culture and its technology (i.e., GGI) both depend upon the explicit manipulation of group norms. Trainees learn how to identify and alter group norms, which norms are especially important to establish (e.g., honesty, helpfulness, confrontation) and challenge (e.g., conning, scapegoating, hurting). While GGI norms relating to the Schools' core values are identical to the broader campus norms, other norms vary. For example, students in GGI do not "watch their language," since this might inhibit free expression of feelings.

The remaining seven training issues of group process are leadership, subgrouping, non-verbal communication, communication patterns, hidden agendas, trust level, and facilitator style. These process points help the trainee to "read" group behavior and shape it so that the peer group becomes a powerful force in altering, rather than reinforcing, delinquent behavior.

In addition to the various process issues, an effective GGI group leader must have a framework for understanding the social system of institutionalized delinquents: the distribution of power and prestige among differing roles. Trainers teach Polsky's "diamond," the graphic representation of a delinquent social system proposed by Howard Polsky based upon eight months of observation in a residential treatment setting (Polsky, 1962). The "diamond" describes the structure of a delinquent social system, where "leaders," "lieutenants," and "con artists" exercise control over the weaker "isolates," "dyads," "bushboys," and "scapegoats" through violence and manipulation (see Exhibit 2.3). The diamond is a graphic representation of the status hierarchy.

Noting that the social structure remains unaltered as individuals move in and out of the various roles, Polsky felt that institutions could not be effective as long as the dysfunctional social system remained intact. A second key insight was that cottage staff, in an effort to maintain control, accommodate their own behavior to the delinquent subculture, in effect strengthening the "diamond" and its underlying delinquent values and skills. Polsky observed that staff norms

Exhibit 2.3
Polsky's Diamond

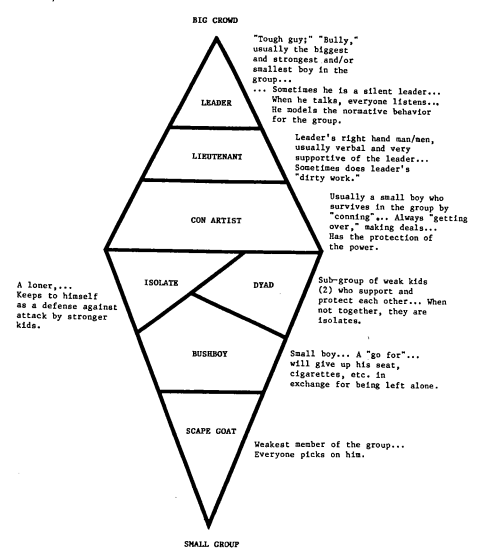

BIG CROWD

LEADER

"Tough guy;" "Bully,"
usually the biggest
and strongest and/or
smallest boy in the
group...
... Sometimes he is a silent leader...
When he talks, everyone listens...
He models the normative behavior
for the group.

LIEUTENANT

Leader's right hand man/men,
usually verbal and very
supportive of the leader...
Sometimes does leader's
"dirty work."

CON ARTIST

Usually a small boy who
survives in the group by
"conning"... Always "getting
over," making deals...
Has the protection of
the power.

A loner,...
Keeps to himself
as a defense against
attack by stronger
kids.

ISOLATE   DYAD

Sub-group of weak kids
(2) who support and
protect each other... When
not together, they are
isolates.

BUSHBOY

Small boy... A "go for"...
will give up his seat,
cigarettes, etc. in
exchange for being left alone.

SCAPE GOAT

Weakest member of the group...
Everyone picks on him.

SMALL GROUP

relating to interpersonal relations with students (e.g., forming informal alliances with delinquent leaders) reinforced the delinquent social structure.

Sam Ferrainola believed that Polsky's research provided the key insights for the development of an effective program. It would be necessary to "crush the diamond," that is, alter the social system so that power and status flowed away from aggressive and manipulative students and toward "positive peers" who modeled the Schools' values and upheld prosocial norms. For two years the "diamond" was the focus of daily cottage staff meetings, where each student in the unit was discussed in relation to the roles Polsky described. The result was posted daily on the cottage bulletin board, where every student could see how he and his peers were seen by staff. Those identified as delinquent leaders knew that the "honor" would mean close observation and frequent confrontation by staff. As these students reacted by keeping a low profile, lower status students began to feel less threatened and stepped out of the "bushboy" and "scapegoat" roles, hastening the collapse of the "diamond."

The establishment of a positive student culture and the Bulls Club signaled the end of the delinquent social system at the Schools. It was no longer possible to gain status through conning and intimidation; delinquent behavior invited confrontation by staff, other students, and the entire Bulls Club. The "diamond," though still a useful training device, was no longer descriptive of the student social system at Glen Mills.

Force-field analysis has replaced the "diamond" as the Schools' primary analytic tool. The technique is Glen Mills' adaptation of Lewinian force-field analysis; the Schools use it to analyze the "force field" of peer pressures within GGI groups and living units. Once weekly all cottage staff discuss the students in their unit until a consensus is reached regarding each boy's influence upon the cottage force field. Each student is rated on ten behaviors:

1. Models positive behavior
2. Confronts negative behavior
3. Accepts confrontation
4. Gives helpful feedback in GGI
5. Supports staff
6. Accepts feedback in GGI
7. Keeps his room and cottage detail clean
8. Supports student confrontation
9. Arrives on time for GGI, Townhouse, and classes
10. Participates in extra-curricular activities

A student who scores 5 or below is regarded as "negative." Those scoring 8 or above are considered "positive"; they are assertive in maintaining positive norms. The remainder are "neutral" students who neither strongly uphold norms nor engage in negative behavior. The cottage force field is a composite of the individual student vectors.

The most favorable force field occurs where the highest status students in the unit are also the most positive; the least favorable where negative students have managed to become leaders. In the latter case, staff mount a concerted effort to elevate the status of positive students with leadership potential while systematically denying status to negative students through sanctions, frequent confrontation, and manipulation of peer group pressures. If this strategy fails, the only recourse is to expel the negative leaders or transfer them to units with strong, positive force fields. This step is always a last resort, since teams which "export" their problem cases lose status within the institution.

The results of each cottage's analysis are communicated to the group living director, whose office maintains a large board with the names of each counselor listed for each cottage. Next to each counselor's name are a series of chips, one for each of his counselees, color-coded to indicate whether the student is positive (green), neutral (yellow), or negative (red). A glance at the board enables the director to quickly assess the campus force field as well as the status of each living unit. The board provides a visual reminder to staff regarding the importance of norms and peer pressures. The information it provides is important to decisions regarding staff or student transfers and serves as an early warning system alerting team leaders to units where the force field may be too weak to maintain positive behavior.

The final training component is a two-day module on the Schools' Performance Evaluation System (PES). Goals are to understand the PES, which covers all staff, and to learn how to write a job description.

Job descriptions at Glen Mills are individualized tools for the measurement of performance. No two are identical. The format includes a summary statement and a list of specific responsibilities with associated standards of performance. The summary statement is a short overview of the position, stating the title, broad responsibilities, supervisor's title, and relationship to the larger organization. The employee's areas of responsibility are each associated with detailed, measurable performance standards. For example, a counselor/specialist's job description includes one-to-one counseling as an area of responsibility; performance standards might include: "Meet with each counselee at least five minutes each day and for at least one hour each week"; "Prepare action plan for each counselee within two weeks of their arrival"; "Read counselee's files within two weeks of their arrival and share all pertinent information at the following staff meeting" etc. A typical counselor/specialist job description is at least three pages long. Each individual literally and figuratively writes his own job description (subject to negotiation with his supervisor), which provides for an objective appraisal of his performance.

The job description and the PES are not designed to reward or punish individual employees. Rather, the goal is to create a working environment that encourages optimum performance by allowing for maximum staff participation in structuring their own roles and developing clear, mutually shared expectations. The process of developing a job description and negotiating performance standards conveys respect for the motivation and unique talents of each employee, while helping to identify any differences in expectations held by the employee and his supervisor.

Performance evaluations are conducted twice a year. An employee's performance is important, but far from the only factor in deciding upon salary increases and promotions. Glen Mills' unusual policies in these areas reflect the Schools' commitment to loyalty and teamwork.

Except for entry level and highly specialized positions (e.g., dentist) all job openings at Glen Mills are filled by promotion from within. All supervisors come up through the ranks. They have demonstrated a high level of skill in all the roles occupied by their subordinates. Thus there is a core group of approximately 40 senior staff who could, if need be, conduct the Schools' program effectively. The ability to absorb, without loss of key staff, the personnel cutbacks which would be necessary if student enrollment were dramatically reduced greatly diminishes Glen Mills' vulnerability to fluctuations in admissions levels. In particular, it has placed the Schools in a strong position to resist attempts by client counties to impose damaging requirements. For example, when Philadelphia (which accounts for 40 percent of the Schools students) refused to pay Glen Mills' regular per diem rate for students during weekend home passes, the Schools notified city officials that this decision would make it necessary to expel all Philadelphia students. The outcome was a negotiated settlement which reduced the frequency of home passes, but not the per diem.

There are four requirements for advancement. First, the candidate must demonstrate a high level of excellence in his current job. Second, he must have voluntarily taken on responsibilities beyond the normal job requirements. These might include coaching an athletic team, organizing a major trip or social event, serving as an advisor to the Bulls Club, or other duties. Third, management must believe that he is capable of performing well in the new role. Finally, he must be committed to both the Glen Mills philosophy and to the administration. The latter requirement is characteristic of many successful organizations, but only rarely made explicit.

An individual who qualifies on all four points may be given an opportunity to show that he can handle the new position. He will be placed in the new role for a three-month probationary period, without any salary increase. The message given to him by his department's senior staff is: "We realize you don't know the new job and will make mistakes. We want you to succeed. Ask lots of questions, because we're behind you and will do everything we can to help you make it." There is no expectation that the candidate will be an instant success in his new role, only that he will do his best and depend on the team for support. Most find themselves with the new title and increased salary after the three months.

Salary increases at all levels are based primarily upon team, not individual, effectiveness. For line staff, individual performance is also factored into the computation. Team leaders and top managers, who are expected to work as a team at all times, receive a uniform raise based upon the performance of the weakest team member. The policy reinforces teamwork norms, insuring that each individual's interest is best served by strengthening the team and actively supporting any members who are struggling.

Academic Education Department

Students enter Glen Mills with a wide range of educational experience and ability. Since 1976 new students' IQs have ranged from 55 to 130, with an average of 88. A few have been high school graduates, but most have completed only nine years of formal education. Standardized tests indicate that the average new student's verbal and computational skills are below the sixth grade level, but the range of scores spans first through twelfth grade. A few have been successful academically; the majority have experienced failure in the traditional classroom setting. Meeting the educational needs of so diverse a population requires not one school, but several. Thus, the name of the institution: Glen Mills Schools for Boys.

Glen Mills' academic program is designed to meet each student at his own level of functioning and to set ambitious, but achievable objectives within an individualized instruction plan. Each student's educational level is assessed during his first week at the Schools. The assessment includes the Metropolitan Achievement Test (MAT), which is readministered after six months to measure the student's progress. Based upon the results of the initial assessment, the student is assigned to one of five educational programs.

The Learning Center Program is designed for students functioning at or below the fourth grade level. Few of these students have ever experienced educational success. The emphasis, accordingly, is upon individualized one-to-one tutoring using high motivational materials designed to hold the student's interest. An Individualized Education Program (IEP) is designed for each student. Objective measures of progress are frequent; effort and improvement are rewarded. At this level, an important goal is to break the cycle of failure and frustration. Meaningful success experiences are as important as content.

The Learning Center is also the site of the Schools' special education program, designed to meet the needs of students classified as "exceptional" under the provisions of Public Law 94–142. The instructional program for these young men is similar to that of their Learning Center peers, except that their teachers are Glen Mills staff certified as special education instructors and their program is monitored by the Chester County Intermediate Unit operating under the auspices of the Pennsylvania Department of Education. In addition, their IEPs are developed and monitored by a multidisciplinary team which includes a teacher, school psychologist, and administrator.

Students functioning between the fourth and eighth grade levels are assigned to the Intermediate Program. Classes are conducted in the student's cottage by a counselor-teacher from his unit. Instruction is provided to groups of 10 to 16 students. Learning is self-paced, with strong emphasis upon basic skills. A student must achieve a grade of 80 or higher on each mastery test before proceeding to the next objective on his IEP. Cottage activities (e.g., field trips, out-of-state travel, projects for homecoming celebrations, programs for cottage or campus audiences) are designed by the counselor-teacher to reinforce formal academic instruction. Rewards for achievement include cottage parties or special meals to celebrate students' progress.

A young man performing well at the Intermediate level becomes eligible for a qualifying test assessing his readiness to move on to one of three courses that comprise the GED Program. The Pre-GED, GED, and Project Help courses each consist of a two-month semester focusing upon mathematics, social studies, science, reading and writing skills. Their common goal is to prepare students for their GED exam, leading to a General Educational Development certificate. Pre-GED and GED are intensive, highly structured courses conducted in Tresa Hall, Glen Mills' school building. Project Help is a supplementary program conducted in the evenings for students falling behind in the other two courses.

The GED program is designed to provide instruction while simultaneously preparing students to maintain their concentration during five hours of GED exams administered on two consecutive days. During the first day of class, students in the GED course are introduced to special class norms:

• Sit up straight at all times
• Do not rest your chin on your hand
• No "side" conversations
• Raise hand for attention
• Raise hand in response to every question posed by the teacher

The GED norms are intended to prevent students' attention from wandering and to maintain concentration and involvement for the entire period. For example, an instructor waits for all hands to go up every time a question is asked. A student who knows the answer should offer his understanding to help his classmates; a student who does not know the answer should always seek help: either way, his hand should be in the air. Most importantly, the norm ensures attentiveness. If called upon, a student must be prepared to give the answer or express his lack of understanding in a way that shows he has been listening.

Combined with motivational ceremonies and the strong support for educational achievement provided by Glen Mills' culture, the courses have made the Schools' GED program extraordinarily successful. During the period 1982–87, 974 (86 percent) of the 1,136 students who took the state GED exam passed.

The College Prep Program is available to students who have earned their GED and express interest in continuing their education. The major emphasis of the curriculum is on preparation for the Scholastic Aptitude Test (SAT). Classroom work includes both individual and group instruction. Additional program components include career counseling and support in completing college admission and financial aid application procedures. During 1982–87,

89 students have been admitted to college following the College Prep Program.

Students who succeed in the College Prep Program are encouraged to enroll in the Schools' College Program. These students take one or two courses per semester at nearby Delaware County Community College and attend regular tutoring sessions at Glen Mills to supplement their classwork. Tutors help the college students to prepare for exams, strengthen study skills, and organize their time so that research papers or other projects are completed on schedule. Twenty-nine students have earned 175 college course credits through the college program.

The Herman Barcus Scholarship Fund enables qualified Glen Mills students to pursue a college education after discharge from the Schools. The fund provides full tuition, room and board, books, and a $200 allowance for the student's first year in any U.S. college. Between 1983 and 1987 44 students received Barcus scholarships.

The Schools' educational programs are the responsibility of Randy Ireson, director of education. Staff resources include 82 counselor-teachers in the Group Living Department who serve as Intermediate Program instructors, and 28 individuals who report to the director of education. The latter group consists of counselor-teachers, educational specialists, and staff members of Academic Hall, Glen Mills' academic honors cottage. All Glen Mills instructors are also counselors in either Tradesman Hall, Academic Hall, or one of the other living units, an arrangement that minimizes staff costs and greatly facilitates working relationships among the vocational, academic, and group living departments.

Glen Mills' program motivates students by rewarding effort and recognizing achievement at several levels of accomplishment. There are numerous ceremonies, each designed to reward and to motivate.

Learning Center students who have achieved their goals are individually honored in front of their peers and presented with a small gift and printed certificate of achievement during a ceremony conducted by the director or a senior administrator. A student who has successfully completed the Learning Center curriculum will usually speak, describing how hard work can overcome self-doubt and a poor academic record, and the satisfaction of being able to read and write. His example and exhortations to strive for the goals carry more weight with his peers than anything staff can add.

At a monthly "MAT assembly" students who have shown a year or more of academic progress during the past six months receive a school jacket; those who demonstrate at least nine months' growth earn a clock radio. Entertainment (mimes, magicians, etc.) is provided to make the assembly fun for all: the effect upon the audience is as important as the experience of the honorees. The Schools' ceremonies are designed to be attractive to its students so that they will have positive associations to academic achievement.

GED ceremonies are scheduled at two-month intervals to coincide with the start of each new GED class. With the incoming students in attendance, each student from the previous class is given a sealed envelope containing the results of his GED exam. Unbeknownst to the students, the 15 percent or so who have failed the test are filtered out by staff prior to the ceremony; the incoming students witness an uninterrupted sequence of smiles, shouts, and "high-fives" as each envelope is opened and a Glen Mills Schools ring presented to the proud "graduate."

The most impressive educational ceremony, Educational Awards Day, occurs annually in June. The entire student body is in attendance, along with the families of many of the students. Transportation for the students' family members is provided by Glen Mills. After a formal academic procession, complete with caps and gowns, the 1987 ceremony featured speeches by the Schools' valedictorian, and an alumnus who had received a four-year scholarship to an area university. A keynote address by Judge Robert Mason of Prince George's County, Maryland, was followed by numerous awards (including a $6,000 scholarship) to outstanding students and staff. The event concludes with a special luncheon for students, staff, and guests.

Cottages also benefit from their students' progress. Each month approximately 15 to 25 percent of the students in each cottage take the MAT exam to determine their rate of academic growth during the past five or six months. The cottage whose students demonstrate the most progress receive a "win" in the form of a pizza party, trip, or some other prize. Thus is the role of staff and peer support in individual achievement recognized and rewarded.

Two important educational principles at Glen Mills are an emphasis upon effort and accountability of instructors for student growth. When Academic Hall, the cottage for scholastic honors students, was opened in 1985 it was decided that admission would be based solely upon academic effort as measured by the combined judgments of the student's teachers and group living staff. Everyone must have the opportunity to obtain status and recognition through academics, regardless of their level of performance. Glen Mills would extend its highest honor to those who apply themselves the most, not to those who achieve the most. Academic Hall houses some Glen Mills students who have been accepted in area colleges. It also houses students functioning at the fourth grade level.

Teacher accountability is a cornerstone of the Glen Mills approach. Results of the MAT tests are of as much interest to instructors as to students because instructors are expected to achieve a growth rate by their students of at least 1.5 grade levels of improvement in basic skills for each nine months of instruction. Those who fail to do so have three months to meet the goal or be removed from their job. At Glen Mills the belief is that students will not fail to make progress unless instructors fail to teach.

In summary, Glen Mills believes that its students have enormous academic potential which can be realized through the development of individualized educational programs within the context of a supportive institutional culture. The academic program is highly innovative, conspicuously rewarding academic effort, holding instructors accountable to achieve strong growth, encouraging creative educational and motivational approaches and, most importantly, establishing supportive peer norms.

Support Services Department

The Support Services Department includes 91 employees assigned to the Schools' business office (10), maintenance (29), farm (8), central receiving (5), and food service (39) units. It is directed by Garry Ipock. Mr. Ipock, who joined Glen Mills' Social Service Department in 1971 under Mr. Ferrainola's predecessor (Mr. Ferrainola disbanded the Social Service Department), has the broadest experience of any Glen Mills manager. Together with the director and Tom Beecher, Garry was one of the gang of three who plotted the Schools' transformation during 1975–76, when they had few allies. His loyalty during Mr. Ferrainola's difficult first year (1975) won the respect and trust of the new director, who appointed Garry director of admissions. With no staff assigned to him, there was little to "direct." But his skilled and aggressive marketing of the Schools to Pennsylvania county courts yielded the new students, and hence the revenue, which fueled the development of a new Glen Mills during 1976–80.

In each support unit, the primary responsibility of staff is the performance of their unit function and their secondary responsibility is support of the cottage units. The latter responsibility is one more manifestation of the priority of teamwork and businesslike operations at the Schools. The jobs of Glen Mills' support staff depend upon the effectiveness of the Group Living Department as surely as the jobs of General Motors' support staff depend upon the success of the assembly line. Responsiveness to cottage needs for special food service, maintenance, etc., is expected of all support staff.

The need for day-to-day interdepartmental teamwork which directly affects students is less for support service managers than for those in the other four departments. Accordingly, the management style and normative cultures in these units are not always reflective of the broader institutional culture. For example, the food services director supervises a unit which in terms of the quality and quantity of the food provided, cost control, and attractiveness of the dining facility is doubtless among the best in the nation. However, he manages with a highly authoritarian style and prefers to work independently of other Glen Mills managers. Clearly operating outside even the broadest interpretation of Glen Mills' principles, the food services director is nonetheless respected for the extraordinary performance of his unit. The Schools' normative culture is sufficiently elastic to accommodate an aberrant manager in a role that is relatively independent of other units, as long as his performance clearly justifies the exception.

Battling Bulls Club

> To build an effective correctional system is not to try to take away the
> power of the inmates, but rather to figure out ways to use inmate power for
> correctional purposes.
>
> Donald Cressey

No discussion of Glen Mills' formal organization could be considered complete
without acknowledging the role of the Bulls Club. The club is the only student
subgroup allowed to exist at Glen Mills. Though not a "department," it has a
powerful impact upon the Schools' normative culture and even its day-to-day
operation.

By 1987 the Bulls Club had been firmly established for more than five years.
It included the most positive students at Glen Mills. The Bulls Club members
in each cottage had their own officers, staff advisor, and weekly meetings. The
campuswide organization was run by "campus executives" including a president,
vice president, treasurer, secretary, and two sergeants at arms—typically the
most mature, positive role models on campus.

Bulls play a major role in the operation of the Schools. They monitor the
dining hall and student union; serve as Big Brothers to new students; dispense
all campus work assignments to students wishing to earn money; assist in providing night coverage in their living units. Executives of the Bulls Club attend
the weekly Resource Team meeting along with the director and all department
heads and team leaders. Most importantly, Bulls act as student leaders and play
the leading role in maintaining the student normative culture through modeling
positive behavior and confronting transgressions of campus norms. The surest
way to reverse a weakening of cottage norms is to transfer strong Bulls into the
unit.

Students are continually urged by Bulls and counselors to work toward membership in the club through serious involvement in the Schools' program and a
willingness to help one's peers. When the cottage Bulls and staff feel a candidate
is ready, he is given a pledge packet. The packet describes the privileges and
responsibilities of membership, provides suggestions regarding the development
of an appropriate confrontation style, and outlines the pledge process. In addition
to modeling positive behavior, the candidate must write an essay explaining
why he wants to become a Battling Bull and complete a confrontation log—14
pages of 15 confrontations apiece. The pledge candidate must complete 210
confrontations within two weeks, describe them in his log, and obtain the
signature of the students confronted to verify their accuracy. During the pledge
period the student is also expected to take on additional responsibilities in his
cottage and on campus. Approximately half of Glen Mills' students are accepted
into the Bulls Club. Membership is the capstone of the Glen Mills experience.
It represents an opportunity to exercise leadership skills in support of positive,

rather than antisocial behavior, and to enjoy peer group status and recognition based upon self-development and helping others. The Battling Bulls are the embodiment of Glen Mills' philosophy that the habilitation of socialized delinquents is best achieved through the harnessing of peer group pressures to promote constructive behavior.

The cottage representatives, campus staff advisor, and the campus executives meet weekly in the Bulls lounge, a posh area open only to Bulls and featuring comfortable furniture, a pool table, and a large stereo/video system. Reports from each cottage representative describe significant events in the unit and the activities and/or problems of the Bulls in his cottage. Problems are discussed and specific commitments to solve them are made and recorded.

After the meeting job interviews are conducted through a serious, formal process. An applicant must address the Bulls' job committee, explain his reasons for wanting a job, and demonstrate that he is able to handle a job in addition to his other responsibilities in the program. Competition is keen. The control over jobs is an important responsibility contributing to Bulls' status on campus. There are approximately 100 student jobs available in cleaning, food service, and maintenance. They require two to three hours per day and pay about $25 per week, representing an important source of labor for the Schools and income for the students. An important "side" effect is the reinforcement of positive behavior. As the club's staff advisor explained to one applicant, "If you want to get paid by us you have to work for our goals—it's that simple."

All campus Bulls, well over 200 students, meet every two weeks in the chapel. Dr. Claus Ottmüller, a researcher from West Germany, describes the meeting which took place on December 14, 1985:

The meetings have a ceremonial character in order to show the importance of the club for the school to the club members. On the stage of the chapel stands a speaker's desk with a microphone, a second is standing on a table on stage where the campus executives sit. After listening to the national anthem and the pledge of allegiance—in an almost churchlike atmosphere—the president addresses the assembly. The executives give their reports on the state of affairs, financial situation and events in the club. After them, the cottage executives give their reports. . . . This is followed by the initiation of new club members. All have to stand in front of the stage, facing the assembly, after having been called by name. One of them then reads his mandatory paper where he puts out why he wanted to become a bull. After long-lasting applause the president explains to the pledgees that they are now Bulls. After renewed applause they sit down and the secretary reports on new tasks of the club. The incident on 69th Street . . . was problematized anew. "The director needs our support that this might not happen again," says the secretary—he really means it. The Bulls share the feeling that the School is *really* dependent on their cooperation for its functioning. This feeling of being "for real for real" responsible for the institution is one of the keys of the success of the Glen Mills Schools. . . . The meeting goes on with the announcement of a festival, the preparations for sports events and the ratings of the "coverage." Every unit, through its Bulls, supports the staff members during coverage and confrontation of norm violations in the arcade and the cafeteria. There is daily another unit in charge, in the evening the staff members rate their performance. The unit rated best in the week receives a prize of $100 for the account of the cottage Bulls. Often there are two or three teams equally good, then money is split. The winners receive a long applause—another reinforcement besides money.

After this rating the two microphones are carried into the crowd and everybody present is allowed to give positive feedback for individuals or groups. The applause after each feedback is in accordance with the value the students attribute to the individual or the group appraised. There is an appraisal for a "good job" in organizing a competition, a sports team gets best wishes for their next game, a student receives congratulations for being named student of the month, a cottage Bulls Club is applauded because the norms in the cottage are upheld better and the Bull receives feedback because he improved in school in spite of difficulties. (Ottmüller, 1987: 133–34)

The effective operation of the Bulls Club is crucial to Glen Mills' normative culture. Great care is taken to promote the cohesiveness of the Club and the status of its members. For example, the Schools provide payments to each cottage Bulls organization in return for the Bulls' routine assistance to cottage staff. These funds are used by the unit's Bulls for a visit to McDonald's, going to movies and other outings. These activities are highly valued by the Bulls. The privilege of off campus group activities is an important "perk" of Club membership and an incentive for new students to strive for their Bulls' log.

The establishment of the Bulls Club is one of the most significant achievements of the Glen Mills Schools. The club represents a powerful tool for the maintenance of the normative culture. The club is, in effect, a cohesive and active cadre of high status students who serve as role models and ensure that peer pressures are both powerful and positive. Each new student is oriented to Glen Mills by a "big brother," a Bulls Club member who indoctrinates him in the "Glen Mills way" and is responsible to his Bulls Club peers for the new student's behavior. This arrangement ensures that the new student is exposed intensively and early to positive, high status peers. The responsibility to advocate the Schools' program to the newcomer also promotes internalization of Glen Mills' values by the big brother.

The Bulls' leadership is responsive to the concerns of the administration, which they learn first hand in the weekly resource team meetings. Pressing concerns are later communicated by the Bulls' leaders to the cottage Bulls Club officers and, through them, to the Bulls in each unit. Within hours a massive campaign is launched by the Bulls to ensure that the issue—drug use, behavior at sports events, or some other problem—is resolved.

The normative culture model could not function without this potent tool for harnessing peer pressure to promote positive behavior. Replication probably requires a similar student organization. Timing of the establishment of the club is critical. The initial step must be to "crush the diamond" (see Personnel Recruiting and Training, this chapter): staff must first achieve sufficient control to deny peer group status to delinquent leaders. This reduces the danger that club leadership will be exercised by negative students, forcing disbandment. Only after staff have gained firm control can the cultivation of appropriate student leadership begin.

Board of Managers

Glen Mills' Board consists of 20 members (see Appendix 2), serving without compensation. Each is assigned to one or more of 10 standing committees: Admissions, Education, Finance, Group Living, Health, Investment, Planning, Property, Recreation, and Vocational Education. The director of each department serves as staff liaison to the corresponding committee, which represents the primary link between one program area and the board. The committees and the full board meet monthly.

The primary role of the board includes approval of major expenditures (the director can authorize payments of up to $5,000 without board approval), decision making with regard to the Schools' legal and financial affairs, and monitoring current program operations. The Planning Committee works with the Schools' administration in the development of major new programs. The board permits the director a great deal of autonomy in personnel matters, development of programs and policies, and of course the day-to-day management of the Schools.

The board's composition and role have changed significantly since Sam Ferrainola's arrival in 1975. They are best understood in the context of changes in the board-administration relationship.

Sam was named executive director largely on the recommendation of Dr. Pilnick. Mr. Ferrainola felt that the board's level of confidence was not great: he was offered a 90-day contract, which he never signed. For the first six months of Sam's tenure, most of the board's time was absorbed in discussion of loan requests for the financially ailing institution. The Schools' survival was very much at issue.

Herman Barcus, a board member who later became its president, worked closely with the new director to help get the Schools on an even keel financially. The director proved remarkably able—within the first year enrollment increased, the flood of red ink stemmed, and the board was able to turn its attention to matters other than seeking loans. Mr. Ferrainola's astute financial performance was a key factor in gaining the confidence and respect of the board.

He needed all the confidence he could muster. As staff became increasingly disaffected, several bypassed the director and secretly took their concerns directly to board members. On several instances board members inadvertently encouraged this by failing to insist that the matters be discussed directly with Mr. Ferrainola, thereby undercutting the new director's authority.

The behind-the-scenes maneuvering culminated with the accusatory letter received by the board in December 1975. Fortunately, the majority of the board were by then persuaded of Mr. Ferrainola's integrity and competence, and supported the decision to fire those responsible. A few months later, when Dr. Pilnick began to criticize Sam to the board, it was faced with yet another crisis relating to Sam's leadership. The board's dedication, integrity, and ability to reach sound decisions under extreme pressure were tested during many hours of fact finding and deliberation. Their decision to support the director signaled a breakthrough in establishing the foundation of trust and respect that enabled Mr. Ferrainola and his board to work together to build a new Glen Mills.

Most board members valued Sam's "business sense" and creativity. Some, concerned with the director's unconventional approach to his job, urged a tight rein lest he stray *too* far from traditional approaches. In one form or another, the central problem of the board's relationship with the director has been how to avoid stifling the creative energies of this extraordinary leader without abdicating the board's ultimate responsibility for the Schools. How tight a rein should the board hold?

Sam served notice early on that his would not be a conventional approach to programming. Persuaded of the educational value of traveling, and wanting to make clear that the new Glen Mills would be a fine prep school and not a prison, the director resolved to send a group of staff and students on a trip to Florida. Their educational program would be built around the trip: they would develop a budget, calculate the number of miles to be traveled each day, study marine biology, and learn about the geography and culture of the South.

The board was skeptical. To some, sending delinquents to Florida smacked of coddling, or at least suggested that crime *does* pay. Fortunately, the director had important allies on the Education Committee, which endorsed his plan. The committee's spokesperson, Dr. Faye Soffen, recognized the educational value of the proposal and championed it. The trip was approved. It was highly successful, as scores of similar trips since have been. One of its by-products was a strengthened relationship between the director and the board.

Not all of the director's initiatives have yielded such positive results. The "Prep" Program, though successful and highly innovative, was discontinued in part because the director had failed to build adequate board support before launching it. Some members' reservations about the appropriateness of the program in relation to the Schools' primary mission were magnified by a perception that the director had not kept the board adequately informed about his plans. There were other factors involved in the decision to discontinue, but the lesson for the director was the need to communicate more effectively with board members.

The committee structure partially meets this need. In addition, the director frequently consults informally with individual board members to seek or provide information, use them as a sounding board for plans and decisions, or to "seed" new program proposals. Above all, he makes certain that members are kept informed of significant developments, that there are no surprises.

Relations between board and administration are extremely good. Indeed, some concern exists that relations are *too* good, that board members are so supportive of the director that they have difficulty remaining objective. At the formal level, the board compensates by stressing accountability. A thorough and detailed planning process is the price of board approval for major expenditures; the board serves as a reality check on administration proposals.

Informally, board members acknowledge their deference to Sam in program development and implementation. They feel his performance warrants their confidence. There is a strong foundation of trust built upon years of experience and a mutual feeling that, despite occasional disagreements, each party is motivated by a love of the Schools and a willingness to work hard on behalf of Glen Mills.

Board-administration relationships have been tested and ultimately strengthened by a series of critical events which required a united response to external threats. Throughout most of his tenure and despite sometimes intense pressures, the board has been steadfast in their support of Sam Ferrainola. The genius of the board has been to provide a context in which the genius of their extraordinary but unconventional executive director could blossom.

In summary, the board, the Bulls, and the various departments at Glen Mills comprise a molecular "whole" functioning in concert. The performance of each is judged in terms of both its effectiveness in meeting its own objectives and its contribution to the effectiveness of the other elements. The major objective of the Bulls and *every* department is the strengthening of the normative culture.

It is essential to recognize that the service Glen Mills provides is not a "program," but a normative culture supported by a *system* of highly interdependent, consciously designed activities and processes. These include far more than the Schools' academic and vocational offerings. Daily cottage meetings, GGI, confrontation, Bulls Club, continual monitoring of behaviors and norms, individual counseling, awards ceremonies, the function of the "big brother," recreation programs: none operate in isolation. Every thread is related to the others; all are intentionally woven into the fabric of the normative culture.

That Glen Mills students are exposed to one unified normative culture may be the Schools' most remarkable achievement. Most institutions have at least four. Values, attitudes and norms of administrators, professional treatment staff, cottage staff and students typically vary markedly, in ways that interfere with institutional effectiveness. The establishment of a single culture spanning all staff and students may have been more fully achieved at Glen Mills than in any other large correctional facility in history. It is unquestionably the key factor in the Schools' success.

CRITICAL EVENTS: 1980–1986

Development of programs occurred against the backdrop of a series of critical events related here because they illustrate important cultural values and administrative policies, and suggest some of the ways Glen Mills has affected Pennsylvania's juvenile justice system.

Glen Mills' unwillingness to compromise on matters relating to the integrity of its program has brought the Schools into conflict with state agencies and individual government officials on several occasions. Four incidents are particularly noteworthy in terms of their system impact and/or significance in strengthening the Schools' programs and culture. Glen Mills fought for passage of Pennsylvania's Act 30 in 1981 to establish the right of private juvenile correctional institutions to retain control over their own educational programs. A state supreme court decision won by Glen Mills in 1986 preserved the right of private institutions to refuse to accept students who do not meet admissions criteria and are a danger to the institution. Glen Mills' defense of a staff person accused of abusing a student illustrates the administration's commitment to its staff and raises questions as to what constitutes "abuse." Finally, the Schools' successful defense against criminal charges brought by the Philadelphia district attorney concluded one of the most traumatic episodes in the Schools' recent history.

The accounts provided below, like those in the preceding chapter, do not purport to be complete descriptions of the incidents. The perspective is solely that of the Glen Mills administration and staff; no one else was interviewed. The goal in discussing them is not to provide a comprehensive analysis of the events, but to better understand the Schools' philosophy and the director's leadership style.

A student essay in the Schools' newspaper once described the director as an "Obstacle. He is the person who stands in the way of people who try to destroy what we have accomplished for ourselves . . . our Director doesn't let anyone stop his school from growing to its highest point" (*Battling Bulletin*, December 23, 1987, p. 8). Sam Ferrainola is Protector of the Faith. An avid student of European history and political struggles, he relishes both the strategic and tactical aspects of fighting for his beliefs and seems to find life a little dull when there are no adversaries in sight. He is most at home on the ramparts rallying his forces against attacks by "The System," usually in the persons of government bureaucrats or entrenched interest groups.

All four of these incidents illustrate the determination of Glen Mills' Board and administration to "stand strong" (an expression heard often at Glen Mills) for its beliefs. The operating principle is easily stated: Be clear about your values and core objectives. When challenged, do everything possible to resolve the dispute in a way satisfactory to both parties. But never betray your principles under the guise of "compromise."

Few would dissent from this position. The following incidents illustrate how it represents far more than a philosophical stance at Glen Mills.

Retaining Control over Programs

During 1979 Glen Mills was requested by the Pennsylvania Department of Public Welfare (DPW), which administers the state's programs for delinquents, to provide an estimate of the Schools' expenditures for education. Sensing that the request may be less innocuous than it appeared, the director learned through a series of inquiries that the funding mechanism for private juvenile correctional facilities would soon be altered in a way that posed a major threat to Glen Mills. Prior to 1979 the Schools' charges for each student were paid by the committing county, which (in the case of Pennsylvania counties) was reimbursed by DPW for 50 percent of the charges. In 1979 DPW decided that it would no longer reimburse the counties for any charges related to education, since this was the responsibility of the Department of Education. Each institution would be required to bill the Department of Education separately for these costs.

The director realized that the new policy caused two problems for Glen Mills. First, when the counties' reimbursement was reduced, they would soon refuse to pay the Schools for the full cost of the program. Second, Glen Mills' only option for recovering the lost revenue would be through the Department of Education. Under state law, this would require that Glen Mills' educational program be subject to the administrative control of the department. The Schools would lose control over teacher recruitment and curriculum.

The consequences would be disastrous. Glen Mills' culture could not be maintained if educational staff were not accountable to the director or if they enjoyed working conditions far superior to other staff. The Schools' staff earn an annual salary below that of most certified teachers. Glen Mills' staff work 12 months per year, including many evenings and weekends. If the "outside" instructors were accepted, a "we-they" atmosphere would soon replace teamwork, especially since the director would have little authority over the new teachers. With no commitment to or experience with the Schools' normative culture approach and little loyalty to its administrative team, the teachers could destroy staff cohesion. Glen Mills' program, which requires a very high level of teamwork among *all* staff, would not survive intact.

Foreseeing the possible consequences, Mr. Ferrainola responded to the DPW inquiry with a question of his own: What constitutes "education"? Broadly conceived, nearly everything that a student experienced at Glen Mills might be considered education. The response was precisely what the director had hoped. DPW would leave it to the administrator's discretion to define the term, though they encouraged a broad interpretation with a correspondingly large cost allocation. This would reduce substantially the monies DPW would have to provide while making the institutions dependent upon the Department of Education. Sam Ferrainola, alone among the area institutional directors to recognize the dangers, reported Glen Mills' costs as $3.27 per student per day, while other institutions submitted charges as high as $20.00. The funding the Schools received from the counties was therefore reduced by only 5 percent, while other institutions came to rely heavily upon the Department of Education.

Glen Mills refused to accept the Department of Education funding, anticipating the need to challenge the department's plan to impose state-accredited personnel upon the institutions. The plan requiring the hiring of certified teachers enjoyed strong support from the teachers' union; the odds on preventing the change were heavily against Glen Mills.

The Schools decided to press for legislation to enable private correctional institutions to conduct their own educational programs. The strategy would be to persuade legislators that the institutions are best able to provide instruction to their youths, most of whom have already failed in conventional classrooms. As evidence of the potential benefits of Glen Mills' alternative approach the Schools produced highly complimentary evaluation reports from Pennsylvania and Maryland in which evaluation teams had pronounced Glen Mills' educational program outstanding. The Schools augmented the report with standardized testing data showing impressive gains in math and verbal skills for Glen Mills' students.

Lobbying hard with political leaders of both parties, Glen Mills persuaded their state representative to introduce Act 30, a bill exempting private correctional institutions from the administrative control of the Department of Education. Act 30 requires the Department of Education, in effect, to reimburse institutions for their educational costs as long as students show adequate progress and the costs do not exceed those that would be required if the local school district provided the instruction. Glen Mills was able to blunt strong opposition by the Department of Education by quietly pointing out to them that their current practice of direct reimbursement to institutions for the services of uncertified teachers, albeit on an interim basis, was illegal. Glen Mills was "clean," having refused to accept the monies, but the Department of Education needed Act 30 to legitimize their current practice.

Despite the resentment of the Department of Education and the opposition of the teachers' union, Act 30 was enacted in 1981 with only one dissenting vote. The battle was won, but the war continued. When the Department of Education audited Glen Mills' records, they set the Schools' educational costs at $4.37 per student per day. In justifying the low rate, the Department cited Glen Mills' original estimate ($3.27). The Schools seemed to have fallen victim to its own stratagem. Meeting with a group of educators to appeal the department's decision, the director began by asking: "Which of you is prepared to state for the public record that it is possible to provide even the most minimal education for $4.37 per day?" No hands went up. Glen Mills' rate was doubled to $8.74, a great improvement but still less than half of the average payment to other institutions.

The director had a contingency plan in the event that Act 30 had not passed. Glen Mills would have refused to allow the department-certified teachers on its campus, opting instead to comply with the law by busing its 300 students to the department's facility each day while operating its own educational program in the evening. While clearly an unsatisfactory option, this would have preserved the Schools' program. Moreover, the daily influx of 300 delinquents would likely have induced the Department of Education to find a way to accommodate Glen Mills' program.

Retaining Control Over Admissions

Among the most significant differences between public and private institutions is the historical right of private schools to refuse to accept students whom they believe to be inappropriate for their programs. This right is particularly important to Glen Mills due to the Schools' reliance upon norms rather than close individual supervision or physical restraints to maintain control. Glen Mills does not accept a student if the safety of the community would require close and continuous monitoring of the boy's behavior. Specifically, Glen Mills admissions criteria exclude fire-setters.

During 1986 Glen Mills accepted a Philadelphia student who they subsequently determined had started several fires, although there was no mention of the incidents in the boy's record. The young man was immediately returned to court, but in an unprecedented action the judge refused to reconsider the commitment and ordered the student back to Glen Mills. Contact by the Schools' staff attorney and later by an outside law firm representing the Schools failed to persuade the judge to reverse his decision.

With two core issues at stake—the safety of the community and the Schools' right to control admissions—the Schools could not accept the judge's decision. Attempts at negotiation having failed, Glen Mills appealed to the state supreme court. The court upheld the institution, securing for all private Pennsylvania institutions a right necessary to the continuation of programs which employ no physical security.

Protecting Students from Abuse

Glen Mills' program model includes strong safeguards to protect against staff abuse of students. Risks of abuse are high due to the emphasis upon confrontation to maintain campus norms. Careful staff selection, training, and monitoring are essential to ensure that confrontations do not result in abuse. Less obvious but equally important is the need to support staff who are unfairly accused of abuse.

An administrator's first responsibility is to protect his students. His second is to be fair to staff. Students will be abused if the administrator ignores either of these. To forget the first responsibility invites abuse by staff. To forget the second invites abuse by students.

Glen Mills' policy is to discharge any staff member who commits or permits abuse, and to strongly support staff when charges are unjustified. The former is necessary to protect the students from staff abuse, the latter to maintain the campus norms which protect students from abuse by other students.

Two incidents illustrate these policies. In the first, an inebriated off-duty cottage counselor arrived in his unit during the evening shift and began to harass several students. He forced one student to stand in a corner while he cursed and berated him, repeatedly insulting both the boy and his family. When the director learned of the incident, he fired both the offending staff and a counselor who had been present but failed to intervene.

The second incident involved an altercation between a student and a counselor that resulted in the student suffering a bloody nose. An inquiry by the state Department of Welfare was followed by a letter to the director advising him that the counselor had abused the student, a conclusion at odds with the findings of Mr. Ferrainola's own investigation. The DPW opinion was based solely upon the boy's statement and the nature of his injuries. Interviewing both the staff member and student witnesses, the director found that the counselor had defended himself against the student whose long record of assaultive behavior included an unprovoked and vicious attack against his own father.

The director believed that the DPW letter, if not contested, represented a threat to both the staff member and Glen Mills. He informed the DPW officials of his own findings, but they refused to rescind their conclusion.

That left Mr. Ferrainola with three options. He could ignore the DPW finding. This action was rejected because it would place the Schools at serious legal risk if the counselor were involved in a second incident resulting in injury to a student. A second option was to fire the counselor. There were three reasons why this would be unacceptable. First, it would be morally wrong since the director believed him to be innocent. Second, it would be unfair because the DPW accusation would prevent the staff member from obtaining other employment in his field. Most importantly, it would place the entire program in danger. When staff members see that the administration is unwilling to defend counselors who are doing their job, they no longer take the risk of intervening in potentially dangerous situations. "Don't get involved" becomes the norm. As staff avoid confronting negative behavior, street norms of bullying and intimidation become established in the institution. Finally, a form of abuse far more common and harmful than staff abuse—the abuse of students by other students—becomes rampant and unchallenged. To fire the counselor would be to sacrifice both staff and, ultimately, the students for the sake of expediency.

The director opted to take the only other course of action available to him. He challenged the DPW findings in court. When DPW acknowledged that it could not substantiate its charge of abuse, Glen Mills accepted the agency's offer to purge its records of the charges.

These incidents raise important policy and procedural questions: What constitutes abuse? What steps can be taken to minimize staff abuse? For what forms of abuse should institutions be held accountable? Glen Mills' program model is especially vulnerable to abuse and to charges of abuse. Confrontations are frequent, sometimes verbally harsh, and occasionally involve physical restraint. Students who choose to file (and at times exaggerate) complaints about staff behavior have ready access to telephones. Mail is not monitored. Inexperienced social service workers unfamiliar with the confrontation model are easily manipulated.

The steps Glen Mills has taken to protect students include:

1. Careful staff selection. Interviewers look for self confidence, self-control, a sense of humor, and a positive attitude toward students.

2. Staff training. Special emphasis is placed upon development of an appropriate confrontation style. Staff are shown how to avoid placing a student in a situation where he must either resist or lose face.

3. Staff norms. The most important protection is the strong norm of showing respect for students, especially during confrontations. The focus of confrontation is the student's behavior, not his character.

4. Monitoring of danger signals. All "level VII" confrontations must be reported to Bulls Club's executives and to the director of group living. It must also be reported to the Resource Team convened every Monday by the executive director. Frequency of "level VII" confrontation, runaways, and other indications of possible abuse are monitored weekly campuswide and in every cottage.

5. Accessibility of top managers. Students with concerns about staff behavior may discuss them with their Bulls Club's representative, counselor or team leader. Any concern which is not resolved to the student's satisfaction at one of these levels is investigated personally by the director of group living.

6. Investigations of all incidents involving physical restraint. An incident report is filed in the Office of the Group Living Director whenever a "level VII" confrontation occurs. All such incidents are investigated by the director of group living, who interviews all students and staff involved. Documentation of the investigation is provided to the student's probation officer.

7. Reassignment of staff. If a staff member is involved in too many "level VII" confrontations, he may be reassigned to avoid a recurrence even though his behavior during each incident was within acceptable limits. In a typical situation, an individual was assigned to work with another counselor and instructed to allow his partner to handle any confrontation beyond level V.

These policies, developed over a period of nearly ten years, have proven effective. There have been 42 student allegations of abuse investigated by outside authorities between 1975 and 1987. None has been sustained.

Staff conduct is the most important factor related to abuse in correctional institutions. Glen Mills' confrontational approach presents the issue sharply: During the first six months of 1987 there were 8 "level VII" confrontations (physical restraint) and an even larger number of "level VI" (touch for attention) incidents. These episodes can be jarring to an outsider. The precipitating behavior may seem inconsequential in relation to the upset associated with a confrontation which progresses beyond level V. The goal is not to avoid conflict, but to insure that negative norms do not gain a foothold on campus. The staff member may appear to be abusive, and if he loses control, may actually become abusive. This risk must be weighed against the risks of not confronting negative behavior. Glen Mills' system is grounded in the belief that the most vicious forms of abuse are those which occur when "street" norms are permitted to take hold, when status is achievable through bullying and manipulation, when the strong are permitted to prey on the weak. Administrators, in their concern over the appearance of staff abuse, can unwittingly encourage a normative climate which makes inevitable far worse forms of victimization. By holding institutions accountable for staff abuse but not the victimization of students by their peers, the system provides an incentive to minimize staff confrontations and thereby makes more probable the victimization it seeks to avoid.

Glen Mills' management believes that the surest protection against abuse is a strong, positive normative culture. In most correctional institutions, staff abuse is a far less significant problem than intimidation at the hands of other students. Rape, extortion, beatings, and less traumatic forms of abuse are common occurrences where staff fail to confront the "street norms" which encourage victimization of students by their peers.

Juvenile institutions should be held accountable for creating an environment where youths do not get hurt—by anyone.

There is a striking absence of tension on Glen Mills' campus. Student injuries of any kind are exceedingly rare. The suicide attempts which plague some institutions are unknown. Glen Mills has demonstrated that a relaxed, humane environment can flourish where staff are held accountable for *all* forms of abuse, not merely staff abuse.

Resistance to "Prosecutorial Vindictiveness"

The only view of Glen Mills' campus most Philadelphians have ever seen was provided by the evening news telecasts on October 24, 1983. The newscasters revealed that the city's popular District Attorney, Edward Rendell, had filed a criminal complaint against the Schools, alleging that Glen Mills had defrauded the city of $243,000 in charges for students who were no longer at the institution. Mr. Rendell's action led the city controller to begin to withhold monies payable to Glen Mills under its existing contract with the city.

The charges stemmed from the Schools' transitional program under which some Philadelphia students were permitted to leave campus and live at home for several weeks prior to discharge. During this period the Schools charged a reduced per diem rate and provided support services in the form of periodic contact by Glen Mills' staff, who helped the student with any problems he experienced in readjusting to the community. Mr. Rendell charged that this amounted to releasing the students without court approval. He further claimed that the services were not being delivered, and noted that some of the boys supposedly in the transitional program had in fact been rearrested and incarcerated. Lacking any evidence of personal profit on the part of individual administrators, he brought charges of unlawful taking, theft by deception, deceptive business practices, and tampering with public records against the institution for the alleged overbillings.

The reactions of the state juvenile justice system ranged from disbelief to outrage, with surprise the common denominator. Newspaper articles carried interviews with probation officers who, stunned by the news, noted that Glen Mills had recovered from major problems to become seemingly the best institution in the state during Mr. Ferrainola's tenure. The headline in the *Philadelphia Inquirer* read "Fraud Charge Darkens Glen Mills' Comeback."

On November 29, 1983, all charges against Glen Mills were dismissed. The court held that the district attorney had failed to establish probable cause to suspect that Glen Mills had committed any crime.

Despite the dismissal of the charges, the district attorney continued to threaten Glen Mills with new charges unless the Schools complied with his demands for payment. Consequently, on February 2, 1984, Glen Mills filed a suit against the district attorney alleging interference with contractual relations, specifically his inducement of the city controller to breach his legal obligation to pay Glen Mills under its current contract with the city.

Through two very intensive years of litigation and continual threats of criminal charges the Schools maintained that it had been entitled to all monies received under the transitional program. The costs of the proceedings were staggering in both monetary and emotional terms. Attorneys' fees paid by the Schools far exceeded the $243,000 sought by the district attorney. The charges were a major distraction for the administration and the Board of Managers, draining off energies which might otherwise have been devoted to program development.

There was a temptation to cut losses by seeking an out-of-court settlement. In a letter to Deputy District Attorney Arthur R. Shuman, Jr., February 14, 1984, Glen Mills' attorney asserted that

On Friday, January 13, 1984 . . . you *specifically stated* that even though based on information you possessed there was no basis for a criminal prosecution you would consider using the powers of your office as well as the powers of a grand jury to develop information warranting the institution of criminal charges, but if Glen Mills would agree to pay the $243,122.23, you would see to it that there was no civil or criminal proceeding for Glen Mills to be concerned about. (Letter from Richard A. Sprague)

The director and a majority of the board felt that the most important issue was not money or time but the integrity and reputation of Glen Mills. To submit to blackmail and buy their way out of the predicament would be to accept the legitimacy of the charges. The Schools' honor would not be sacrificed to expediency. "Integrity," Mr. Ferrainola said, "is like virginity: you can only lose it once."

Any possibility of compromise vanished in April 1985 when the director, Tom Beecher, and several other Glen Mills managers were led out of the Schools' Administration Building in handcuffs to a caravan of state police cars. The district attorney had filed criminal charges against six individuals and ordered their arrest. As students and staff witnessed what they regarded as the district attorney's attempt to intimidate and degrade their leadership, the support of the community for the board's position became total and unshakable. Loyalty and pride are deeply rooted in Glen Mills' culture; Mr. Rendell's action had made compromise unthinkable.

The arrests compounded the strain upon all concerned, but particularly the director, who felt responsible to maintain an upbeat and confident public image. Hardly a day went by without some stressful event related to the court action. Some jurisdictions were hesitant to commit students to the Schools. There were endless meetings and discussions with (expensive) attorneys. The trauma spilled over onto Mr. Ferrainola's family, as when his daughter came home from school crying because her classmates wanted to know if her father was a thief. Late at night the director would sometimes walk alone around the Schools' athletic fields. As in 1975, he wondered whether the struggle was worth the stress his colleagues and family were experiencing.

On the face of it, the district attorney's charge that the director and Glen Mills had sought to defraud Philadelphia's taxpayers seemed ludicrous. During Mr. Ferrainola's tenure the Schools' per diem charge was reduced by more than 40 percent; this would appear to be a poor strategy for defrauding taxpayers. The district attorney was never able to identify a single contractual provision violated by the Schools. The city controller's office conducted an audit covering the period when the alleged overbilling had occurred, and determined that the Schools had not overbilled the city. Indeed, Glen Mills had provided many thousands of dollars of service to the city for which it had not received payment. Furthermore, the district attorney's office was aware that Glen Mills had not misled the city regarding the placement status of its students. Mr. Frank Davis of the Community Related Institutional Probation (CRIP) Unit of the Philadelphia Juvenile Probation Office had informed them that Glen Mills had fully complied with its obligation to notify CRIP prior to placing students in the Transitional Program; failure to notify the committing judges was the responsibility of the CRIP staff and not Glen Mills. Nonetheless, as the district attorney pursued Glen Mills many outside the Schools' community assumed that there must be some basis for his allegations. Mr. Rendell was widely perceived to be a politically ambitious but hard working and honest prosecutor. If he saw smoke there must be fire.

Sam Ferrainola believed that political ambition underlay the vendetta. Mr. Rendell had taken a politically popular hard line on juvenile crime, urging the state to expand its capacity for secure confinement of juveniles. Glen Mills had strongly resisted the district attorney's proposal in the belief that secure confinement was not only unnecessary but counterproductive for the large majority of serious offenders. The Schools went so far as to offer to accept 20 randomly selected offenders currently placed in secure institutions, at no cost, in order to demonstrate that construction of a new maximum security facility was not necessary. The combination of state budgetary concerns and arguments such as Glen Mills' had blocked the prosecutor's proposals.

Glen Mills' officials believed Mr. Rendell's initial charges were due to the Schools' opposition to his "get tough" stance; miscommunication between the court, the CRIP Unit, and the district attorney; or perhaps an honest mistake. In any case, they felt that the district attorney was surprised by the Schools' refusal to negotiate a settlement and found himself too publicly committed to the Glen Mills litigation to back off without losing face.

After two years of legal maneuvering the dispute was finally resolved in court on May 20, 1985. After hearing the testimony from both sides, the judge dismissed all charges against Glen Mills. His ruling, which included the finding that the district attorney's conduct amounted to "prosecutorial vindictiveness," has few precedents in American jurisprudence in its condemnation of abuse of power by public officials.

Thus vindicated, Glen Mills' Board of Managers and director faced a difficult decision: Should they pursue their own litigation against the district attorney or negotiate a settlement to their lawsuit? Sam Ferrainola's personal feelings were clear: Mr. Rendell had sought to destroy his Schools' reputation and his honor. He had abused his power as a public official, causing injury to Glen Mills, Sam Ferrainola, and his family. The director wanted justice. He wanted the public to know that their district attorney was a man of very little integrity. He wanted Mr. Rendell to experience the public humiliation he himself had suffered.

But he also realized that his personal feelings must not be permitted to interfere with his decisions on behalf of the Schools. In emotionally charged situations it is particularly important to keep one's objective clearly in mind. Glen Mills' position had been strongly supported by the court, whose decision was tantamount to an abuse of power charge against a district attorney who claimed a reputation for integrity. The Schools' integrity had been successfully defended, though at great cost. How would prolonging the most stressful episode in Glen Mills' modern history help the Schools? With great ambivalence the director acquiesced in the board's decision to reach a settlement with the city and reestablish positive relations with the Schools' largest client.

The settlement agreement, dated April 30, 1986, recognizes "the high quality of services" and "exemplary results" achieved by Glen Mills. It provides for an increase in city funding to Glen Mills of $1,300,000 to accommodate additional Philadelphia offenders; stipulates that the Schools' per diem rate is "fair and reasonable," and agrees to drop all criminal and civil charges against Glen Mills in return for the Schools' withdrawal of all claims against the city. Appended to the agreement was a letter from City Controller Joseph Vignola stating that a review of the case by his office " . . . indicated that Glen Mills was entitled to all payments made by the city to it" during the period of the alleged over-billing.

Sam and Gerda Ferrainola

Weekly Resource Team meeting of a $16 million organization: chaired by Mr. Ferrainola, the meeting includes all department heads, team leaders, and Bulls Club (student) executives.

Graduation Day at Glen Mills

Aerial view of Glen Mills' campus. The main quadrangle is bordered by six cottages and the student union building, with the chapel and the Administration Building at either end.

Bulls Club executive officers

3

The Glen Mills

Experience

What's it like at Glen Mills? You wouldn't believe it if I told you.
Part of a conversation reported by a student during a homepass

By 1988 Glen Mills' program had been shaped, refined, and tested during more than a decade of Mr. Ferrainola's tenure. A new student arriving on campus finds one of the most carefully managed, highly structured, and controlled living environments he will ever experience. Control, however, does not imply regimentation and is not evident. In fact, there is a striking absence of the usual instruments of control. There is no physical security, disciplinary units, or careful monitoring of movement by staff. Few new arrivals guess that Glen Mills' primary mechanism for maintaining order resides where they would least expect to find it—in the other students. Paradoxically, it is the behavioral control achieved by the Schools' powerful normative culture which will make possible the flowering of his individual abilities during the student's stay at Glen Mills.

The new student is placed in a cottage using a rotational assignment system. With the exception of Academic and Tradesman Halls the Schools' cottages are not "typed." Socialization begins as he walks to his cottage when he notices how students and staff interact, witnesses a confrontation or is himself confronted in a friendly but firm way to tuck in his shirt, avoid walking on the grass, etc.

Arriving at his cottage the student meets his counselor, other unit staff, and his "big brother," a cottage Bull who will orient him to the Schools. His counselor provides him with an information packet describing the program, the daily routine, and the seven levels of confrontation. He explains the process for resolving problems or concerns: Raise them first with peers during GGI, then with a cottage Bull or an executive Bull. Later options include the counselor, cottage team leader, and group living director.

During the evening cottage meeting ("Townhouse"), his big brother introduces him to the other students in the unit, each of whom gives his name and recites one norm. Students, more than the staff, will show the new student around the campus, talk to him about the program, and explain what is expected of him.

The first two weeks are very busy as the student learns the daily routine, how to do various cottage chores, visits several vocational shops, becomes acquainted with his peers and staff, adjusts to GGI, etc. A visit to the Schools' clothing warehouse is arranged; the student selects a (free) complete outfit from among a wide variety of new, stylish, top quality articles of clothing. The Schools' health care staff conduct a complete medical and dental exam. Academic placement follows completion of MAT testing. All the while he is consciously and unconsciously absorbing the messages of Glen Mills' culture: the values and expectations that will shape the way he interacts with peers and staff, the amount of effort he devotes to his studies, the way he dresses, and even the way he walks.

Students who have been in other institutions are surprised to find that the strongest leaders among the students, the campus Bulls Club members, are the most vocal in support of the program and play a key role in day-to-day operations. Rather than model negative behavior, Bulls confront it—indeed misbehavior is more often confronted by students than by staff. Whereas in some institutions the more powerful students are allied in opposition to staff values, Bulls often speak to their peers about school pride, how fortunate they are to be at Glen Mills rather than a lock-up, their responsibility to take care of Schools property, the importance of giving others respect, the need to take advantage of educational opportunities, to strive for membership in the Bulls Club, etc. Needing to feel secure and accepted in this strange environment, looking to peers for cues as to how to get along, and realizing that the Bulls hold real power at Glen Mills, new students usually decide to work with them rather than against them. The decision to seek peer group acceptance through positive behavior is the first step in a successful experience at the Schools.

Once the initial weeks of orientation are behind him, the student settles into a daily routine offering a variety of program options within a highly structured schedule. The school day begins at 6:30 A.M. when all students wishing to go to breakfast are awakened by a cottage Bull. Students who choose not to go to breakfast may sleep until 7:45 A.M.

Responsibility for dining hall supervision rotates among the cottages. Battling Bulls and staff from the cottage meet at the Administration Building at 6:45 A.M. to discuss the areas of coverage during the breakfast meal. At 7:45 the Battling Bulls and staff return to their cottages and wake up all students. From 8:00 to 8:30 all students must shower, dress, and make their bed. From 8:30 to 9:00 students perform their morning detail of cottage cleanliness. The leadership of the Battling Bulls continues as they monitor, confront, and keep the norms intact. During detail time each student is required to perform a specific chore in the cottage, as well as being responsible for the cleanliness of his individual room. The cleanliness norm is very important in teaching students how to work and interact socially while helping one another achieve a common goal: cottage pride.

The Glen Mills Schools Daily Schedule

6:30 A.M.	Wake-up
7:15 A.M.	Breakfast
8:00 A.M.	Clean cottage
9:00 A.M.	GGI
10:00 A.M.	Class
12:00 noon	Lunch
1:00 P.M.	Class
3:00 P.M.	Free time
5:00 P.M.	Dinner
6:00 P.M.	Evening program
8:00 P.M.	Snacks
9:15 P.M.	Curfew
9:30 P.M.	Townhouse
10:00 P.M.	Free time
11:15 P.M.	Bed
12:00 Midnight	Lights out

GGI is held every day Monday through Friday at 9:00 A.M. in each living unit except for Academic and Tradesman Halls, the two honors units. Each group is run basically the same way. A group consists of 10 to 12 students sitting in a tight circle in their unit's living room along with a cottage staff member who is also in the circle and participates in the group process. Also, any number of observers may sit outside the circle but do not interact with the group. These may include visitors, senior counselors, team leaders, the group living director or members of the training staff who observe the group and provide feedback to the staff facilitator on at least a weekly basis.

During GGI the student learns to confront and to accept confrontation; to both give and receive feedback from his peers; to read and understand non-verbals, hidden agendas, subgroups and leadership struggles; and to expose and confront issues before his peers. Along with these skills he experiences the development of a trusting relationship with his peer group. The tools developed during the hour of GGI will be vital to the student's entire Glen Mills experience.

Class time extends from 10:00 A.M. to 12:00 noon and from 1:00 P.M. to

3:00 P.M. daily. Depending on the student's academic history and his performance on standardized achievement tests, he will be assigned to the Learning Center, Intermediate Program, Pre-GED, GED, or College Prep class. The majority of students enter with basic skills competencies between the fourth and eighth grade levels and are initially assigned to the Intermediate Program. Since these classes are conducted in the student's cottage by a counselor-teacher from his unit, the educational experience further strengthens the identification with the cottage and relationships with the cottage peer group.

Between noon and 1:00 P.M., all students eat lunch in the campus dining hall. Mealtime is important not only for its nutritional value but also for its social value. The four meals (breakfast, lunch, dinner, and evening snacks) are used as a time to develop a family atmosphere between the students and the staff. This is done by having the staff and students eat together, at tables seating four, for the development of personal relationships in an informal atmosphere.

Food is plentiful and of good quality; cleanliness and orderliness are stressed in the dining area. Cafeteria norms include no loud talking, no talking between tables, presenting a neat appearance, returning your tray when finished eating, cleaning up your table when you complete your meal, and no smoking in the cafeteria. There are also designated doors that students enter and exit through in the dining area. Students form single file lines when receiving food. Everyone is allowed to eat as much as they like but food cannot be taken out of the cafeteria. These norms are supported through confrontation by staff and Bulls assigned to monitor the dining hall during each meal.

Academic and advanced vocational classes are in session from 1:00 P.M. to 3:00 P.M., followed by a free period until dinner at 5:00 P.M. During free time various activities are available to the students. The Schools' athletic teams practice during this time; an intramural program is also offered. Parent-student communication and letter writing is encouraged. Students may call their parents in the student union where phones are provided. Free time provides an opportunity to visit with friends from other cottages in the student union over snacks and refreshments, or socialize with staff members working in other cottages on campus. A student may also schedule a meeting with his cottage counselor during this time.

A variety of academic, athletic, and vocational programs are offered during the evening immediately after dinner. It is expected that all students will participate. Students are expected to be present at their program at 6:00 P.M. Evening program activities at the gym expose students to various athletics, sports, training methods, and general physical conditioning. The Chess Club provides basic instruction as well as an opportunity for competition and tournaments. Swimming and bowling are popular options. Sports and Society is a program designed for the more serious athletes interested in learning the fine points of certain sports, as well as their relationship to society. The campus Learning Center and library are open in the evening to give students the chance to brush up on their school work and/or to explore new areas of interest. Project Help provides tutoring for GED students who need extra help in preparing for their GED exam. A silkscreening program enables students to learn the basics of silkscreen printing. The key characteristic of the evening program is diversity. There are well over 20 options a student may choose, including the full com-plement of vocational offerings.

A positive normative environment is as crucial to the evening as to the daytime programs. Without a strict and consistent normative environment, no vocation can be learned, no subject can be studied, and no sport can be mastered. If a student disrupts the normative environment in his area he is held accountable by his instructor and also by the counselors and peers in his living unit.

At the end of the evening program each student receives a pass signed by the instructor, which must be presented to his cottage staff when he returns to the cottage at curfew.

The dining hall reopens between 8:00 and 9:00 P.M. to provide "snacks," which might include hot dogs, milk shakes, hamburgers, hoagies, steak sand-wiches, etc. Glen Mills' managers credit the snack period as an important factor in the nearly total elimination of disruptive behavior during the evening shift.

Between 9:15 and 9:30 P.M., a campuswide curfew is enacted. Students who have been at the dining hall or the various vocational and recreational areas report back to their units. Cottage staff monitor the students' evening program pass to determine which program was attended. Many counselors set individual counselee goals concerning which program they should attend. These are usually based upon a mutual agreement between the counselor and counselee concerning his vocational and educational needs. A student who has agreed with his coun-selor to attend an evening welding class but submits a basketball or recreational pass will surely be confronted.

The curfew also provides a security check. Since all students are required to be in their respective units, students who do not report are of immediate concern. If a student is found to be truant, his name will be called into the switchboard for "in house" communication and the State Police notified.

During the curfew period staff are expected to observe individual students who have had problems through the day. If staff feel that a student who had been confronted earlier is currently showing a negative attitude, he can be counseled accordingly.

In summary, the curfew period is an important phase of the Schools' overall program. It involves census, staff/student accountability, monitoring of voca-tional and educational progress, one-to-one counseling, and campus-community security.

The Townhouse meeting occurs every night at 9:30. An additional Town-house also may be called when staff deem necessary for unit or campus com-munication. The meeting consists of the entire cottage staff and student population. Students assemble in the largest room of the unit, sitting in a close group on the floor while staff and perhaps the cottage Bulls Club officers stand around the periphery.

In most cases a Townhouse will begin with a staff facilitator sharing general information involving the campus or the unit. This can include the weekly sports schedule, upcoming campus events, holiday home pass dates, and unit responsibilities. A second important function involves giving positive recognition to specific individuals or groups within the unit. This would include students who have earned vocational or educational awards, Bulls Club's accomplishments, sports accomplishments, and individual student growth.

A third process begins when a staff member or Bull invites students to "own up." Several hands are raised. After he is recognized the student stands and says "I want to own up and apologize to my peers and staff for. . . . " He will then bring up any negative behavior he was involved in during the day. This might include disrespect to staff, failure to attend the evening program or being ejected from the student union.

After a student has brought up an issue, he will receive feedback from his peers and staff. If he is not receptive to feedback the staff will recommend that the normative issue be dealt with on an individual or smaller group basis. This would include one-to-one counseling, GGI, or receiving feedback from the Battling Bulls Club.

Other issues brought up during this period include conflicts that occur on student floors within the unit. Examples would be roomate conflict, floor cleanliness, and not respecting each other's privacy. All students are expected to accept responsiblity for their misbehavior. A young man who does not voluntarily "own up" loses status when another student calls him on it.

Finally, at the end of each Townhouse new staff and students are introduced and all students are assigned nightly cleaning details. Details involve areas in the unit such as bathrooms, floor, recreational rooms and classrooms which must be cleaned each evening. In conclusion, the Townhouse serves an important role in building cohesion, communication, confrontation, and motivation.

At 10:00 P.M., after everyone is accounted for in the unit, the switchboard operator is called, and the population count is logged. During the next hour students who have completed their cleaning details may shower, watch TV, listen to radios, write letters, work on school projects, read, have one-on-one counseling sessions with their counselors, or spend their free time in any other acceptable manner. Staff work on recording systems such as census charts, student daily logs, and information sharing for the morning shift.

Students are required to be in their own rooms by 11:00 P.M. during the week; on weekends this time varies depending on the behavior of the students. While students are required to be in their own rooms, they are allowed to leave to discuss any problems with staff or Battling Bulls Club members on duty. Battling Bulls Club members check to make sure norms pertaining to bedtime are followed. These include being in one's own room, keeping the noise level down, and making certain students are getting ready for bed.

At 11:15 the Bulls and staff instruct the students to turn off their lights and get into bed. They are allowed to listen to their radios or watch their own TVs until midnight, when everything is turned off. From 11:15 to 12:00 the coun-selors monitor the unit and finish any paperwork begun earlier. Bulls assigned to night duty are responsible for checking various areas of the unit and initialing their check sheets if everything is found to be satisfactory. Checkpoints include: fire extinguishers filled, fire doors closed, fire hoses in place, noise level down, all students in bed, a head count, and any additional comments that may be necessary.

Just before midnight the night counselor who covers the 12 to 8 shift arrives, and is briefed about any issues of which he should be made particularly aware. An inspection of the unit and head count is made before the 4 to 12 shift leaves. After everything is checked out, the 4 to 12 staff leave the night Bulls in charge of the unit with the back up of the night counselor. Between midnight and 6:00 A.M. night counselors make rounds and are responsible for checking on the units. At 6:00 A.M. the night counselor awakens the night Bulls who in turn wake up the other students for breakfast.

The new student must spend his first six weekends on campus before he becomes eligible for a home pass. The campus begins to empty out on Friday afternoon, as Glen Mills' buses take students with home passes to train stations. With the most positive students gone home and those left behind faced with possible depression and the prospect of long hours of unscheduled time with little to do, weekends can be stressful in many institutions.

At Glen Mills, the weekend is never dull. On a rotational basis, the staff of each cottage take responsibility for weekend activities. They deprive the Devil of the opportunity to make work for idle hands. On Friday afternoon

there is often a sports event, furthermore the arcade is opened from 3:00 to 4:00 P.M. Dinner from 4:00 to 5:00 is especially good. From 5:30 to 9:00 P.M. there are video films shown on the Betamax below the chapel. At the same time there are four competitions in the arcade, for example, drinking a Coca-Cola in the shortest time, special pool contests, blowing balloons until they burst—events similar to small children's birthday games. Winners receive small prizes.

There are also four activities in the gym. These are a little more sportive, but here, too, they have a playful character—jumping in a sack, shooting baskets and the like. It was observable that the playful activities even got "tough" juveniles out of their role of "coolness." These activities continue throughout the afternoon and evening, except for the 7:00–8:00 snack time.

Saturday morning is free for sleeping late. From 1:00 to 4:00 and 5:00 to 9:00 there are eight more activities in the arcade and gym. The Betamax is also open.

Sunday morning is also free, with yet more activities and the Betamax available in the afternoon. There is a bingo tournament, with prizes, from 5:00 to 8:00. During this time bingo is the only activity, as staff members are needed on the buses which bring students back to school from their homepasses. (Ottmüller, 1987: 135–36)

All students are expected to participate in at least nine activities during the weekend. There is a great deal of positive interaction with peers and scant opportunity for boredom, brooding or the "Devil's work."

Weekend planning is a good example of the Glen Mills approach to problem solving. The goal is clearly defined: making the weekend experience an enjoyable one that strengthens the normative culture while reducing the likelihood of boredom, depression, and mischief. Responsibility for achieving the goal is assigned to a unit. Exceedingly detailed planning is followed by task assignments and the total support of on-duty staff from all units. Finally, the success of the weekend plan is evaluated each Monday morning during the Resource Team meeting, with liberal praise directed toward the team leader whose unit was responsible for a job well done.

All aspects of the program structure encourage immersion in peer group involvement. Accountability to one's peers, the primacy of the "help others" norm and the sheer time spent in group activities ensures frequent interaction. It is not possible to remain a "loner."

Most students are initially bewildered by the normative culture. Glen Mills seems like a different planet, where the things which seemed important back in the neighborhood—race, fighting skill, gang membership—no longer mean anything. As one Bulls Club executive put it: "There are no black students or white students at Glen Mills. We're all gold (referring to the School's colors)." With the help of his "big brother," counselor and most of all, his cottage peer group the new student soon begins to feel at home in this bizarre world.

As the days and weeks go by, the new student adjusts to the daily routine. He begins to notice subtle changes in himself. On the street he had felt uneasy and on guard around the tougher boys, who would "rank" him with half-teasing insults (or worse) to remind him of his place. He had done the same to others when he thought he could get away with it; it made him feel like he was somebody important. At Glen Mills he begins to feel safe. It is clear that staff and Bulls are the most powerful "gang" on campus and they never allow any student to be pushed around or even disrespected. Maybe that is why he feels less on edge now.

When he first arrived, he was not sure what to make of all the talk about acting like a gentleman; he guessed the Bulls were just "fronting" for the benefit of the staff. He had been surprised to find himself saying "hello" to a stranger on campus. It just felt like a natural thing to do, he had seen so many students do it and been greeted so many times himself. The man looked like he might be a judge or something; it had felt strangely satisfying to look him in the eye as he greeted him.

He first heard about norms from his counselor and cottage peers on the night of his arrival, but he had been too nervous to pay much attention. Mostly, he learned how to get along by noticing what the other students on campus did. Accepting confrontation had been easy for him: it was never intimidating or hostile, and he was eager to fit in.

He learned in GGI that merely getting along was not what Glen Mills was all about. Active involvement was required. Like many boys who had been followers before coming to Glen Mills, he had been afraid to confront negative behavior by his stronger peers. Consequently, he was himself confronted: Didn't he care enough about his peers to give them honest feedback about negative attitudes? How could he respect himself if he wouldn't stand up for himself? Didn't he trust his peers to support him? Led by the cottage Bulls, each GGI group member let him know that they expected him not just to "get along," but to actively support campus leaders and confront those who showed disrespect for their peers or the Schools. It sounded risky, but it helped to know that the strongest student leaders would support him if he tried (and continue to confront him if he didn't!). He soon came to feel secure upholding Glen Mills' norms. His counselor had remarked that he seemed to have grown—or was he just standing taller now?

School feels *really* different. Out on the streets no one really cared whether he went or not; it seemed that the teachers preferred "not." At Glen Mills, if he is even a few minutes late, he is confronted by his instructor. Then by his cottage counselor. Then even his peers get on him about it. (Back on the streets his friends hadn't been very interested in school. Few even bothered to go). It is easier to be on time.

In his public school he had always been behind the rest of his class. He had been promoted every year even though he had not completed the work. He had stopped trying: no one noticed, and the papers all came back covered with red marks even if he did his best. At Glen Mills the other students in his class are all on his level; he had even been able to help some of them with a math problem. The teachers notice him; in fact they have developed an individualized education program, complete with a series of realistic objectives, just for him. His first two tests were pretty bad, with 15 of 20 questions wrong on the first and 12 of 20 wrong on the second. But even that feels different than it used to. Instead of ignoring the student or harping about all the mistakes, the teacher had seemed genuinely excited about the improvement, and spoke to him about what he could achieve if he did a little bit better each week.

His cottage staff had remarked about his progress and one of the Bulls, a MAT award winner, talked to him about his own experiences in the Learning Center. He told the student that if he continued to apply himself he might be recommended for Academic Hall, even if he did not get the best grades. At Glen Mills, he said, you earn respect for personal effort and helping your peers.

As the student removed his glasses, he realized there had been another important change in him. He was thinking about what he might do with his life. Before coming to Glen Mills no one ever thought he would amount to much. But he had made these glasses in the Schools' optical shop. In a few weeks he had learned to read prescriptions and operated the half dozen machines required to prepare the lenses, and produce and test the eyeglasses. What else might he be able to do? Some of his classmates were learning to build houses. Others wrote and printed the Schools' newspaper. His roommate, who had not even been involved in gymnastics before coming to Glen Mills, earned a place on the Glen Mills' team which won the state championship. Best in the whole

Commonwealth of Pennsylvania! Before Glen Mills, no one had even noticed that his roommate might be a good gymnast, or encouraged him to try out.

College might not be for him, but he felt proud that dozens of Glen Mills students had gone on to attend college. The only thing that they had in common was that before they came to the Schools, absolutely no one—not their teachers, not their families, not they themselves—thought they were college material. Glen Mills is the kind of place which makes you believe you can become something.

The last change he noticed in himself was hard to put his finger on, but he seemed to feel less angry. Many people—even his own family, sometimes—had treated him like dirt. He guessed he deserved it; he had done some bad things. But Glen Mills had given him a fine room with nice furniture, asking only that he take care of it. The Schools had allowed him to pick out a sharp outfit of clothing, asking only that he keep his appearance neat. The food, served in a clean, well lit and nicely furnished dining hall, was as good as he had ever eaten and there was as much for him as he wanted; the Schools only asked that he not waste it and that he treat others in the dining hall courteously. The Schools' doctor and dentist had taken care of all his medical needs. They had treated him not like an inmate, but like a patient; it seemed to matter to them that he feel good and have strong teeth. The track shoes he was given when he made the team were the finest available. His cottage would be traveling to Florida in the spring. When his radio was stolen the entire staff had stayed until 1:00 A.M. questioning students until it was recovered. The radio was nothing to them, they could have shrugged their shoulders and gone home. The incident helped him to understand what his counselor meant when he said "When one of us has a problem, we *all* have a problem."

All these things had somehow affected the way he felt about himself, and the way he treated others.

Cottage staff and Bulls were well aware of the student's progress. Several had urged him to try for his Bull's log. The student had been helped by the Bulls since the day he arrived. Now he himself would be initiated into the club. He would assume his place among the Schools' student leaders. He would see to it that new students get off to a good start in their own experience at Glen Mills.

The Bulls take pride in the Schools and in their role as student leaders. At the end of every weekly Resource Team meeting, with the entire administrative team present, the executive director turns toward the Bulls Club representative and asks "What are we going to do this week?" The reply is always "Make Glen Mills a little better than it was last week."

The Schools had taught him that surprising and wonderful things happened when he worked to make his own life a little better each week. It is a lesson he will hold onto for life.

4

Program Effectiveness

Although the current concern of correctional evaluators is that "nothing works," an important question is what they would do if something did work. It is likely that they would be hard-pressed to repeat past performances if there is little accurate and coherent description of what treatment was delivered.

Eva Lantos Rezmovic

Does Glen Mills' program "work"? What is the evidence of the Schools' effectiveness? These are the questions that determine whether the model warrants the attention of the nation's policymakers, researchers, and correctional administrators.

Numerous research designs might be used to assess a program's effectiveness. An experimental design, in which subjects are randomly assigned to two or more treatment conditions and outcomes compared, is usually considered the approach of choice. However, the appropriateness of experimental designs has too often been assumed by investigators whose efforts might more fruitfully have been directed toward field studies and time-series experiments. This is not an argument in favor of weak methodologies, but a recognition that the level of knowledge and theory development in correctional research is not nearly advanced enough to warrant a primary emphasis upon experimental designs.

In the search for "what works" the current state of the art requires a dominant emphasis upon the judgments of experienced practitioners, combined with careful documentation and analysis of existing programs to identify factors associated with effectiveness (or lack of it). This should be followed by research involving planned variations and taking maximum advantage of naturally occurring ex-

periments. Experimental designs are appropriate in the later stages of the knowledge development process, as confirmatory procedures when there are sound
reasons to believe that a program model is more effective than available alternatives. At present, however, it is doubtful that the major variables associated
with program effectiveness have been identified; theory development is not well
advanced; and documentation of existing programs is sparse at best.

Premature use of experimental designs is wasteful in that, relative to strategies
more appropriate to the stage of knowledge development, they contribute very
little to our understanding of program effectiveness. Worse, the failure of controlled experiments to consistently demonstrate the effectiveness of any program
model has contributed to the impression that "nothing works," which is all too
often taken to mean that nothing can work. Where a critical mass of policymakers adopt this view, there is a danger that institutional rehabilitation efforts
will be dismantled entirely, a terrible and wholly unwarranted step for which
both juvenile offenders and society would pay dearly.

A well reasoned strategy for knowledge development in juvenile corrections
has been proposed by Dale Mann (1976). Noting that "evaluators have done
much that furthers confusion by focusing upon arcane issues of methodology
and measurement," Mann urges an approach relying heavily upon documentation and analysis. He concludes with a summary of a paper by Robert Yin of
the Rand Corporation, stressing the need to develop

soundly based knowledge directly related to the problems faced by practitioners. In that
regard Yin recommends supporting work that will aggregate individual evaluation studies
and case analyses. He points out that single studies do not establish credible facts (nor
should they be expected to). Only replication, refinement, and aggregation lead to sound
knowledge that can be expected to inform practice. (Mann, 1976: 92)

The evaluation of Glen Mills' effectiveness contributes to an aggregation which
informs practice—and thereby moves the field one step closer to something that
works.

In an excellent discussion of methodological issues relating to the evaluation
of correctional programs, Rezmovic (1979) notes that many evaluations contribute little to our understanding of the requisites for effective programming
because they provide few clues as to the nature of the treatment: What services
were provided? By whom? How often? How well? To whom? Why? Without
this information, it is difficult or impossible to gain insight into the reasons for
program effectiveness, or to replicate promising approaches. In the case of
evaluations that fail to yield evidence of effectiveness, inadequate discussion of
the treatment process makes it impossible to distinguish between failures due
to an ineffective treatment model and those due to poor program implementation. A useful analysis must include a description of the treatment model, its
implementation, and impact.

The first two chapters provided details regarding the Schools' staff, culture, and programs—the nature of the treatment. This chapter discusses first the theoretical and philosophical foundations of Glen Mills' model, the "why" of the program. Next it describes "to whom" by profiling the students admitted between 1976 and 1983. Finally, follow-up data for nine annual admissions cohorts are presented, and evidence of both the near-term and long-range effectiveness of the program model is discussed.

THEORETICAL FRAMEWORK

Glen Mills' program is grounded in sociological theories of delinquency. As articulated by the Schools' managers, their belief is that the majority of delinquent behavior, like much adolescent behavior, is motivated by a need to gain peer group acceptance or status.

That is not to say delinquency is caused by social factors alone, or even that these are the root causes of most delinquency. There is compelling evidence that numerous factors are involved. Academicians have examined genetic, biochemical, emotional, developmental, familial, and societal contributions with varying degrees of interaction and relatedness to social-psychological, peer group pressures as causative factors. The point is made by Leonard Bernstein's Jets in *West Side Story*, who present Officer Krupke with a bewildering array of explanations for their behavior. Their delinquency is due to mothers who are junkies, fathers who are drunks, psychological disturbance, lack of love and understanding, problems of adolescence, laziness, alcoholism, limited career opportunities, and a "deep down inside" badness.

In short, peer group pressures may or may not be a primary cause of delinquency; affiliation with a delinquent peer group may be as much a consequence as a cause of an individual's delinquency. But the architects of Glen Mills' normative culture believe that the key to effective intervention is to be found among sociological theories of delinquency causation.

Glen Mills' program took shape during a five-year trial and error process guided by the values, instincts, and experience of the director and his top managers. The most important theoretical perspectives influencing their work were the three major classes of sociological theories of delinquency: structural/ strain, cultural, and control theories. Confrontation, the key tool for maintaining norms and changing individual behavior, is grounded in learning and behavioral theories.

Underlying Theoretical Perspectives

Structural/strain theorists attribute a major role in delinquency causation to the discrepancies between socially induced aspirations and legitimate avenues to their realization (Cloward and Ohlin, 1960). Aspiration-opportunity disjunction leads to frustrations and alienation from mainstream society.

Two aspects of the Glen Mills model alleviate the strains postulated by the theory. The first is the strong emphasis upon gradual improvement, the surprising results that can be achieved by striving to be just "a little bit better" each day. By narrowing the gap between aspiration and actuality (or, by breaking up the long journey into smaller, achievable steps), the chances of success are greatly improved.

The second element is the targeting of programs to individual needs. The Schools' high enrollment makes possible a broad range of offerings. Athletic teams are formed to accommodate students of widely different levels of ability. Academic instruction is carefully geared to each student's level of functioning. A variety of vocational opportunities are offered to accommodate students' interests and aptitudes. Everything possible is done to build a bridge between the ground where a student stands and the destination he would like to reach, coupled with encouragement at each step along the way. The diversity of Glen Mills' programs and the Schools' one step at a time philosophy are responsive to the issues raised by structural/strain theory.

Cultural explanations of delinquency point to the role of a subculture of delinquency in promoting antisocial behavior. In one formulation, Cohen (1955) claimed that working-class males who are unequipped to compete with their middle-class peers draw together in a delinquent subculture having its own standards, values, and status structure. The values and expectations of the group become all important:

It is not the individual delinquent but the gang that is autonomous. For many of our subcultural delinquents the claims of the home are very real and very compelling. *The* point is that the gang is a separate, distinct and often irresistible focus of attraction, loyalty and solidarity. (Cohen, 1955: 31)

Later research confirmed the role of the subculture in eliciting delinquent behavior (Wolfgang and Ferracuti, 1967) and identified self-esteem as a critical variable affecting susceptibility to delinquent social pressures (Clark, 1959).

Differential association theory (Southerland and Cressey, 1970), a first cousin of subculture theory, stresses the role and importance of small group affiliations (i.e., as opposed to the larger social system focus of subcultural theorists) in the causation of delinquency.

The primacy of peer group norms in molding delinquent behavior is the central principle underlying the normative culture. Institutional settings provide a unique opportunity to manipulate all elements of the students' psychosocial environment. Most miss this opportunity and find their best therapeutic efforts subverted by the powerful imperatives of the delinquent peer group.

Glen Mills, on the other hand, systematically works to eradicate the delinquent subculture and replace it with prosocial values, beliefs, and norms communicated through the cottage peer group. It combats delinquency by harnessing and redirecting the forces that played so large a role in its development.

Finally, by establishing a norm of group support and recognition for initiative and achievement at all levels of functioning, Glen Mills promotes the development of self-esteem, which buffers the student against negative peer pressures upon his return to the community.

Control theorists postulate a link between delinquent behavior and weak ties to conventional values and beliefs. One reviewer, summarizing Hirschi's statement of control theory, stresses the importance of conventional attachments:

attachment to conventional persons, commitment to conventional pursuits, involvement in conventional activities, and belief in conventional values reduce the likelihood that a youth will engage in delinquent conduct. (Office of Juvenile Justice and Delinquency Prevention, 1981: 19)

Control theorists hold that delinquency results when socialization processes do not establish bonds of sufficient strength to reinforce the values and norms of mainstream society, leaving the individual vulnerable to recruitment into a delinquent peer group.

From the moment a new student arrives on campus his experiences with his peers and the Schools' staff are designed to encourage his acceptance of prosocial values. Cottage staff are selected on the basis of their ability to model core values: respect, teamwork, cleanliness, hard work, commitment, pride. There are no high status, negative role models; both formal and informal status is systematically denied to all but those exhibiting positive behavior. At Glen Mills, to belong means to embrace conventional values; helping others, modeling positive behavior, and striving to succeed in educational, athletic, and vocational programs are the routes to recognition.

The final theoretical perspective that is important to the Schools' model is social learning theory. Learning theorists believe that antisocial behavior is usually not evidence of psychological disturbance, but develops in much the same way as the more acceptable behavior of nondelinquents: through observation, imitation, and reinforced practice (Bandura, 1969).

In order to combat delinquency, it is necessary to extinguish antisocial behaviors and reinforce prosocial actions. This is achieved most directly through confrontation and rewards/recognition. In accordance with learning theory, Glen Mills' trainers stress the importance of confronting all negative behaviors, since every failure to confront signals acceptance and makes the offending behavior more difficult to extinguish. Conversely, staff are instructed to be alert to even the smallest positive steps and support them by word or gesture. The most positive students are rewarded with membership in the powerful Bulls Club. Awards for both effort and achievement are frequent; those involving material goods (e.g., jackets, rings, radios) are of top quality and prized by recipients. The "lesson" is clear—prosocial effort brings status, recognition, and reward; antisocial behavior brings relentless confrontation by staff and peers.

The architects of Glen Mills' model turned not to delinquency theorists but to their own values, instincts, and experience in establishing the normative culture. However, their understanding of delinquency and their judgments as to the tools required to combat it are faithful to the views advanced by sociological and social learning theorists. It is significant that these are integral to most correctional programs found effective (Cullen and Gendreau, 1988).

In the final analysis the Schools' model requires no judgments about the root causes of delinquency. Inner city youths who fear for their safety and seek protection, boys who feel rejected by mainstream society due to poverty or educational deficits, youths who have never experienced competent parenting, young men frustrated by a perceived lack of legitimate avenues to a desired lifestyle, those made cynical by the well-publicized moral failures of the culture's political and business leaders, teenagers inundated in the nihilistic messages of punk rock and the uninterrupted violence and deceit of many motion pictures: few are "crazy"; all are prime candidates for recruitment into a delinquent peer group. Psychopathology excluded, Glen Mills' model holds that the common factor in most delinquency is a living environment where threats to personal safety and security are widespread, and antisocial behavior is an effective route to acceptance and status among one's age mates.

The antidote, therefore is immersion in an environment where respect and physical safety are assured and where peer group acceptance and material rewards are contingent upon prosocial behavior.

In summary, Glen Mills' program is grounded in the following set of assumptions regarding the nature of delinquency:

1. The large majority of delinquents are not emotionally disturbed. Students accepted by Glen Mills are psychologically healthy young men whose delinquency reflects their need to protect themselves and secure peer group acceptance and status.

2. Delinquent behavior will not persist in a community where staff and student leaders are unified in consistently rewarding prosocial behavior and sanctioning antisocial behavior.

3. As a group, delinquents have substantial undeveloped academic, athletic, and vocational potential, which can be realized in a supportive and challenging psychosocial environment that provides a range of programs broad enough to accommodate diverse student skills and interests.

4. Students who return to their home communities armed with an awareness of the powerful role of peer pressures; an acceptance of personal responsibility for their own success or failure; the experience of acclaim for academic, vocational, and personal growth; the pride of being a respected student at a respected prep school; the habit of seeking and offering help in time of need; and educational, social, and vocational skills adequate to compete in the job market can withstand the considerable negative influences which once engulfed them in delinquency.

These assumptions about delinquents and delinquency do not, however, entirely account for the structure of Glen Mills' culture and programs.

Core Beliefs

As indicated in Chapter 1, the "why" of Glen Mills' approach reflects three core beliefs beyond an acceptance of a sociological model of delinquency. These are held so unequivocally by Glen Mills' administration that they can be considered fundamental axioms in the Schools' habilitation system.

First, students are not regarded as morally inferior to nondelinquent adolescents. They have done *bad things*, but they are *not bad* people. They are no less deserving of respect and dignity than any other human being; specifically, they do not "deserve" to be deprived or punished any more than the students at prestigious private academies.

Acceptance of this principle resolves the role conflict experienced almost universally by institutional child care workers. No Glen Mills staff ever needs to rationalize the act of escorting a young man to an isolation cell. Isolation units, restraints, and other forms of punishment commonly employed as instruments of control in institutions have no place at the Schools.

Glen Mills' normative culture permits no action intended to physically or psychologically injure a student. It does, of course, require policies that prevent students from abusing others or the normative culture. A young man unwilling to conform to dining unit norms is not deprived of food, for every Glen Mills student has an inalienable right to top quality food. He is, however, deprived of the privilege of eating his food in the dining hall. A student who persists in unacceptable classroom behavior is not denied an education, for a good education is an inviolable right of every Glen Mills student. He is, however, deprived of the privilege of receiving the education in the classroom. A young man whose behavior in the cottage is consistently unacceptable to his peers or staff is not locked in an isolation cell "to let him think about it," as the standard rationalization puts it. Rather, he is required to find a living unit willing to accept him. If he is unable to do so he suffers Glen Mills' ultimate sanction: expulsion. Custody, the preoccupying concern of most institutions, is of minimal concern to staff since Glen Mills' philosophy requires that custody goals be achieved through the creation of a program that students will feel proud to call their own. The primary impediment to escape at Glen Mills is the student's realization that, if he leaves, the Schools may not accept him back.

A second core belief is that given an appropriate normative culture, habilitation is best achieved when program and facilities are of top quality. Glen Mills' leadership seeks to provide the finest programs, facilities, and services possible in *all* areas; not merely those normally considered "treatment." Just as parents who send their child to college expect strong programs and an attractive facility, the taxpayer (who pays a far higher "tuition") is entitled to the same expectation regarding juvenile offenders.

Since Glen Mills regards its students as no less deserving than the denizens of Harvard, the Schools' administrators are not deterred by the desire—which in some institutions is either overt or unconscious and couched in "it's for their own good" rhetoric—to deprive or punish them.

This factor is of utmost significance in understanding Glen Mills' model. It is one of the elements which most clearly distinguishes it from most programs for juvenile offenders. It accounts not only for the computers in the classrooms and the state-of-the-art vocational assessment equipment, but also for the well-tended shrubbery; steak dinners; stylish, noninstitutional clothing; and student trips to Florida. The impact upon students' pride and self-esteem is incalculable.

Like all organizations, Glen Mills operates with a finite budget. Priorities must be established. Recognition of a need for a new or upgraded program can seldom be followed immediately by an allocation of monies to meet the need. The difference between Glen Mills and most other institutions is that the Schools' board and administration, when reviewing a program that would improve Glen Mills, very rarely say "We can't do this, it's too costly." Rather, they say "We can't do *all* of this *now*," and develop a plan that will, over time, yield the desired result. The Schools' board and managers are very cost-conscious, but only *after* deciding upon their objective. The question then becomes "How can we do this most economically?" The quality of the end product is never compromised; Glen Mills is not a "settle for" type of organization.

Glen Mills does not merely seek to be the best school for juvenile offenders in the country. It seeks to be the best "prep" school in the country. With programs, staff, and facilities second to none, Glen Mills seeks to become the nation's leading school for preparing young men for life—providing them with a new vision and hope for the future as well as the academic, vocational, and personal requisites for realizing their potential to live a satisfying and law-abiding life. In the director's words, a place "where Rockefeller would want to send his kids."

The Schools' dual emphases upon accepting responsibility for one's behavior while helping others to grow derive from the final "axiom," the belief that staff and students *alike* have enormous potential for growth. When a student rises during the daily cottage Townhouse meeting and says "I want to own up and apologize to my peers and staff for . . . ," he is acting out a ritual which is core to the Glen Mills experience. It is far more than an admission of misbehavior. It is an expression of obligation to the community and an acknowledgment that it is he himself who is responsible for his own behavior. As his staff and peers refuse to accept the usual excuses for delinquency—poverty, an uncaring family, racism, etc.—the student becomes alert to his own rationalizations, and their disempowering effects. And as his admissions are answered by offers of help and exhortation to change his ways he begins to realize, as Karl Menninger (1973) pointed out, that recognition of personal responsibility is a cause for hope, not despair. If he had the power (with a little help) to foul up his life, perhaps he also has the power (with a little help) to straighten it out.

The call to growth—to accept the challenges life presents and to support one another in overcoming obstacles—pervades every aspect of Glen Mills' program.

Obstacles and setbacks, far from being negatively valued reasons for discouragement, are viewed as opportunities for improvement. On the athletic fields and in GGI, in classrooms and counseling sessions, in staff training and senior staff meetings the message is the same: Let's work to become a little bit better today than we were yesterday. Don't strive for perfection. The only people who make it to the top of the mountain are those who set out to climb small mountains; these unfortunates now have nowhere to go but down.

A good institution is one that teaches both its staff and its students to become good mountain climbers: to risk leaving the security of the ledge you stand upon and, through personal effort and accepting the help of others, experience the satisfaction of reaching the next higher ledge. For the Glen Mills community it is the process of the climb—the triumph over obstacles—which gives life its satisfactions and its meaning, not conquering the peak.

THE GLEN MILLS STUDENT: A STATISTICAL PROFILE

Program models are likely to be more effective with some types of students than with others, hence the importance of describing "to whom" services are provided. As discussed in Chapter 2, Glen Mills excludes offenders for whom its group-focused habilitation program appears contraindicated: arsonists, overt homosexuals, and the mentally ill. There is a strong preference for older, "socialized" delinquents for whom peer pressures have played a significant role in misbehavior.

Whenever possible, data are presented in this chapter for the 3,038 students who were admitted to the Schools' residential program between January 1, 1976 and December 31, 1984. Exhibit 4.1 indicates the growth in enrollment during the period, and Exhibit 4.2 provides a statistical profile of the 2,795 students admitted 1976–83. Due to missing data and rounding, totals may not sum to 100 percent in all cases.

Several terms used in Exhibit 4.2 require further elaboration. "Grade level functioning" is the average of new students' scores on the Metropolitan Achievement Test, administered within two weeks of admission. "Age at first court appearance" is the age at which the student first appeared in family court charged with delinquency. "Previous institutionalizations" include any court-mandated placement in an institution. "Reason for commitment" is the most serious delinquent act leading to placement at Glen Mills (students are frequently charged with more than one offense). "Property crime" includes theft, breaking and entering, receiving stolen property, criminal trespass, purse snatching, and destruction of public property. "Authority" includes violation of probation, escape, possession of firearms, disorderly conduct, malicious mischief, and resisting arrest. Finally, a student is considered "Peer oriented" if he is a gang member or committed a crime in the company of his peers, otherwise he is considered a "loner."

Exhibits 4.3 through 4.7 show trends in admission cohorts regarding their

Exhibit 4.1
New Admissions to Glen Mills Schools Residential Program: 1976–1984

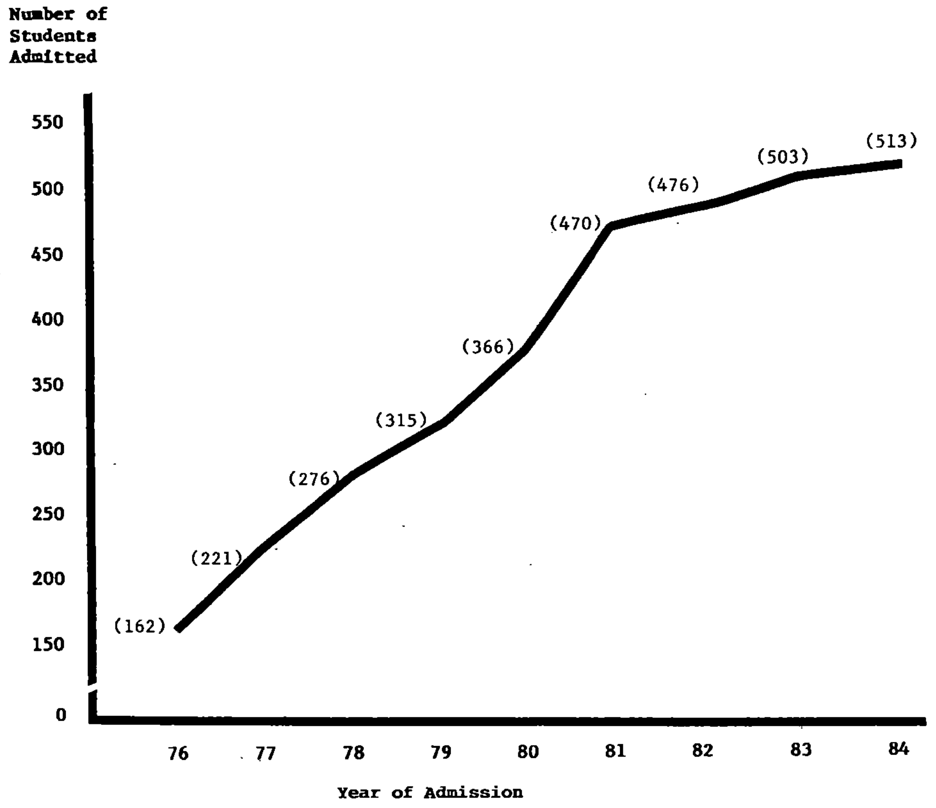

Number of
Students
Admitted

550 — 500 — 450 — 400 — 350 — 300 — 250 — 200 — 150 — 0

(162) (221) (276) (315) (366) (470) (476) (503) (513)

76 77 78 79 80 81 82 83 84

Year of Admission

county of origin, racial distribution, family composition, offense for which committed, and history of assaultive behavior.

As these data indicate, the model new student at Glen Mills during the period 1976–1983 was an urban, black gang member, between 16 and 17 years old. He came from a single-parent household headed by his mother and had three brothers and sisters. Upon admission his math and verbal skills functioning were at the sixth grade level. He had first appeared in court charged with a delinquent offense at about 14 years of age. He had been arrested, though not institutionalized, several times.

EVALUATION FINDINGS

Glen Mills' goal is to provide effective programs at reasonable cost in a humane environment, enabling students to live a crime-free life after discharge. The evaluation plan is designed to assess the Schools' effectiveness in achieving these goals by reviewing institutional records and conducting a survey of all students approximately two years post-discharge.

Data Sources

Data are collected for all students at several points during and after their residency at Glen Mills. The major data collection points are intake, discharge, and two years post-discharge. Data sources include:

Intake

- Court records: Demographic and history of delinquency data are available for all new students.
- Medical exam: Height, weight, body type, and eyesight measurements for all new students.
- Tests of cognitive functioning: Every new student takes an IQ test and the Metropolitan Achievement Test within two weeks of admission. The Metropolitan is readministered to all students approximately six months after admission to assess growth in basic skills.

Discharge

- Administrative data: This includes program participation information, awards, reason for discharge, and placement.
- Counselor ratings: Every student is rated by his counselor regarding his level of involvement in the program, the quality of his relationships with peers and staff, and his conformity to the Schools' norms.

Follow-up. During the summer of the third year following the year of admission an attempt is made to locate and interview each student in the admissions cohort, including those who did not complete the School's program. For ex-

Exhibit 4.2
Student Population Profile: 1976–1983 Admissions (N = 2,795)

	Number	Percent
COUNTY		
Allegheny (Inc. Pittsburgh)	561	21
Philadelphia	1,148	42
Other Pennsylvania Counties	1,015	36
Out of State	69	2
RACE		
Black	1,844	66
White	856	31
Hispanic	85	3
Other	7	--
FAMILY COMPOSITION		
Head of Family		
Both parents	729	26
Mother	1,609	58
Father	170	6
Relative	165	6
Other guardian	114	4
Birth Order		
Only child	121	6
Oldest	384	18
Youngest	443	21
Middle	1,171	55
Number of Siblings		
0	169	6
1	260	10
2	482	18
3	500	18
4	478	18
5	299	11
6	197	7
7 or more	332	12

Exhibit 4.2 (continued)

	Number	Percent

HOME AREA

	Number	Percent
Urban	1,830	78
Suburban	397	17
Rural	114	5

PHYSICAL

Body Type

	Number	Percent
Stout	111	5
Average	1,906	90
Slight	107	5

Eyesight

	Number	Percent
Owns corrective lenses	312	14
Requires (but does not own) corrective lenses	134	6
Does not require lenses	1,799	80

Height Average = 5 ft., 8 inches

Weight Average = 145 pounds

AGE AT ADMISSION TO GLEN MILLS

Average = 16 years, 6 months

(Std. Dev. = 11.4 months)

BASIC SKILLS

Grade Level Functioning when Admitted

Verbal: Average = 5.9
          (Std. Dev. = 3.2)

Math: Average = 5.8
          (Std. Dev. = 2.5)

Exhibit 4.2 (continued)

	Number	Percent

HISTORY OF DELINQUENCY

Age at First Court Appearance

	Number	Percent
10 or under	145	7
11 - 12	311	14
13	344	15
14	492	22
15	527	23
16	339	15
17	87	4

Estimated Number of Arrests Prior to Placement*

	Number	Percent
1 - 2	18	33
3 - 4	23	43
5 or more	13	24

Number of Previous Institutionalizations

	Number	Percent
0	1,307	64
1	480	24
2	155	8
3 or more	89	4

Record of Assaultive Behavior

	Number	Percent
Yes	941	40
No	1,428	60

Reason for Commitment to Glen Mills

	Number	Percent
Murder	14	0.5
Forcible rape	38	1
Assault	427	16
Armed robbery	472	17
Burglary	635	23
Auto theft	199	7
Drug related	32	1
Property crime	460	17
Authority	365	13
All other	98	4

Exhibit 4.2 (continued)

	Number	**Percent**
Peer Orientation		
Loner	574	28
Peer oriented	1,456	72

* These data were unavailable for the 1976-1983 cohorts.
  The estimates shown are based on a study by Goodstein
  and Sontheimer (1987) of 54 randomly selected students
  admitted to Glen Mills in 1984.

ample, in the summer of 1986 follow-up data were sought for every student admitted to Glen Mills' residential program during 1983. On average, the follow-up interview occurs 27 months after discharge. This period was selected because most recidivism occurs within two years following discharge. However, due to variation in the month of admission and the length of stay, the follow-up period ranges from 12 to 40 months, with data collected for two-thirds of the cohort between 18 months and 36 months post-discharge.

Interviews are conducted in person or by telephone. Whenever possible the student himself is interviewed. When this is not possible, information is sought from a family member:

• In-person interviews: Individual, confidential, hour-long structured interviews are conducted with at least 30 randomly selected former students from each admission cohort. Topics covered include both the student's recollection of Glen Mills and his experiences since discharge.

• Telephone interviews: Brief telephone interviews are conducted with all former students in the admission cohort who can be located, or with a family member. Respondents are asked about employment, education, training, and recidivism experiences since discharge from Glen Mills.

Intake and discharge data are available for all 3,308 students admitted to the Schools' residential program during 1976–84. Follow-up data were obtained for 1,398 students, or 42 percent of those admitted. Of the remaining 1,910 students, 19 refused to be interviewed and 1,891 could not be located.

Interview Method

The interview process was employed for the first time during the summer of 1979 to collect follow-up data on the 1976 admissions cohort. It has been used with only slight modification in each succeeding summer. The goals of the interview process are to conduct in-depth, individual interviews with a random

Exhibit 4.3
Percent of Admissions by County, 1976–1984

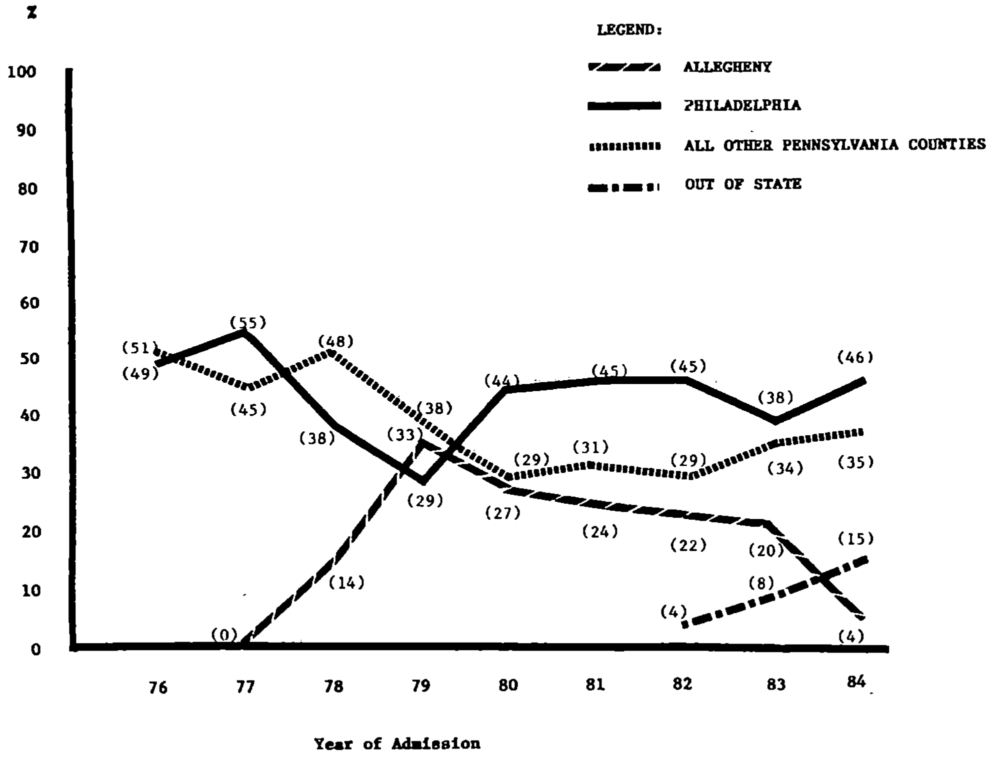

LEGEND:

▨ ALLEGHENY

▬ PHILADELPHIA

░░░ ALL OTHER PENNSYLVANIA COUNTIES

▬▪▬ OUT OF STATE

%

100
90
80
70
60
50
40
30
20
10
0

(51)
(49)
(55)
(48)
(45)
(38)
(46)
(38)
(33)
(29)
(46)
(45)
(31)
(29)
(45)
(29)
(38)
(34)
(35)
(15)
(20)
(22)
(24)
(27)
(29)
(14)
(0)
(4)
(8)
(4)

76   77   78   79   80   81   82   83   84

Year of Admission

120

Exhibit 4.4
Percent of Admissions by Race, 1976–1984

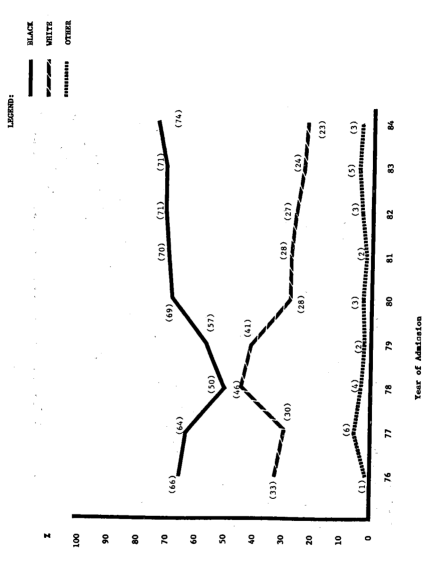

Exhibit 4.5
Family Composition (Head of Family), 1976–1984

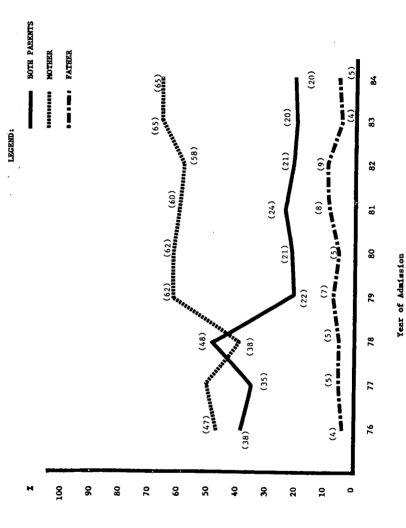

Exhibit 4.6
Percent of Admissions by Offense, 1976–1984

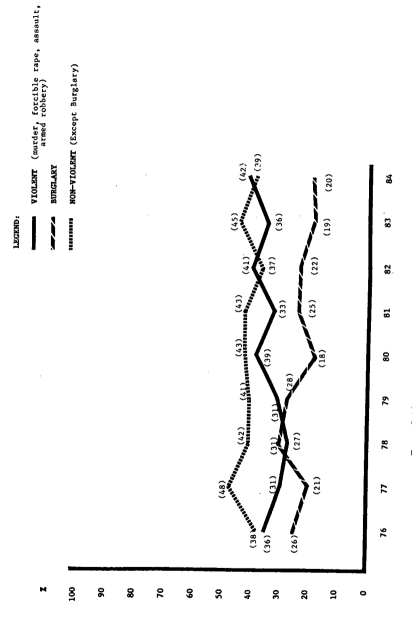

Exhibit 4.7
Percent of Admissions Having History of Assaultive Behavior, 1976–1984

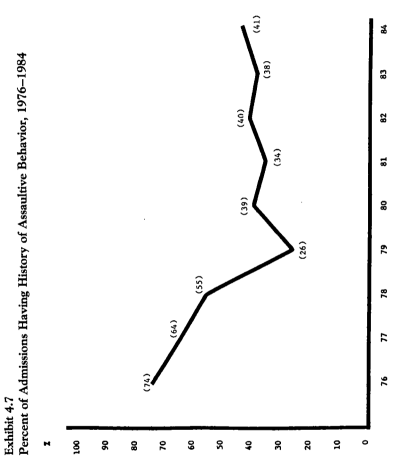

Year of Admission

Exhibit 4.8
Follow-up Sample

Admission Cohort	Students in Cohort	In-Person Interview with Student (%)		Telephone Interview with Student (%)		Telephone Interview with Student's Relative (%)	
1976	162	42	(26%)	14	(9%)	9	(6%)
1977	221	34	(16%)	38	(17%)	42	(19%)
1978	276	40	(15%)	31	(11%)	56	(20%)
1979	315	42	(13%)	27	(9%)	96	(30%)
1980	366	48	(13%)	19	(5%)	87	(24%)
1981	470	32	(7%)	47	(10%)	123	(26%)
1982	476	39	(8%)	45	(9%)	126	(26%)
1983	503	34	(7%)	36	(7%)	133	(26%)
1984	513	40	(8%)	23	(5%)	119	(23%)
TOTALS	3,302*	351	(11%)	280	(8%)	791	(24%)

*Total admission = 3,308 and follow-up sample = 1,398
 Year-of-Admission data were missing for six students in the follow-up
 sample.

sample of at least 30 students from each admissions cohort; and to determine the post-discharge experience of as many of the remaining students as possible through telephone interviews with the students themselves, or where this is not possible, with the students' family members.

The initial step of the follow-up process is the construction of a list of all students in the admissions cohort, together with their last known addresses and telephone numbers, by the Schools' Admission Department. Random numbers are assigned to each student on the list, and these determine the subsample targeted for the in-depth, face-to-face interviews. Where it proves impossible to locate and interview one of the students from this subsample, the individual is replaced by the boy having the next lowest random number until at least 30 interviews have been completed.

The attempt to locate a former student begins with a telephone call and/or visit to his last known address. Since this address is typically two years or more out of date, several telephone calls and visits are often necessary to contact the student. In all cases, efforts are continued until the boy is located or until there are no further leads as to his whereabouts. Typically, three to five phone calls and at least one visit are required, though in some cases more than ten phone calls and five on-site attempts are necessary to locate a subject or remove him from the interview sample.

In many cases a visit to the last known address produces information from former neighbors which is instrumental in locating the boy. One case, though not typical, illustrates the detective work involved. The subject's last known phone number having been disconnected, a visit was made to the address that had been current at the time of discharge. The subject's family had moved, but a neighbor indicated that the boy's grandfather worked in a nearby grocery store. Contact with the grandfather indicated that he had lost touch with his grandson, but believed the boy had gone to Collegeville. Finding no trace of the subject in Collegeville, a small town 15 miles from Philadelphia, it was decided to contact the state penitentiary near State College, Pennsylvania. The hunch proved accurate; the boy was located and interviewed in the prison.

Since the inception of the research all follow-up interviews have been conducted by Dr. William Dubnov. The size of the face-to-face sample was constrained by budgetary considerations and Dr. Dubnov's availability, which required that all data be collected during May to September of each year. The average of the face-to-face sample size is 39. Refusals are rare; less than 2 percent of students located during the research have refused to be interviewed. The problem is finding them.

When contact is made with the subject, Dr. Dubnov introduces himself and explains the purpose of the research—to help Glen Mills to improve its programs. Assuring the subject of confidentiality and anonymity, Dr. Dubnov offers him five dollars to participate as an interviewee. The fee is paid prior to the interview. It is stressed that honest answers are crucial to the usefulness of the research; the boy is told that he may decline to answer any questions he would prefer not to discuss.

Subjects are often initially suspicious of the purposes of the interviewer. Time spent in establishing rapport prior to the interview has proven to be important. All interviews are conducted in private and on the subject's "turf"—his home, a local fast food restaurant, near his worksite, etc. For those who are incarcerated, it is necessary to conduct the interview in the correctional facility.

The in-person interview follows a structured protocol of 40 questions pertaining to the subject's recollections of his experience at Glen Mills and events since his discharge. On average the interview requires one hour. Some require no more than 45 minutes, others as long as 90 minutes.

In addition to the sample of former students with whom in-person interviews are conducted, information is also sought regarding all other students in the cohort. This is achieved through brief telephone interviews with all other subjects who can be located, or with a parent or relative. Efforts to locate these students are less intensive, in most cases restricted to phone calls. Whenever possible, the boy himself is interviewed. However, in many cases family members do not know or are unwilling to divulge his whereabouts, but do have sporadic contact with the subject and are able to provide some or all of the information sought. The interview consists of five questions regarding the subject's experience since discharge: Has he returned to school? Completed a training program? Been employed? Arrested? Reincarcerated? Despite the difficulties of establishing rapport over the telephone lines, respondents are usually cooperative after the purposes and conditions of the interview are explained. The average interview time is seven minutes, but in some cases individuals have remained on the phone for more than an hour.

This methodology has yielded follow-up data for 42 percent of all Glen Mills students, provided during face-to-face (11 percent) or telephone interviews with the subjects (8 percent) or relatives (24 percent). This success rate compares favorably with other large-scale studies which attempt to locate juvenile offenders after discharge from correctional supervision. For example in a post-discharge telephone follow-up study of delinquents released from a wilderness program (STEP, 1984) researchers attempted to contact and interview 1,442 former students, using only "last known phone number" data from agency records. The project was terminated after 3,040 calls, with 218 (15 percent) students interviewed and contact established with the families of 195 (13 percent) others. The median follow-up period (approximately 28 months) was similar to that of the Glen Mills study, though the average time between discharge and follow-up of STEP students was several months longer. The Glen Mills and STEP success rates in locating former students and their families indicate the relative effectiveness of the two methods in terms of response rate. The benefits of the more rigorous (and more costly) Glen Mills methodology include the improved response rate and, in all likelihood, a more representative interview sample.

Quality of Follow-up Data: Validity and Generalizability

Two important issues bearing upon interpretation of the follow-up data are the representativeness of the interview samples and the accuracy of interviewees' responses. Two samples are of particular concern: the sample of former students ("in-person" sample) with whom individual, face-to-face interviews were conducted, and the total sample comprised of the in-person sample together with former students and family members of former students who agreed to brief telephone interviews. Information regarding the quality of Glen Mills' environment was sought only during in-person interviews. Recidivism estimates were based upon total sample responses.

There are several concerns regarding the accuracy of interview data. The first is poor recall. Former students interviewed in person were asked about events which had occurred nearly three years in the past; their recollections may not be accurate. A second is lack of information. For example, a parent whose contact with a son is sporadic may believe and report that the son has not been arrested since being discharged from Glen Mills, even though one or more arrests had in fact occurred. Finally some interviewees may have deliberately lied, due to embarrassment, suspicion of the interviewer's motives, concern regarding the confidentiality or uses of the data, hesitancy to appear critical of the Schools, or other reasons.

The interview procedure described above was designed to establish the conditions known to encourage accurate reporting. In addition, respondents were told that they could skip questions if they were uncertain of the answer or for any reason felt uncomfortable responding. In rare cases (less than 2 percent) interview data were discarded when Dr. Dubnov felt that the necessary level of trust had not been established and the accuracy of the information was in serious doubt. In Dr. Dubnov's opinion, the large majority of in-person subjects took the interview seriously and responded honestly to the questions. The level of candor of respondents interviewed by phone is more difficult to assess, due to the additional difficulties involved in establishing rapport and the inability to watch for and respond to non-verbal cues.

Sample Representativeness and Generalizability of Findings. Sample representativeness is an important issue in its own right, independent of validity. Even if reporting were completely accurate, interview data could be misleading if the subjects in the sample were not typical of Glen Mills students as a whole.

Two questions must be asked in relation to each of the samples: (1) Is the sample representative of the Glen Mills student population with respect to available demographic, delinquent history, and program participation characteristics? (2) What is the likelihood that nonrepresentativeness, where it occurs, restricts the generalizability of the findings, that is, do the differences matter?

Data analyses indicate that the samples are statistically similar to the Glen Mills population on most characteristics. The "in-person" sample was statistically representative on 27 of 33 background variables; the total interview sample on 19 of 33. In every instance where a statistically significant difference was found, its magnitude seemed inconsequential (e.g., the mean I.Q. of the sample differed from that of the overall population by a single point, 88 versus 89).

A separate study was conducted to determine whether the recidivism experience of the interview sample differed from that of the Glen Mills students who were not interviewed. Court records for a random sample (N = 463) of students from Philadelphia were reviewed to compare the recidivism of those who had been interviewed with that of students who could not be located for interview. There was less than 1 percent difference between the two groups. Accordingly, it is likely that the total interview sample is representative with respect to recidivism, that estimates based upon the interview sample are generalizable to all Glen Mills students.

Validity. Prior research on the validity of self-report by delinquents and substance abusers has identified several conditions under which survey data have been found to exhibit good validity (Polich, 1982; Sobell and Sobell, 1982; Skinner, 1984; NIDA, 1985). Accurate responses can be expected when subjects are assured of confidentiality, not drunk or high, and understand the purposes of the survey. All of these conditions prevailed during the face-to-face interviews, which were conducted by an experienced researcher expert in establishing rapport.

Data collected during in-person interviews were consistent with similar information from other sources. For example, respondents in later cohorts provided increasingly favorable assessments of their Glen Mills experience, which corresponded closely with the researchers' observations at the Schools during the period 1976–84, interviews with staff, and the quantitative data (e.g., on runaways, behavioral incidents, etc.) collected by the Schools.

A variety of consistency checks indicated that students were accurate in their self-report. For example, when compared to recidivists, students who had made a good adjustment to the community were significantly more likely to feel that Glen Mills had helped them. These factors justify confidence regarding the validity of data collected in person.

Generally, self-reported arrest and incarceration data have been found to be particularly reliable, possibly because interviewees realize that their responses are easily checked against official records. Greenfeld (1985) found that in large-scale studies estimates of prison return rates based upon offender self-report and official records vary by less than 1 percent. Studies of inmates' self-report show that prisoners' accounts include more arrests than, and as many convictions as, their official records (Marquis, 1981).

Glen Mills' self-reported recidivism data were closely scrutinized for three reasons. First, the issue is more sensitive than most of the other interview topics, reflecting directly on the boy's success or failure post-discharge. Second, of the interview data upon which recidivism estimates were based, only one-fourth were collected during in-person interviews. Establishment of rapport—a crucial factor in eliciting accurate responses—is far more difficult on the telephone, a factor which may adversely affect validity. Finally, in many cases the telephone interviews were conducted with a parent of the former student, introducing the possibility of inaccurate reporting due to lack of knowledge.

For these reasons, a detailed study of the validity of the self-reported recidivism data was conducted. Philadelphia juvenile and adult court records were reviewed during 1986 for a random sample of 463 Philadelphia students admitted to Glen Mills during the period 1976–81. The sample includes 60 percent of the 770 students admitted from Philadelphia during these six years, and represents more than one-fourth of all admissions (N = 1,810). Slightly more than half of the sample (54 percent) had completed Glen Mills' program; one-third had absconded or been discharged for failure to adjust to the program.

Court data obtained for each subject included the number of arrests, convictions, and incarcerations within 27 months of discharge from Glen Mills. This period was selected to coincide with the average follow-up interval for the interview sample. In addition, data relating to justice system involvement occurring more than 27 months post-discharge were collected. The range of follow-up periods reflected in the court data was three to eight years, with a mean of six years.

Court records were located for 417 individuals, representing 91 percent of the original sample. Juvenile records for 46 boys had been lost or expunged, and they had no arrests as adults. These 46 cases were dropped from the sample. Excluding them provides a conservative bias to recidivism estimates. Since these students had no adult arrests, it is very likely that their post-discharge adjustment was more favorable than that of the remaining 417 boys.

The primary objective in collecting the court data was to validate the interview data. However, several findings are of general interest:

1. Of the 417 cases, 360 (86 percent) had been rearrested and 229 (55 percent) re-incarcerated during the six years following their discharge from Glen Mills.
2. Within 27 months of discharge from Glen Mills, 345 subjects (83 percent) had been arrested in Philadelphia. Fifteen subjects experienced their first post-discharge arrest more than 27 months post-discharge. Of the 360 individuals rearrested within six years post-discharge, 96 percent were arrested within the first 27 months.
3. Within 27 months of discharge from Glen Mills, 184 subjects (44 percent) had been incarcerated in a juvenile or adult facility for a new crime. Forty-five students (11 percent) were reincarcerated for the first time more than 27 months post-discharge. Of the 229 individuals reincarcerated within six years of discharge, 80 percent were incarcerated within the first 27 months.
4. Within six years after discharge from Glen Mills, 189 subjects (45 percent) were convicted of a Part I offense (murder, rape, aggravated assault, armed robbery, burglary, larceny, motor vehicle theft, arson).

These findings are based upon the experience of Philadelphia students who attended Glen Mills during the developmental phase of the Schools' normative culture. However, they suggest recidivism rates, especially for rearrest, that are significantly higher than those based upon survey data.

Detailed study of these findings, to be published in a later paper, indicate that data from the follow-up interviews of Glen Mills students underestimate the actual levels of recidivism, and that the distortion is greatest with respect to rearrest. Estimates based upon follow-up interviews require adjustment. Specifically, estimation of actual 27-month recidivism requires upward adjustment of the rearrest rate based upon interview data by a factor of 1.55 and the reincarceration rate by 1.26. The adjustment compensates for:

1. Deliberate underreporting. It is likely that at least 80 percent of respondents were honest. But some of the underreporting of recidivism was probably deliberate.
2. Lack of information. Interview data from family members is subject to error because, lacking daily contact with the student, these individuals may believe that no justice system contact has occured when in fact this is not the case.
3. Forgetfulness. Asked about events which in many cases occurred two or more years in the past, some respondents may simply have forgotten whether or when they occurred.

4. Timing of the follow-up interview. Although the average follow-up period is 27 months, some interviews occur as early as 12 months post-discharge and some as late as 40 months. Since the large majority of recidivism occurs within the first 27 months (96 percent of rearrests and 80 percent of reincarcerations), this causes the actual 27-month recidivism rate to be underestimated by a process whose *average* follow-up period is 27 months. The number of individuals whose initial recidivism occurs *after* their interview but *before* 27 months substantially exceeds those who recidivate *after* 27 months but *before* their interview.

Reflecting both self report and official records, recidivism estimates (Exhibits 4.19, 4.20) derived using the adjustment factors are higher than those which would be derived from either source independently. They are very conservative, particularly when used to compare Glen Mills' recidivism with rates from studies that utilize only official records or only self-report.

Glen Mills' success in providing effective programs at reasonable cost in a humane environment is assessed in the following four sections. Finally, the significance of the recidivism findings is discussed in relation to the findings of other studies.

Unless otherwise stated, findings presented in this section are based upon the experiences of all students admitted during 1976–84. During the nine-year period of evaluation two-thirds of the 3,308 admissions completed Glen Mills' program; that is, they were discharged upon the Schools' recommendation following a successful stay. In addition, 14 percent were discharged by court order against the Schools' recommendation; 12 percent were discharged after running away; and 8 percent were sent back to court after having failed to adjust to the program.

Since an institution which accepts a student also accepts responsibility for helping him, evaluation based upon data for all students (regardless of whether they compeleted the program) provides the most accurate assessment of program effectiveness. However, since it is not unusual for evaluations to restrict their scope to program completers, these data are sometimes presented separately to facilitate comparison to other studies.

Short-term Effectiveness

The average length of stay for Glen Mills students was 9.5 months (11 months for program completers). The impact of academic, vocational, athletic, and GGI programs during the period of residency was assessed through standardized tests and individual interviews.

Evidence for the effectiveness of *educational programs* comes primarily from two sources: Metropolitan Achievement Test scores measuring improvement in basic skills, and success on the GED exam entitling the student to a high school equivalence diploma.

Improvement in MAT math and reading scores is shown for each admission cohort in Exhibit 4.10. Average growth over a six-month period is measured

Exhibit 4.9

Percent of Admissions by Reason for Discharge, 1976–1984

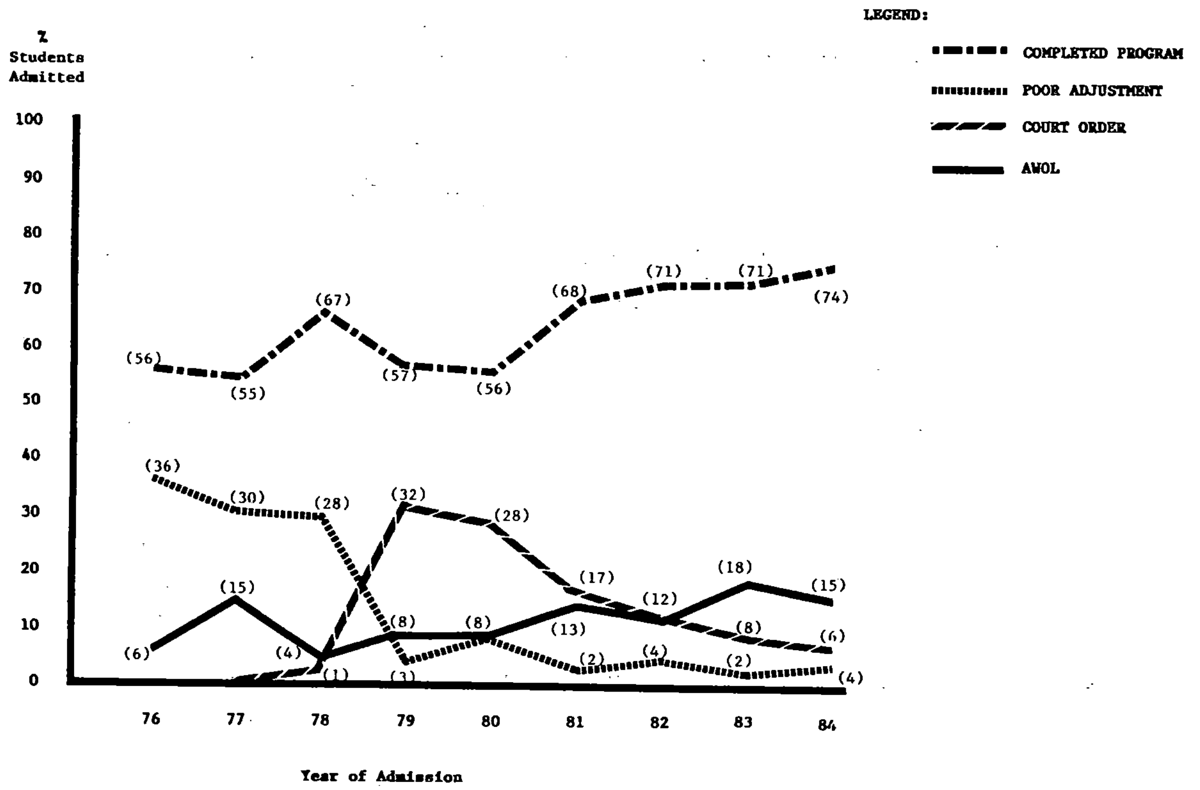

% Students Admitted
100
90
80
70
60
50
40
30
20
10
0
76
77
78
79
80
81
82
83
84
Year of Admission
LEGEND:
COMPLETED PROGRAM
POOR ADJUSTMENT
COURT ORDER
AWOL
(56)
(55)
(67)
(57)
(56)
(68)
(71)
(71)
(74)
(36)
(30)
(28)
(32)
(28)
(17)
(12)
(18)
(15)
(6)
(15)
(4)
(1)
(3)
(8)
(8)
(13)
(2)
(4)
(2)
(8)
(6)
(4)

Exhibit 4.10
Grade Level Improvement in MAT Math and Reading Scores by Year of Admission, 1976–1984

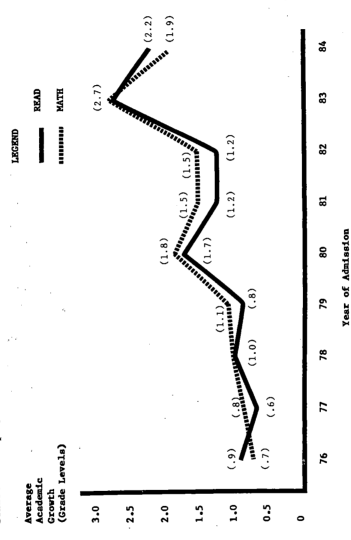

for each student for each student using pre-post MAT testings. These data are then extrapolated to estimate the improvement in grade level functioning during the nine-month academic year. Glen Mills' educational programs operate year-round; the nine-month data are presented to allow comparison to traditional, nine-month programs such as public school systems.

On average, Glen Mills' students have completed 10 years of formal schooling and function on the sixth grade level upon admission to the Schools, indicating a rate of growth of .6 years in skills development for each (academic) year of schooling prior to Glen Mills. By comparison, in the years 1976–84 the average student gained 1.4 grade levels in reading and 1.6 grade levels in math for each nine months of instruction at Glen Mills; the gains for 1983 and 1984 averaged above 2.0. These figures exclude individuals whose test scores declined or showed improbably large gains (i.e., five grade levels or more), to partially control for distortions caused by some students who do not exert their best efforts on the test and thereby distort the average gain scores. Allowing for the likelihood of some residual bias due to this phenomenon, the dramatic gains in basic skills nonetheless suggest a highly effective educational program.

Exhibit 4.11 shows the number of students attempting and passing the GED exam in each admissions cohort. Both the number and proportion passing increase over the eight-year period; by 1983 nearly 200 Glen Mills students per year were successful in earning their high school diplomas despite long histories of failure in the public schools. Glen Mills' achievement in this area has never been matched by any other Pennsylvania correctional facility.

The 72 students who, having earned their GED at Glen Mills, went on to enroll in college are a further indication of the quality of education at the Schools. Individuals' achievements, while not representative, attest to the capacity of the Schools' program to meet the needs of students along the entire continuum of ability. Four percent of new admissions are high school graduates; 15 percent arrive with reading skills below the third grade level and math skills below the fourth grade level. Some of the latter have enormous unrealized potential. The most dramatic example is a "special ed" student who arrived with an educational history suggesting that he may be uneducable. After three years at Glen Mills he accepted an offer of a full scholarship from Dartmouth College.

The quality of the Schools' athletic programs may be unrivaled among juvenile correctional institutions in the United States. The majority of students participate in at least one sport, although very few have been involved in organized athletics prior to Glen Mills. One-third of the students admitted between 1976 and 1984 played on a varsity team. Individual and team achievements since 1976 include:

- A national high school championship in powerlifting.
- Victories by Glen Mills' "Prep" football team, comprised of students and staff, over freshman teams from major colleges, including Penn State.

Exhibit 4.11
GED Testing, 1975–1986

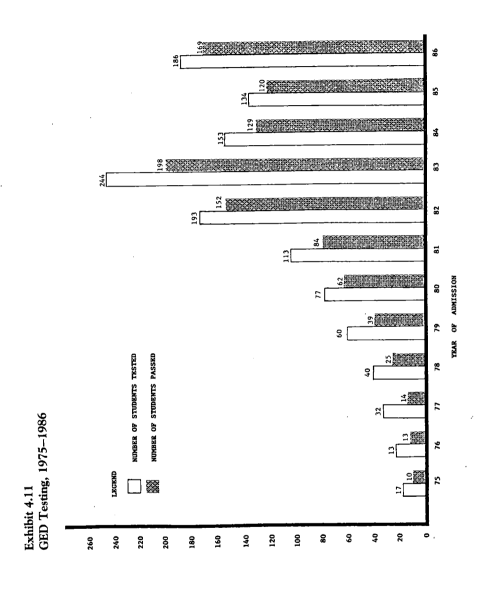

- Glen Mills' athletes have been awarded athletic scholarships to major universities including Temple, Maryland, West Virginia, Syracuse, and Virginia Tech.
- A staff member of Glen Mills' "Prep" team went on to become an All-American running back at the University of Maryland and to play professionally for the Washington Redskins.
- Glen Mills has won Eastern Pennsylvania District championships in gymnastics and basketball, and league championships in football, track and field, cross-country, and basketball.
- The cross-country team is undefeated in 40 consecutive dual meets.
- Glen Mills has produced state championship teams in gymnastics, powerlifting, and track and field, as well as individual powerlifting, discus, and shotput state champions.

With few exceptions, Glen Mills' 14 varsity teams are competitive against opponents in one of the strongest athletic divisions in the state. This despite the ability of competing districts to "groom" their athletes during three years of middle school and four years of high school competition.

Evidence for the effectiveness of Guided Group Interaction (GGI) comes from earlier research by the senior author and from interviews with students after discharge. One objective of GGI is to create and sustain a prosocial peer group normative culture. Prior research (Grissom, 1977) confirms that students experience the GGI norms as significantly more prosocial than the "street" norms of their home communities. During in-person follow-up interviews two years post-discharge, three out of four (77 percent) students recall "liking" GGI and 86 percent felt that the GGI sessions had helped them. Indirect evidence of the effectiveness of GGI in promoting positive norms comes from interviewees' assessments of the Schools' culture: as the GGI program became more refined and better established, norms regarding aggression and manipulation improved. (Note, however, that these trends reflected broader organizational development—e.g., staff training and cohesiveness—and were not due entirely to increased effectiveness of GGI.) The proportion of interviewees from each admissions cohort that felt that manipulativeness was a viable strategy for students declined sharply and rather continuously between 1976 and 1984 (See Exhibit 4.18).

As the most recently established program, evidence for the effectiveness of vocational training is sparsest. Since 1980, when the first shops became operational, 1,244 students have successfully completed vocational programs. Of these, 51 have gone on to further formal training after leaving Glen Mills and 14 were placed in jobs.

Follow-up data for the 1980–83 admissions cohorts also suggest a positive effect. Of students who took vocational courses, 95 percent reported liking them; 94 percent felt the courses had been helpful. The proportion of students who found employment during the first 27 months post-discharge increased from 63 percent (1980 cohort) to 85 percent (1984 cohort). These data reflect the quality of Glen Mills' training and other factors, most importantly a general improvement in overall regional employment.

In summary, there is compelling evidence regarding the short-term effectiveness of Glen Mills' educational, athletic, and GGI programs. Available data for the vocational offerings is encouraging, though less conclusive than for the other areas.

Cost

The per diem cost of Glen Mills' residential program in 1988 is $70. This represents a 42 percent *reduction* from the 1975 rate of $121, despite the high inflation of the late 1970s. Glen Mills has not increased its per diem during the 13 years of Mr. Ferrainola's tenure.

Data for the most recent year for which information is available indicate that the average per diem costs nationally for private juvenile correctional facilities was $58 (U.S. Department of Justice, 1986) in 1982. The vast majority of the 1,877 private institutions were small programs; the average population served was 17. Few offered a range of programs comparable to those provided by Glen Mills. Assuming that average costs have kept pace with inflation, Glen Mills' program is today among the less expensive programs nationally. Pennsylvania data provided in the Justice Department report indicate that, in 1982 the Commonwealth's 56 private facilities charged an average per diem of $59 and the 34 public facilities averaged $103, suggesting that Glen Mills' charges in 1987 place the Schools among the least expensive local options. Average per diem rates for Pennsylvania large public institutions in 1987 was $150.

Significantly, the Glen Mills rates cover all the services traditionally provided by correctional institutions plus substantial "extras":

- Most students take at least one extended trip during their period of commitment, usually to Florida.
- The Schools pay the transportation costs for all home visits. In the case of out of state students (e.g., Iowa, Michigan) these are substantial.
- Scholarship funds covering full tuition and books have been provided to 44 students who were admitted to area colleges following their stay at Glen Mills.
- Glen Mills provides its program free of charge to an average of 20 "returning students" who wish to return to the Schools after discharge to complete academic or vocational programs, or compete on athletic teams.
- Each student may eat four meals per day.
- Most students receive one or more achievement awards during their stay. These may include clock radios, a Schools ring, Glen Mills jacket, or other award.
- The Schools provide a comprehensive physical exam and pay the cost of all necessary medical or dental treatment.
- Eyeglasses were provided at no cost to 134 students in the period 1976–83.

• Upon admission, each new student is taken to a warehouse full of new clothing of various styles, and permitted to select a complete outfit of his choice.

The Schools' low per diem reflects four factors: the role of the Bulls Club, careful attention to cost control, inherent cost-effectiveness of Glen Mills' normative culture, and the productivity of its staff.

The Bulls Club, whose members include roughly one-half of the student population, plays a valuable role in program operation. Direct "services" include monitoring student behavior in the dining hall and student union; allocating paying jobs on campus to students in need of extra income; serving as "big brothers" to new students and assisting staff responsible for night time coverage in their living units. Most importantly, Bulls provide positive student leadership and share responsibility with staff for maintaining the normative culture. The current culture could probably not be sustained without the Bulls. The dollar value of their contribution to Glen Mills' effectiveness is substantial.

In terms of its business principles and *attention to cost control* Glen Mills bears a closer resemblance to corporate America than to a human services agency. Operating costs are continually reviewed by the Schools' business office and Board of Managers, resulting in numerous economies. Some examples: the Schools' annual costs related to unemployment insurance decreased from $140,000 to $35,000 when a self-insurance plan was developed. Costs for medical and dental care (insurance and services) for students and staff were reduced by several hundred thousand dollars annually, and the quality of care substantially improved, through a combination of self-insurance and the hiring of a full-time physician and two dentists. Food services costs were minimized through the construction of large freezers, enabling the Schools to purchase food in "ton" quantities and take advantage of bulk purchasing discounts. A portion of Glen Mills' land is leased to area farmers to the mutual benefit of Glen Mills and its neighbors. Most of the Schools vocational shops provide goods or services of value to its program: eyeglasses, printing, auto repair, etc. Glen Mills has taken full advantage of the economies of scale made possible by its large student and staff population.

A third factor in cost-effectiveness is the normative culture model itself, which requires neither security staff nor social service personnel. The security function is distributed across the entire community; all staff and students are expected to confront negative behavior whenever it occurs. Since delinquency itself is not a psychiatric syndrome and Glen Mills does not admit emotionally disturbed students, the Schools have no greater need for mental health professionals than any other high school. Requiring neither social service nor security departments the Schools' normative culture model is at least $600,000 per year less expensive to operate than a clinically oriented program of comparable size.

The model is inherently cost-effective in its focus upon norms and systems, as opposed to staffing levels, in providing security and student growth. In more traditional programs, the first response to crises is often "We need more staff," not "This system isn't working." At Glen Mills, the opposite is true.

The fourth and most significant factor in Glen Mills' cost equation is the contribution of staff, whose numbers are small, productivity high, and salaries modest. The Schools are able to operate effectively with a low staff complement because staff serve in multiple roles. All academic and vocational instructors are also cottage staff. In addition, staff work tens of thousands of hours of overtime per year to coach athletic teams, tutor students, direct cottage projects, and lead student trips. None receive overtime pay. Salaries are modest at all levels.

Recruitment policies, staff norms, and a compensation policy linking rewards to the Schools' overall fiscal performance are key factors in staff productivity. Individuals who are too quick to ask "What's in it for me?" are not hired, however strong their qualifications. Norms of teamwork, pride, and doing more than your share all contribute to productivity.

Finally, all staff are kept informed of the Schools' fiscal situation and all understand that "profits" do not go to stockholders or to an expensive and bloated administrative staff, but are passed on to them in the form of additional program resources and very substantial fringe benefits (see Chapter 2). The latter has included a "match" of up to 50 percent of employee contributions to the retirement plan, and Christmas bonuses. Attractive housing is provided for senior staff, minimizing turnover among key personnel. In good years, the value of fringe benefits can be very substantial. Poor years bring austerity but seldom layoffs, since the basic salary burden is not great.

All staff have a stake in the efficient operation of the Schools and in working together as a team, since raises and bonuses are not individualized but based upon team performance. Together, these policies encourage strong staff commitment, high morale, and productivity levels rarely achieved in nonprofit organizations.

Humane Environment

In the juvenile justice system incarceration is recognized as a legitimate response to some forms of delinquency, intended to incapacitate and rehabilitate the offender. Punishment in the form of unnecessarily harsh conditions of confinement makes rehabilitation more difficult and has, therefore, no place in juvenile correctional programs. Administrators should be held accountable for maintaining an environment as free as possible of all forms of physical and psychological abuse. Effectiveness in achieving this objective is a central issue in the evaluation of any correctional program.

The low incidence of abuse at Glen Mills reflects the Schools' valuing of its students and the effectiveness of the confrontation process. Abuse is most common in environments where individuals are demeaned. It is rampant in institutions where delinquents are regarded as "bad" and unworthy of respect. These views provide a rationalization for abusive treatment, usually under the guise of "security needs." Staff abuse, whether physical or psychological, in turn creates a climate of deprecation, anger, and fear—fertile soil for aggression by students who seek to recover their self-respect through intimidation of weaker peers. When abuse goes unchallenged it becomes the norm: accepted, expected behavior.

Glen Mills' core value of respect is manifested in its norms governing interactions among staff and peers, and in the quality of medical/dental care, food, clothing, furniture, and program facilities provided to its students. The message is clear and consistent: Your health matters. Your appearance matters. The nurturing of your mind and body matters. *You matter.* These messages are the stuff of which self-esteem is made. They are as essential to a humane environment as sunlight to a green garden.

It would be a very serious mistake to confuse respect and the high quality of Glen Mills' environment with "coddling" of delinquents. "Coddling" involves rewarding, or at least tolerating self-centered and irresponsible behavior. Selfishness, in the form of lack of concern for one's peer group, and irresponsible behavior are *never* accepted at Glen Mills. The probability that these behaviors will be challenged is very high.

The confrontation process is inextricably linked to the quality of the environment. When confrontation is effective, students will respect property and each other. Feelings and behavior associated with an abusive environment—fear, vandalism, fighting, suicide attempts, runaways, etc.—will be uncommon. Conversely, when consistent and appropriate confrontation of negative behavior does not occur, "street" norms quickly become established and negative students become powerful through manipulation of staff and intimidation of peers; that is, the culture reinforces delinquent behavior. Therefore, core issues pertaining to the quality of the institutional environment include the strength of implementation of the confrontation process and indications of physical or psychological abuse. Specifically:

- How frequently do confrontations occur? Are the nature of the confrontations appropriate to the behavior which led to the confrontation? Do staff and students share responsibility for confronting negative behavior? Do staff monitor and control student confrontations to guard against abuse of the process by students seeking to dominate their peers?

- Does the institution demonstrate a commitment to minimizing abuse by monitoring related behaviors and implementing appropriate policies and procedures? What formal mechanisms exist to detect and eliminate abuse? How effective is the attempt to establish a humane environment, as reflected in the prevalence of feelings and behaviors related to abuse?

In a correctional facility where nearly half the residents have a history of assaultive behavior, emotionally charged interactions are frequent and the potential for abuse high. Glen Mills' administration believes that its confrontation process is an alternative to the usual tools employed by correctional staff to prevent abuse: physical restraint (i.e., handcuffs, isolation cells, etc.) and drug therapy. When applied to adolescents who evidence no significant emotional disturbance, physical restraint and medications can themselves become forms of abuse which, in the long run, may be more harmful than the behaviors they are invoked to prevent. Evaluation data presented below strongly suggest that the confrontation model, properly implemented, is a humane and effective alternative to other forms of behavioral control for student populations similar to Glen Mills'.

An effective confrontation process must be consistent and respectful of the individual confronted: negative behavior that is not confronted is thereby reinforced; disrespectful confrontation creates hostility and conflict, ultimately encouraging more abusive behavior than it prevents. Evidence of the frequency and appropriateness of confrontations comes from the Schools' administrative records and from in-person interviews with former students two years after discharge.

Maintenance of the normative culture requires constant staff vigilance and involvement. On average, staff in the Group Living Department report approximately 100 confrontations per day; or approximately 10,000 daily confrontations by the department as a whole.

A key indicator of an effective normative culture is frequent confrontations *by students.* Of a random sample of 310 former students, 145 (46 percent) reported that they were more often confronted by students than by staff while they were at Glen Mills. When confrontations by staff in all departments and by students are included, the total number of confrontations per day is well over 10,000; that is, an average of at least 16 confrontations per student per day.

During face-to-face follow-up interviews students report far lower levels of confrontation. Three-fourths say they were confronted less than once per week outside of GGI and less than once per week in GGI during their last three months at Glen Mills. Even during their initial three months in the program, when confrontation is heaviest, nearly half report that they were confronted less than once per week in GGI and less than once per week outside GGI.

The discrepancy between the frequency of confrontation as reported by Glen Mills staff and students is due to at least two factors. First, confrontation is focused disproportionately upon "negative" students. When a boy's behavior is consistently unacceptable he becomes the target of a coordinated campaign by teachers, coaches, cottage staff, Bulls, etc. to insure that his behavior results in loss of status, that he does not "get over" (get away with negative behavior). Second, most confrontations are so subtle or minor that the student does not experience them as "confrontations"; the vast majority are forgotten by the end of the day or at least over the course of the two years between discharge and interview. Only a very few are serious enough to warrant much attention. There were only nine level VII confrontations during all of 1986, despite an average daily population over 500. Confrontations of level V and above are infrequent and tend to be concentrated upon a very small percent of the most negative students (see Exhibit 2.2).

Data from follow-up, in-person interviews indicate that confrontation by staff is experienced as appropriate and helpful by most students. Four out of five (81 percent) said that confrontations by staff were appropriate; 9 percent felt staff confrontations were usually not harsh enough and 10 percent felt they were too harsh. A large majority (92 percent) characterized staff confrontations as having been "helpful" to them. Perceptions of confrontations by students are less positive. One-fourth (24 percent) recalled confrontations by students as having been too harsh and one-fifth (19 percent) as too mild, though three out of four (74 percent) said that confrontations by students had generally been helpful to them. Overall, these data suggest that staff confrontations are almost uniformly experienced as constructive; confrontation by students is experienced as less effective but, on the whole, plays a positive role at the Schools. No interviewees felt that confrontation was used by students to intimidate or degrade their peers, confirming that student confrontations are carefully monitored and controlled by staff who are alert to abuses of the process.

Glen Mills' director of group living monitors indicators of abuse and has established policies and procedures to prevent it. All level VII (physical restraint) confrontations must be reported by staff to their senior counselor and team leader. The senior counselor records the incident in the cottage log and the team leader individually interviews all students and staff involved in the incident. His report and recommendations are forwarded to the director of group living, who interviews the student involved and the team leader and notifies both the student's parents and the court of the incident. Finally, the executive director receives a report from Group Living describing the incident, the actions taken, and any recommendations for additional steps. It is the Schools' policy to investigate all incidents of possible abuse, whether related to a confrontation or reported independently by students or staff. Staff who are found to be abusive or to have failed to intervene to prevent abuse are subject to immediate dismissal, though this has been necessary on only four occasions during the past decade. Staff who are involved in repeated level VII confrontations are instructed to seek support from other staff and then withdraw from future serious confrontations. Finally, to ensure that the confrontation process is maintained, Glen Mills commits the full support of the Schools up to and including legal action to defend any staff found to have been unjustly accused of abuse. The latter policy is crucial to ensure that staff feel secure in their interventions and do not hesitate to confront negative behavior.

A strong normative culture is the surest protection against most forms of abuse. In order to detect threats to the culture as soon as possible, the Group Living Department monitors numerous "vital signs" on a monthly basis. The department's information system is a crucial management tool, allowing staff to track critical indices and to alert the director, team leaders, and Bulls when troubling trends emerge. The director then meets with the staff and student leaders to plan a strategy and obtain commitments to implement the agreed-upon plan. Failure to monitor key trends risks allowing negative norms to obtain a foothold before managers recognize the danger. Once established, these norms are far more resistant to change. Negative norms are the cancerous tumors of a normative culture; early detection and strong confrontation the best protection against malignancy.

Exhibits 4.12 through 4.16 show the average daily student population and the incidence of various negative behaviors for six-month intervals from 1982 through June 1987. In each case the number of incidents in each six-month period is traced from the time the Schools' monitoring system was established (January 1982; monitoring of "stealing" and "physical restraints" began in 1984). "Break-ins" refers to any forced entry to a campus building: kitchen, student union, etc. "Truancy" is any unauthorized absence from campus; the majority of these cases involve students who return late from weekend home visits. Students are due back on grounds at 6 P.M. on Sunday and are considered truant if they have not arrived by midnight. Most of these students return on their own within a day or two. "Assaults" refer to physical assaults. "Stealing" refers to any theft of property, including inexpensive items such as cigarettes, socks, etc. The strongest indicators of an abusive environment, suicide attempts, are not shown because there have been none during the past 10 years.

Both the overall trend and the pattern of the data are noteworthy. The general trend in the incidence of all negative behaviors except graffiti is down, despite a nearly 50 percent increase in the student population during the 1982–87 time frame. This suggests a significant strengthening of the normative culture con-temporaneous with a sharp increase in enrollment. This finding is striking in relation to the belief that larger programs are necessarily more negative in their effects, an assumption that gained wide currency during the past two decades but requires reexamination. Note also that virtually every significant increase in a negative behavior is followed immediately by a downturn during the fol-lowing six-month period, providing strong evidence that the management team is successful in detecting and responding effectively to troublesome trends before these reach crisis proportions or become established and resistant to change.

Exhibit 4.13, which bears most directly upon abuse, indicates that the known incidents of physical assault upon students reached a high of 54 during the period from January to June of 1985, when the average daily population was 435. Were these random incidents, the typical student would have roughly one chance in eight of suffering an attack during the six-month period. During the first six months of 1987, when there were an average of 570 students on campus, there were only seven incidents of assault. The probability of victimization had de-clined to less than one chance in 80.

Individual, in-person follow-up interviews are a rich source of information regarding the quality of Glen Mills' environment. Exhibit 1.1 presented the responses of 311 subjects from eight admissions cohorts to the questions: Were

Exhibit 4.12
Average Daily Student Population, 1982–1987

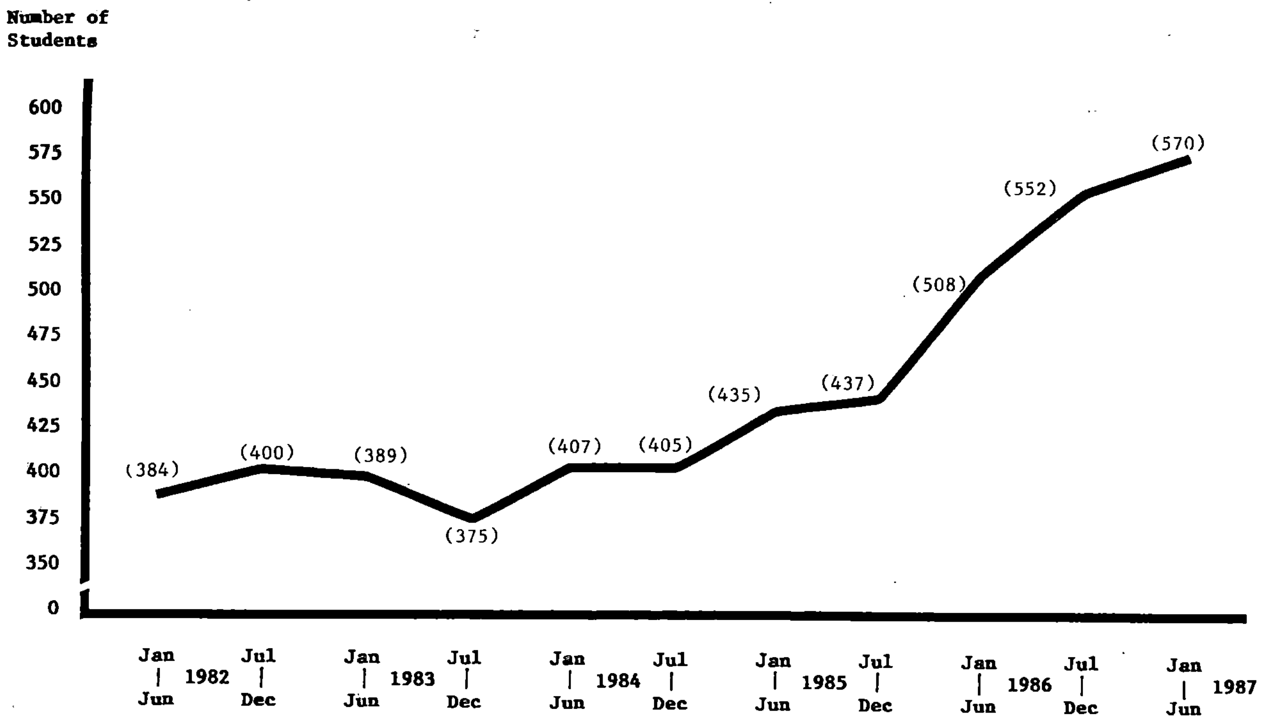

Number of
Students

Exhibit 4.13
Incidents of Assault on Staff and Students, 1982–1987

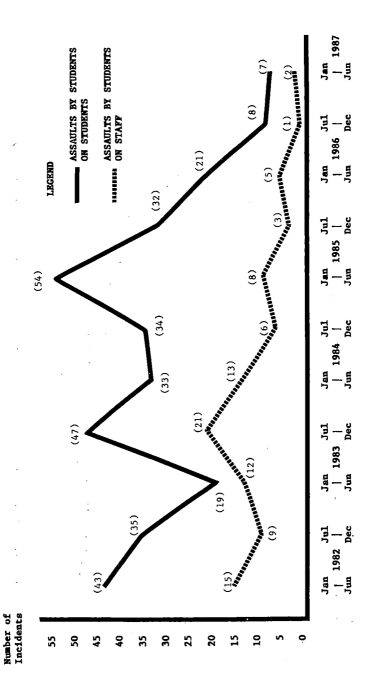

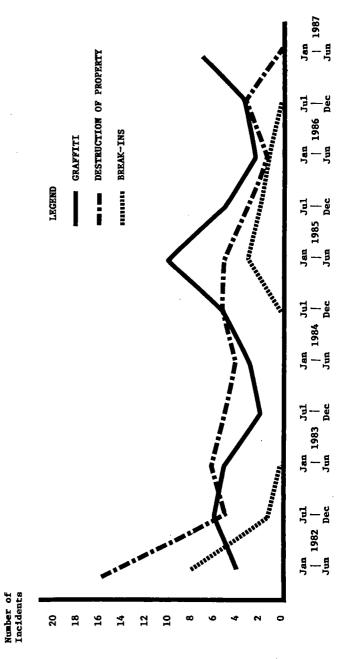

Exhibit 4.14
Incidents Involving Graffiti, Break-ins, Destruction of School Property, 1982–1987

Number of
Incidents

LEGEND

GRAFFITI

DESTRUCTION OF PROPERTY

BREAK-INS

Exhibit 4.15
Incidents of Truancy and Drug/Alcohol "Highs," 1982–1987

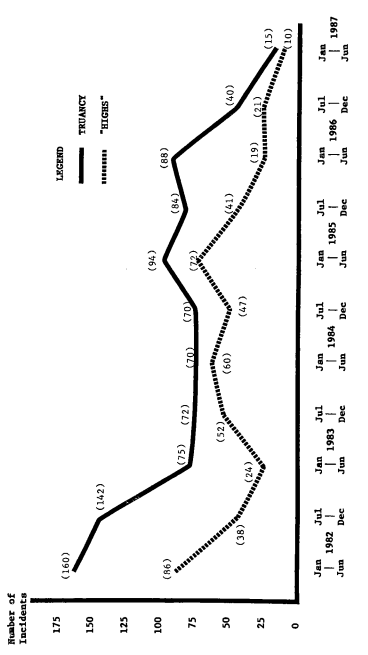

Exhibit 4.16
Incidents of Stealing, Physical Restraints, 1984–1987

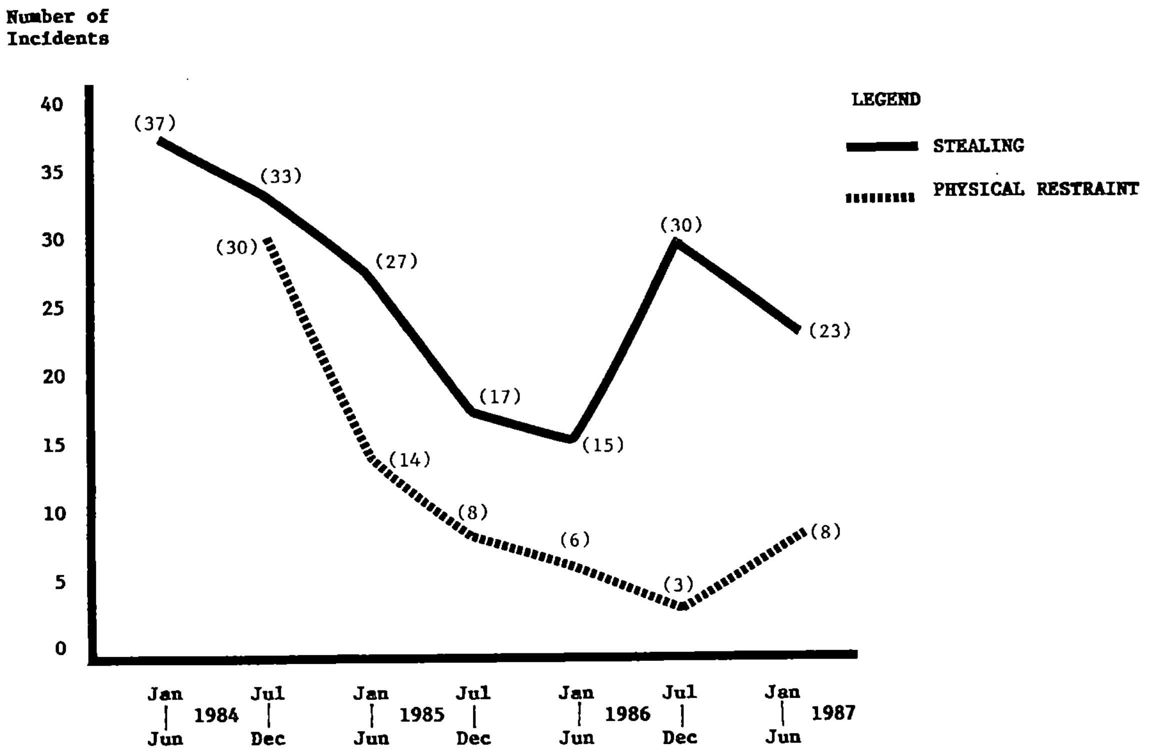

Number of
Incidents

LEGEND

━━━ STEALING
▪▪▪▪▪▪▪ PHYSICAL RESTRAINT

40

35

30

25

20

15

10

5

0

(37) (33) (27) (17) (15) (30) (23)

(30) (14) (8) (6) (3) (8)

| Jan 1984 | Jul | Jan 1985 | Jul | Jan 1986 | Jul | Jan 1987 |
| Jun | Dec | Jun | Dec | Jun | Dec | Jun |

you ever hit by another student while at Glen Mills? Were you ever hit by a staff member? If so, did the staff member strike out in anger or was he acting in defense of himself or others? The data indicate clearly the effects of the establishment of the normative culture during the period 1977–80: a sharp increase in staff involvement and confrontations led to more frequent physical confrontations between staff and students but a concomitant, steady reduction in student abuse of their peers as staff took control away from negative student leaders. With the normative culture established, 1980–84 brought a reduction in all forms of physical confrontation. These data attest to both the effectiveness of the staff campaign to wrest control of the Schools from negative student leaders (1976–80) and the immense power of the normative culture to preserve order without physical confrontations (Exhibits 1.1 and 4.16).

Exhibit 4.17 presents respondents' self-report in response to the question "Were you ever truant from Glen Mills?" Once again, the pattern of reduced truancy is consistent with the continual improvement in the Schools' normative culture. Significantly, students rarely went truant because of aversive conditions at Glen Mills. Nearly half (49 percent) wanted to be with their family, an additional third (34 percent) wanted to be with their friends. Relatively few said they went truant because of problems with staff (11 percent) or other students (13 percent). The total is greater than 100 percent because a few students gave more than one reason for their truancy.

Interviewees, when asked about their recollections of Glen Mills, provided consistently favorable responses. Nearly all said they liked the academic (89 percent), athletic (98 percent), and vocational programs (95 percent). Large majorities liked the staff (92 percent), believed that staff cared about the students (92 percent), felt that staff could be trusted to treat students fairly (89 percent), and were helpful (97 percent).

Perhaps the strongest indication that the Schools have largely succeeded in eliminating the intimidation of students by their peers, which plagues many correctional institutions, is the finding that 282 (92 percent) of 305 interviewees said they were "never" afraid of other students at Glen Mills. Nine (3 percent) said they were "sometime" or "often" afraid, the remainder (5 percent) "rarely." Exhibit 4.18 shows that manipulativeness, as measured during follow-up interviews, declined steadily as the new culture matured.

The most unusual evidence of a humane environment comes from students who "vote with their feet"—to return! There are always a minimum of 20 "returning students" on campus who have requested scholarships to return and complete an academic program or participate in athletics. These young men are treated exactly like any other student, except that the Schools receive no money for them.

Finally, global assessments of Glen Mills by former students are very positive. More than two-thirds (69 percent) strongly disagreed with the statement that they "would have been better off had they not been sent to Glen Mills"; 7 percent strongly agreed. Ninety-two percent said that they would want a close

Exhibit 4.17
Percent of Students Who Went AWOL Once or More by Year of Admission, 1976–1984

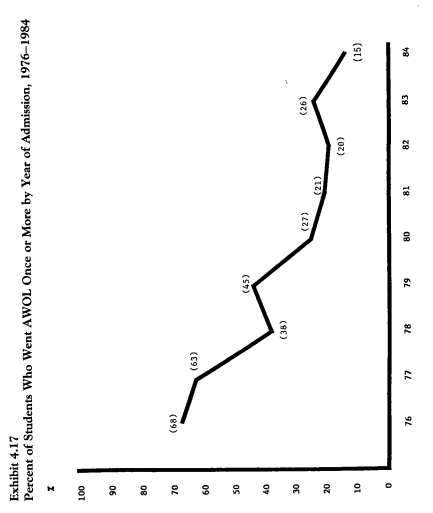

Year of Admission

Exhibit 4.18
Percent of Students Who Agreed that "You Could Get Along Well at GMS if You
Were Slick," 1976–1984

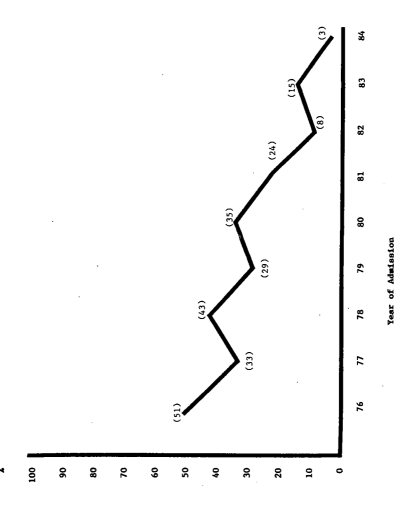

Year of Admission

friend to be sent to Glen Mills if a judge decided to institutionalize him. Less than 4 percent felt that their stay at Glen Mills did not help them.

In summary, Glen Mills has developed and implemented policies and procedures to minimize all forms of abuse. Data from the Schools' information system indicate that, as these policies were put in place and the normative culture strengthened, the incidence of behavior associated with abuse declined. This conclusion is independently corroborated through interviews with students after their discharge. The low level of fear and tensions among students is evident to the on-site observer and confirmed by the total absence of suicide attempts for more than a decade, and by the overwhelmingly positive assessments of the Schools by former students more than two years after their discharge. Assaults upon students do occur, but there is no evidence of formal *or informal* support for abusive behavior among staff or students.

Long-Term Effectiveness

Many consider an institution's long-term impact to be the most important measure of its effectiveness. Relevant questions include: Are there any reasons to suppose that a program will have lasting effects? Where do students go following discharge? What do they do? What support services are available to them? How many continue to commit serious crimes?

There are several reasons to expect that the effects of the Glen Mills experience might be long lasting. Upon discharge, a student has typically achieved significant academic or vocational success, making him better prepared to complete his schooling or find employment. He has learned and practiced positive, considerate behaviors governing his interactions with peers and staff; they "come natural" to him now. He has earned status through actions which benefit himself and do not harm others. This new behavioral repertoire is wholly incongruent with the "street" delinquent subculture. Finally, the Glen Mills experience has powerfully affected his self-concept and self-esteem.

As in standard behavior modification, Glen Mills applies the principles of learning theory to achieve behavior change. If that were the Schools' only achievement, there would be good reasons to suspect that the new behaviors might be specific to Glen Mills, not generalizable to the student's home community where the behavioral contingencies are vastly different. However, a student at Glen Mills experiences not only rewards, as in a token economy, but feels *valued.* The power of the normative culture lies in its ability to insure that those upholding the norms will experience affirming *informal* as well as formal "messages" from both staff and peers. This is the stuff of which true self-esteem is made.

The change in students' on-campus behavior is obvious and important. Less obvious, but perhaps even more important, are the impact of significant achievement, conditional rewards and unconditional valuing upon the young man's self-concept and self-esteem. He is not "bad" or a "loser." He has learned through direct experience that he can play within society's rules and achieve far more than he had thought possible, including the respect of his peers. These outcomes do not add up to an impenetrable shield against the pressures and temptations of the delinquent subculture. But they provide reasons to believe that the Schools' impact will, for many, be both positive and enduring.

What becomes of Glen Mills' students after they are discharged? Interviews with former students indicate that five out of six (85 percent) return to the same community where they had lived prior to their commitment. Most said that their friends were the same group they had associated with prior to attending Glen Mills (42 percent), or at least some of their friends were the same (42 percent).

Most boys (84 percent) returned to live with their families after discharge. Others went to live with relatives (5 percent), friends (3 percent) or alone (2 percent). The remainder of those interviewed went directly from Glen Mills to a group or foster home (1 percent) or to another large correctional institution (5 percent). The latter group is comprised entirely of students who were discharged by Glen Mills after running away or failing to adjust to the Schools' program.

Follow-up interviews were conducted, on average, 27 months following discharge. At the time of the interview three-fourths (74 percent) of the former students continued to live with their families, 5 percent with a relative, 4 percent with friends, and 4 percent alone. One in eight (13 percent) was incarcerated. Of course, these living arrangements may not be representative of all former students, more than half of whom could not be located.

There was a wide variation in the activities reported during the months immediately following discharge. One in six (17 percent) returned to school, 18 percent worked at a full time job, 16 percent worked part time, 2 percent enlisted in the military, and the remainder (except for those transferred to another institution) were idle or tried unsuccessfully to find a job.

During the period between discharge and the interview 27 percent of the respondents had spent at least some time in public school, 5 percent had graduated, and 23 percent had earned a General Equivalence Diploma. Nearly one-third (29 percent) had enrolled in a training program; 13 percent had completed it. More than three out of four (77 percent) had been employed at least once. Twenty of the 310 interviewees (6 percent) had married; ninety (29 percent) had fathered children.

At the time of the interview, six individuals (2 percent) were in high school, two (1 percent) in college, thirteen (4 percent) in a vocational training program, and four (1 percent) in the military. One in four (27 percent) was employed full time, one in seven (15 percent) part time. More than one-third (39 percent) were unemployed; 13 percent were incarcerated.

In keeping with their generally positive associations to Glen Mills, more than half (54 percent) had maintained contact with other Glen Mills students following discharge. One out of three (32 percent) kept in touch with Glen Mills staff. These contacts do not constitute a formal aftercare program. Aftercare services are provided by juvenile probation officers from the committing counties. The quality and scope of these services vary greatly from county to county. In particular, due to caseloads frequently exceeding 50, the quality of aftercare services provided by Philadelphia during 1975–87 was extremely poor.

Aftercare and community reintegration are serious concerns for Glen Mills' students. There is general agreement that the status quo is unacceptable and contributes to recidivism. Options under consideration by the Schools are discussed in the final chapter.

Glen Mills Recidivism in Context. Recidivism estimates for each admissions cohort were based upon follow-up interview data adjusted to correct for underreporting (See Quality of Follow-up Data, this chapter). Exhibits 4.19 and 4.20 present the findings relating to rearrest and reincarceration, respectively.

Interpreting recidivism findings requires great caution. There are two common misconceptions. The first is that two people talking about "recidivism" are talking about the same thing. In fact, this is only rarely the case. Definitions abound, including:

- Rearrest
- Reconviction
- Reincarceration
- Rearrest for a nontraffic offense
- Rearrest for a felony offense
- Rearrest for a felony offense or serious misdemeanor
- Reappearance in court on a new charge
- Reconviction for a Part I crime
- Reincarceration for more than one year
- Reincarceration by the releasing correctional agency
- Reincarceration, except for violation of parole or probation.

There are many others. In general, the deeper the justice system penetration required by the definition of recidivism, the lower the recidivism rate will be. For any sample of ex-offenders, studies defining recidivism as "rearrest" will nearly always yield a higher recidivism rate than those defining recidivism to be "reincarceration," for example.

In addition to the plethora of definitions which refer to the level of reoffending by individuals released from correctional supervision, agencies sometimes use the term "recidivism" to refer to the proportion of inmates having prior convictions—a fundamentally different concept. In a survey of 47 correctional agencies that conduct "recidivism" research, Miller (1984) discovered that 14

Exhibit 4.19
Rearrests within 27 Months of Discharge by Year of Admission* (1976–1984)

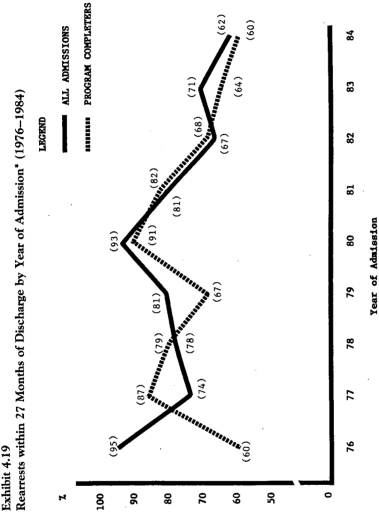

*Based upon Adjusted Self–report

Exhibit 4.20
Reincarceration within 27 Months of Discharge, by Year of Admission* (1976–1984)

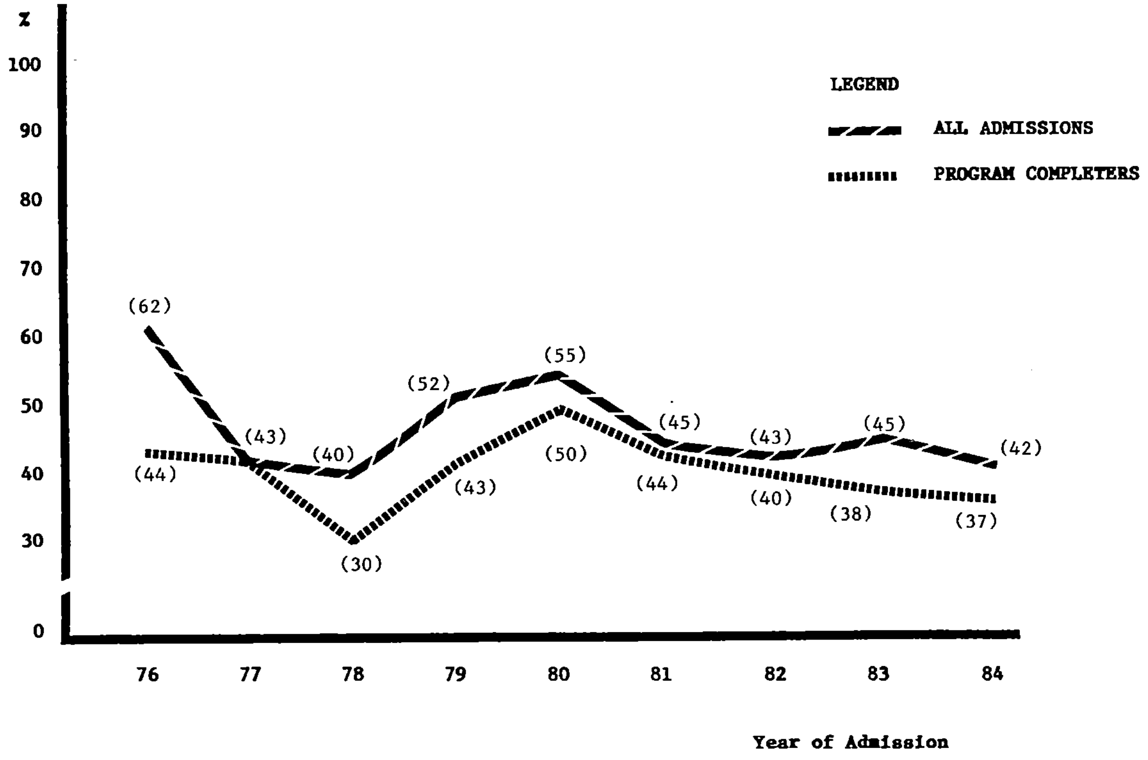

*Based upon Adjusted Self-report

used the term to refer to prior convictions. Naturally, when the same term is used to refer to different phenomena, much confusion results. Illustrating the problem, Miller notes that "Massachusetts in 1980 had a recidivism [reoffending] rate of 26 percent while 52 percent of 1980 commitments had prior adult incarceration." With a wave of the definitional wand, the recidivism rate doubles before your eyes.

Incomparability due to definitional differences is often compounded by differences in the follow-up period. Recidivism rates computed on the basis of a shorter period will be less than those based on a longer period; differences may be substantial when the periods involved are less than three years. This phenomenon can be stated in mathematical terms as follows: the recidivism rate R_T based upon follow-up period T approaches zero as T approaches zero, regardless of the level of offending.

A final confusion regarding follow-up periods is ambiguity in the meaning of a "one year follow-up period." For some studies this indicates that the follow-up period is one year from the date of discharge, while in other cases it refers to data collected in the calendar year following the year of discharge. In the latter case, the actual period at risk varies from a few days to two years.

Data sources accessed in the research also affect recidivism estimates. Estimates based upon agency records, local police files, court data, state police records, self-report, FBI records, etc., will tend to differ, with less comprehensive or poorly maintained sources yielding lower recidivism. An incomplete record-keeping system can make any institution's recidivism rate look good. Of the agencies surveyed by Miller, 32 used their own agency records, 14 used parole records, 8 used probation records, 4 used police records or self-report, 3 used court or FBI records, and 1 used county records.

Finally, studies frequently differ in the composition of the follow-up pool. Juvenile estimates are sometimes based on all releasees, sometimes only on those who have successfully completed the program. Still others exclude from follow-up individuals who were in the program for less than some minimum number of weeks. In the adult system studies are sometimes restricted to those released on parole, for whom there is continuing correctional supervision.

In summary, operational definitions of "recidivism" vary so widely that comparisons between studies are sometimes less a matter of comparing apples and oranges than apples and airplanes; there simply may be no common elements.

The second misconception regarding recidivism is that it is solely a reflection of the quality of an institution's program. While it is true that a well-designed and implemented program staffed by trained and committed individuals will normally yield lower recidivism than its less worthy counterparts, this is by no means always the case. Characteristics of the population served are important: a flawed program for first-time offenders may well experience lower recidivism than even the strongest program for serious and habitual offenders. There are additional factors over which the institution has little or no control: quality of aftercare programs, court practices relating to use of the incarceration sanction, and level of unemployment in the area served all affect recidivism.

In view of these misconceptions, the significance of recidivism data is frequently misinterpreted. "What's the recidivism rate?" is not, in itself, a meaningful question.

It might be noted with tongue (partially) in cheek that the murkiness in the meaning of "recidivism" offers administrators an opportunity to manipulate matters in such a way as to reflect favorably upon their programs. Low recidivism rates gladden the hearts of politicians, board members, and project monitors of funding agencies. Institutional directors are usually desirous of accommodating these important stakeholders. The observations made above suggest a wide range of strategies for the administrator who would like to substantially improve his facility's recidivism rate without going to the expense and bother of upgrading his program:

1. Define "recidivism" in terms of very deep justice system penetration. "Conviction followed by execution" is good, since it holds promise of a low recidivism rate and insures that the offending scoundrel will not be a further embarrassment to the program.

2. Restrict data sources to those least likely to record offenses by former inmates. The sports section of an out-of-state newspaper will do nicely.

3. Restrict intake to those least likely to become repeat offenders. Send back to court any bad actors who make it past the intake screening, and then base recidivism estimates only on program completers.

4. If all else fails, the following corollary to the mathematical theorem stated earlier suggests a sure-fire method for achieving any recidivism rate: Given any recidivism rate R there exists a follow-up period T such that R_T, the recidivism rate based upon T, will be less than R. In less mathematical terms: it is always possible to achieve a satisfactory recidivism rate by reducing the follow-up period.

In summary "recidivism," though appropriately considered to be the most important outcome measure in evaluating the effectiveness of correctional programs, does not lend itself to easy interpretation. Comparisons across studies are particularly hazardous.

Ideally, Glen Mills' data should be interpreted within the context of studies of programs serving similar students and employing identical or nearly identical definitions of "recidivism." To the extent that other studies of juvenile recidivism are dissimilar, comparisons to Glen Mills' data will be strained and conclusions about the effectiveness of Glen Mills' program tenuous.

Recidivism studies are reported in research journals; publications in libraries maintained by the National Criminal Justice Reference Service, the National Center for Juvenile Justice, and the National Center for Crime and Delinquency; and various other sources. Most are of little use in interpreting Glen Mills' data.

In many cases the operational definition of "recidivism" is incompletely described or differs significantly from that adopted at Glen Mills. In other cases the populations studied are dissimilar to Glen Mills'. In still others the findings are based upon samples too small to be meaningful. The range of difficulties in using prior research to guide the interpretation of the Schools' recidivism data is suggested by Neithercutt's (1978) overview of findings regarding the effectiveness of programs for violent juvenile offenders:

> There is mammoth variation in the reported results. . . . In the early 1900's some programs reported failures (return rates) approaching 90% and today's critics often say 2/3 or 3/4 of youth who enter correctional programs recidivate. . . . Project New Pride . . . is plagued by evaluation problems. The Minnesota Serious Offender Project has been operative too short a time to give useful results. . . . [Camp Hill] follow-up data do not address recidivism sufficiently. . . . The Outward Bound programs give too little, and too diverse, results. . . . The Florida Oceanographic reports are laudatory but the data that buttress them are insufficiently reported. . . . [Downeyside] is almost bereft of recidivism data . . . conclusions [regarding behavior modification programs] are restricted by methodological weaknesses. (Neithercutt, 1978: 109–10)

Little of the vast body of recidivism research is of use to the correctional administrator seeking to plan or evaluate his program. Review of scores of recidivism studies confirm that the question of Glen Mills' effectiveness in relation to other programs is not easily answered; directly comparable data are not available. However, the literature includes several relevant studies of statewide or national recidivism which provide a framework for assessing the Schools effectiveness. Representing a composite of program types and delinquent populations, these studies are the best available points of comparison for Glen Mills' data.

Available nationwide data pertaining to juvenile recidivism are of little value in relation to Glen Mills. The single study identified (Vinter, 1976; Barton and Sarri, 1979) was completed more than a decade ago. Its findings are based upon a mailed questionnaire follow-up of 1,837 youth, only 194 (10.5 percent) of whom returned usable questionnaires. No validity checks of the self-report data are reported by the authors. Finally, the sample was dissimilar to Glen Mills' population; female offenders and male status offenders comprised more than half of the sample.

Studies of adult and young adult recidivism are relevant in that they provide a lower bound for estimates of juvenile recidivism. Three of the major factors that distinguish juvenile and adult offending operate to increase the rate for juveniles. First, the force of peer group pressures in encouraging law-breaking is far stronger for juvenile than adult offenders. Second, the consequences of apprehension are usually far less harsh for juveniles than for adults committing similar offenses. Likelihood of confinement, length, and conditions of incarceration all favor the juvenile offender. Third, juveniles are, of course, younger than adults. This obvious fact is significant in view of studies in both adult and juvenile systems indicating a strong, inverse relationship between age and likelihood of recidivism: those who are younger at time of discharge are more likely to recidivate. Data for the adult system are presented below. With regard to juvenile data, Goodstein and Sontheimer (1987), in a study of 527 delinquents discharged from Pennsylvania institutions in 1984, found that younger releasees were far more likely to recidivate than older releasees.

Studies showing an inverse relationship between age and recidivism for the adult and juvenile systems separately do not necessarily establish the conclusion that juvenile recidivism is higher than adult rates. It is possible that recidivism declines during the juvenile years, increases sharply during the early adult years, and declines thereafter. But in view of the factors discussed above, the absence of any data supporting this alternative proposition, and the research evidence (Ariessohn, 1981) it seems most probable that juvenile recidivism rates exceed those of adults, probably by a substantial margin.

Two studies published by the Bureau of Justice Statistics provide estimates of reincarceration rates for males released from correctional institutions. In the first, Greenfeld (1985) estimates that 29.4 percent of state prisoners return to prison within a three-year period. The aggregate data mask a strong relationship between age at release and subsequent recidivism. Of the 18 to 24 age group, 41 percent return to prison within three years of release. Greenfeld's data further indicate that approximately 37 percent of this age group returns to prison within 27 months. Recidivism rates for juveniles in the 15 to 17 age group are likely to be considerably higher.

A later study, (Beck and Shipley, 1987) of 4,000 parolees between the ages of 17 and 22 who were released from prisons in 1978 found that 50 percent were rearrested for a serious crime and 32 percent returned to prison within 27 months of release. The authors note that "recidivism was higher among offenders who were paroled at a younger age"; rates for the 17 to 19 age group were approximately 10 percent higher than the average. The resulting estimate of a 27-month reincarceration rate of 35 to 36% for the youngest adult age group is similar to that found by Greenfeld.

In addition to the studies of adult recidivism, several juvenile studies warrant discussion. Most useful are those examining recidivism across multiple programs. Findings from experimental and quasi-experimental studies comparing single institutions or programs with one another typically focus upon outcome measures at the expense of even minimally adequate descriptions of the treatment environment. Those that do provide descriptive data often focus upon the formal treatment activities. It is now thought likely that the formal treatment component is of no more importance in determining program outcomes than a range of other program characteristics (Greenwood and Zimring, 1985). Staff and student norms; the range of opportunities for academic, vocational, and social development; availability of positive role models; frequency, accuracy, and timeliness of feedback for both positive and negative behavior: all are at least as important as the formal treatment component, yet the majority of research reports are silent regarding these crucial factors. One should not attach much

Exhibit 4.21
Percent of Prison Releasees Reincarcerated within 3 Years, by Age Group

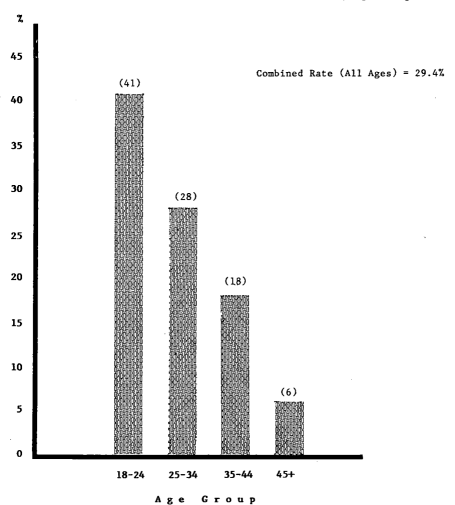

Summary of Data Reported by Greenfeld (1985)

importance to an experimental study demonstrating the superiority of program A over program B in reducing recidivism unless there is sufficient information about the two programs to provide some clues as to the factors behind A's success, or at least some basis for deciding whether program A is unusually effective or merely less ineffective than B. Evaluators have so often asked the wrong questions that their much heralded conclusion that "nothing works" is more descriptive of the evaluations than the programs.

The advantage in combining outcomes of multiple programs (e.g., for state-wide correctional systems) lies in the opportunity to decide what constitutes good performance by examining individual program outcomes in relation to the system as a whole. It is, of course, necessary to take into consideration the characteristics of the population served. A program for habitual offenders which succeeded in reducing recidivism to the system average might deserve national replication, whereas a program for first-time minor offenders which did not consistently outperform the system average would have to be considered ineffective. But for programs serving youth who are not atypical regarding their history of delinquency and social circumstances, the system average provides a useful benchmark for evaluation.

Systemwide studies of recidivism in Florida, Massachusetts, Illinois, Wisconsin, New York, and Pennsylvania provide useful composite data regarding expected levels of reoffending.

During 1984 a study (Lavine and McAlpin, 1985) was conducted to determine the recidivism rates (i.e., reincarceration) for juveniles admitted to Florida correctional programs between January 1976 and May 1983. Included are random samples of juveniles from Florida's residential, noncommunity-based programs, which include training schools and "START" centers for juveniles who are less serious offenders but requiring more supervision than that provided in community-based programs. Follow-up data regarding reincarceration in either the juvenile or adult systems were collected in 1984. The Florida Department of Health and Rehabilitative Services files were the source of data regarding juvenile recommitments. For those not recidivating in the juvenile system, arrest records were sought in Florida Department of Law Enforcement files and traced through the criminal courts to determine whether an adult incarceration had occurred.

Findings indicated that 70 percent of the training school sample and 62 percent of the START sample were reincarcerated during the follow-up period, with roughly 80 percent of the recidivism occurring during the first 24 months post-discharge. The estimated composite recidivism (reincarceration) for the combined programs during the first 24 months post-discharge is in the 50 to 55 percent range; the 27-month figure is somewhat higher.

Among the most rigorous and comprehensive studies of systemwide recidivism ever undertaken is the study of correctional reform in Massachusetts (Ohlin et al., 1977; Smith et al., 1980). The study, designed to examine the effects of replacing traditional training schools with community-based programs, included a sample of 236 boys paroled from five Department of Youth Services institutions in 1967 and 1968 (prior to the close of the training schools) and a second sample of 395 boys entering the (deinstitutionalized) system in 1973 and 1974. Two criteria were employed for recidivism: (1) reappearance in court on any charge other than a traffic offense, and (2) placement on probation, or commitment to the Department of Youth Services or an adult institution. Data were collected from the centralized records system maintained by the Massachusetts

Department of Probation, which includes both juvenile and adult court appearances and dispositions. The authors indicated that the system was not computerized and express concerns about its completeness; recidivism estimates based upon such records presumably tend to underestimate actual recidivism.

Findings indicate that 66 percent of the 1968 sample and 74 percent of the 1974 sample reappeared in court charged with a nontraffic offense within 12 months of release. Of the first sample, 47 percent were placed on probation or committed, as were 55 percent of the second sample.

For purposes of comparison to other studies, the latter results can be extrapolated using Lavine and McAlpin's findings (1985) regarding Florida delinquents, to produce a rough estimate of 24-month recidivism. Lavine and McAlpin's data indicate that the percentage of releases reincarcerated within 24 months is approximately 1.3 times the 12 month percentage. Application of this estimate to the Massachusetts data yields a 24-month recidivism (i.e., probation or commitment) estimate of 61 percent for the first sample and 71 percent for the second. These estimates are imprecise since the timing of recidivism in Massachusetts may not coincide with Florida's experience, and the definitions of "recidivism" in the Massachusetts study was broader in that it included probation. Beck and Shipley's findings (1987) regarding recidivism patterns based upon a national sample of youthful offenders suggest a higher multiplier than 1.3. They found that the 24-month reincarceration rate was 1.6 times the 12-month rate. Taking all the various factors including the incompleteness of the original records system into account, it is reasonable to conclude that the 24-month recidivism (probation or recommitment) rate for the Massachusetts combined samples is at least 65 percent and possibly as high as 80 percent or more. A similar analysis applying Beck and Shipley's rearrest trend data to the Massachusetts sample indicates that the 24-month rearrest rate (note that "appearance in court" underestimates rearrest) for Massachusetts delinquents is at least 75 percent.

An extensive study of recidivism was included in the evaluation of Chicago's Unified Delinquency Intervention Services (UDIS) program, designed to serve the chronic inner-city delinquent (Murray et al., 1978). The study involved three random samples of juvenile offenders committed to UDIS or the Department of Corrections. The baseline sample consisted of 130 males committed to DOC during the period January 1973 through September 1974. The DOC sample consisted of 104 males and the UDIS sample 144 males committed between October 1974 and June 1976.

Findings are based upon official records and reported for police contact, reappearance in court, and reinstitutionalizations within 12 months after release. The researchers found that 64 percent of the baseline sample, 65 percent of the UDIS sample, and 69 percent of the DOC sample had police contact during the first twelve months post-release. Corresponding figures for reappearance in court were 58 percent, 56 percent, and 58 percent for the three samples; and for reinstitutionalization 27 percent, 37 percent, and 25 percent. Regarding the

UDIS police contact data, the authors note that inclusion of boys who went directly from UDIS to DOC increases the 12-month figure from 65 percent to 78 percent. They further note that the 12-month reincarceration rates are based upon less than half the sample and are expected to increase. Extrapolations of the arrest data based upon Beck and Shipley's findings (1987) for young adult offenders suggest a 24-month rearrest rate above 80 percent. These estimates are not directly comparable to the Glen Mills data since they reflect a different jurisdiction and time period. More importantly, the three samples are poorer prospects than Glen Mills students due to their chronic offense histories: on average, subjects in all three samples had been arrested more than ten times prior to the commitment which gained them entry to the study sample. As part of the framework for evaluating Glen Mills' effectiveness the UDIS data are useful in providing an estimate of the effectiveness of juvenile corrections when intervening with the least promising urban delinquents.

A Wisconsin study by Sharon Nachman (1977) focuses upon institutionalized delinquents with relatively favorable prognoses. Her subjects were a random sample (N = 432) which included half of the boys admitted for the first time to Wisconsin juvenile institutions in 1965. Average post-discharge follow-up for subsequent juvenile system involvement was approximately two years. During this period 61 percent were reincarcerated in a juvenile facility. The overall reincarceration rate, including placement in adult facilities, is not reported. In a second study Babst and Hubble (1965) found that of 753 boys first released from Wisconsin institutions during 1964, 43 percent were reincarcerated during the first year. Both studies suggest a 27-month reincarceration rate above 60 percent for students having no prior institutional placements.

As part of an effort to evaluate the impact of New York's juvenile correctional programs, the state legislature conducted an assessment whose findings were published in 1982 (Legislative Commission on Expenditure Review, 1982). The authors note that their attempts to obtain juvenile recidivism data from other states for purposes of comparison to New York yielded usable information from only two states, Florida and California. After the usual cautions regarding the hazards of cross-study comparisons, the report concluded that the reincarceration rate for all three states was "roughly 50 percent." It is not clear what follow-up period was employed or whether these data include all reincarcerations or only those occurring in the juvenile justice system.

Juvenile recidivism in Pennsylvania is the most directly relevant point of comparison for Glen Mills' effectiveness. A recent statewide study (Goodstein and Sontheimer, 1987) examined a sample of 527 juveniles committed to ten public and private correctional institutions (including Glen Mills) during 1983–85. Data sources included probation files, state police records, and a data base maintained by the Pennsylvania Juvenile Court Judges Commission. For the sample as a whole, 47.7 percent were arrested within 12 months of release, including 51.8 percent of the Glen Mills subsample. Twelve-month incarceration rates were not reported, but during the follow-up period (median follow-up interval was approximately 20 months) 16.7 percent of the Glen Mills sample was reincarcerated, versus 24.1 percent of the subjects from the other nine institutions. The authors conducted an analysis of covariance to control for five factors relating to recidivism (prior arrest rate, prior placements, time at risk, institutional adjustment, age at release). Glen Mills' adjusted reincarceration rate (.31 versus .37 for the entire sample) which was adversely affected by the use of "institutional adjustment" as a covariate, was nonetheless the second lowest among the ten institutions. The authors note that interprogram differences were not statistically significant, owing to the small sample size and high intraprogram variation on the recidivism measures.

Comparisons to other jurisdictions would be invalid if Glen Mills students had an unusually favorable prognosis for recidivism. Recidivism rates have been found to vary by race, age at first offense, prior arrest history, and type of offense. The likelihood of recidivism is greatest for blacks (Ohlin et al., 1977; Beck and Shipley, 1987; Hamparian et al., 1985); property offenders (Beck and Shipley, 1987); those with extensive prior arrest histories (Goodstein and Sontheimer, 1987; Tracy et al., 1985); and those whose delinquent careers began at an early age (Goodstein and Sontheimer, 1987). Students admitted to Glen Mills do not have particularly favorable prognoses. Comparison with Goodstein and Sontheimer's sample of ten Pennsylvania institutions indicates that Glen Mills' students began their delinquent careers at about the same age as other Pennsylvania delinquents. Twenty-one percent of the Glen Mills sample (See Exhibit 4.2) were less than 13 years old when they first appeared in court; 26 percent of the Goodstein sample were less than 13 when first arrested. Since some proportion of the latter group would not appear in court until their teen years, these figures are comparable. Glen Mills' students had fewer prior arrests, but the difference is not great: based upon Goodstein's data, 33.3 percent had less than three prior arrests, versus 29.4 percent for the sample as a whole. Glen Mills admits more black students (66.0 percent versus 60.2 percent for the ten institutions combined) and far more property offenders (57.4 percent versus 34.5 percent). On balance, characteristics of its student population provide little reason to expect that Glen Mills' success rate would significantly exceed that of the system average.

Comparison with national data (Bureau of Justice Statistics, 1986) suggests that Glen Mills' residents may be poorer prospects for recidivism than the typical institutionalized delinquent. Of all delinquents held in correctional facilities in 1983, 32 percent were black and 49.4 percent were property offenders. Thus two groups for whom recidivism rates are highest were overrepresented in Glen Mills' population. Furthermore, Glen Mills' population is all male whereas several of the studies described above included females, who tend to have lower recidivism (Ohlin et al., 1977; Beck and Shipley, 1987).

It remains possible that Florida, Illinois, Wisconsin, New York, and Massachusetts delinquents are atypical in having unusually high probability of recidivism. If so, use of data from those states for purposes of comparison to Glen

Mills would bias findings in favor of the Schools. However, nationwide studies of adult recidivism show only very little regional variation (Beck and Shipley, 1987). The available evidence suggests that a regional effect, if it exists, is slight.

Prior research supports the general conclusion that Glen Mills' recidivism rate for rearrest is typical while the Schools' rate for reincarceration is low in relation to national norms for institutionalized delinquents. With regard to rearrest, the Philadelphia birth cohort studies (Tracy et al., 1985) are particularly relevant in that well over one-third of Glen Mills students come from Philadelphia. Data from the 1958 birth cohort, when analyzed in relation to the delinquency histories of students entering Glen Mills, suggest an expected rearrest rate of 70 to 85 percent. The (adjusted) Glen Mills data shown in Exhibit 4.19 are generally in that range.

Based upon the research reported above, it seems likely that, for delinquents similar to Glen Mills' students, the true national rate of reincarceration for a new offense within 27 months of release is at least 50 percent. In comparison, the reincarceration rate experienced by Glen Mills students in nine admissions cohorts has remained generally in the 40 to 50 percent range (37 to 44 percent for program completers) since the establishment of the Schools' normative culture. As discussed earlier, Glen Mills' students do not arrive with a particularly favorable prognosis, and the Schools' recidivism estimates are conservative in that they include a substantial adjustment compensating for an observed bias in estimates based solely on self-report.

These findings indicate that the Schools are effective in reducing reincarceration rates. Glen Mills' reincarceration rate is at least 10 percent (and possibly as much as 35 percent) lower than would be expected on the basis of national averages. This degree of improvement in recidivism would be expected to yield a large reduction in the number of crimes committed by Glen Mills' students (Blumstein and Larson, 1969) and the costs of subsequent justice system processing.

Since 1980, when the normative culture was firmly established, each annual admissions cohort has fared better than its predecessor with regard to recidivism. That this improvement has coincided with a continuous strengthening of the School's culture and programs suggests the possibility that the improvement in recidivism is due to the strengthened program. This cannot be claimed with certainty. But it is possible to rule out three competing interpretations of the data.

First, the improvement is not due to changes in admissions policy. If the Schools began accepting "easier" cases (i.e., students having more favorable prognoses vis-à-vis recidivism) this might account for the improved recidivism. However, there was no change in Glen Mills' admissions policy, and the characteristics of new students were quite stable after 1980 (See Exhibits 4.4–4.7).

Second, the improvement was not due to any lessening of the Schools' commitment to salvaging difficult students. When institutions transfer out their problem cases, they improve the recidivism rate for those who complete the program. As indicated in Exhibit 4.9, the Schools transferred out only a very small proportion of its students during 1980–84; the percentage of new admissions who completed the program rose.

Most significantly, the improvement in recidivism does not reflect a trend toward more lenient treatment of offenders by the courts. Reduction in Glen Mills' recidivism has been achieved during a period when many of the jurisdictions served by the Schools adopted a "get tough" posture toward juvenile crime. Exhibit 4.22 shows the volume of cases and institutionalizations annually during 1976–84 in Philadelphia, by far Glen Mills' largest "client." During this period the number of delinquents institutionalized by Philadelphia's Family Court judges increased by 140 percent while the number of cases heard *declined* by 17 percent. In 1977, 4.8 percent of all cases resulted in institutionalization; by 1984 the figure had climbed to 13.9 percent, an increase of 190 percent in the rate of institutionalization.

Glen Mills achievement of a relatively low reincarceration rate assumes a new significance against the backdrop of so dramatic a change in incarceration policies. A Philadelphia juvenile brought to court in 1984 was nearly three times as likely to be incarcerated as his counterpart in 1977.

The likelihood of incarceration for offenders charged in the adult system also increased dramatically. During the period 1977 to 1984, while the total of arrests in Philadelphia *declined* by 22.5 percent from 129,235 to 100,108, the number of inmates in Philadelphia's prisons *increased* by 79.3 percent, from 1,950 to 3,496 (Citizens Crime Commission, 1985).

In conclusion, the recidivism trends shown in Exhibits 4.19 and 4.20, achieved in the face of a major crackdown on Philadelphia juvenile and adult offenders, do not fully reflect the magnitude of improvement in Glen Mills' programs. Even the increase in Glen Mills' recidivism during the transitional 1976–80 period was less than might have been expected, given the context of the sharply more punitive posture of the courts.

In summary, evaluation of Glen Mills' effectiveness has not been unidimensional, but has analyzed patterns of outcome data from a wide range of sources. Interviews with current and former students, on-site observation, standardized test scores, staff interviews, and official records of recidivism consistently indicate that Glen Mills' is a strong implementation of a cost-effective program model which has achieved remarkably positive short and long term results.

Glen Mills has established a humane environment where students achieve academic, personal, and vocational growth in an atmosphere of respect. The normative culture model has enabled the Schools' administration to achieve these results at remarkably low cost. Glen Mills' per diem rate is among the lowest in the state for programs of similar scope. Finally, former students are unusually successful in avoiding future serious justice system involvement.

It is often the case that extraordinary programs are built upon the vision, commitment, energy, and charisma of a single leader. Glen Mills is a case in

Exhibit 4.22
Philadelphia Juvenile Court Cases and Institutionalizations, 1977–1984

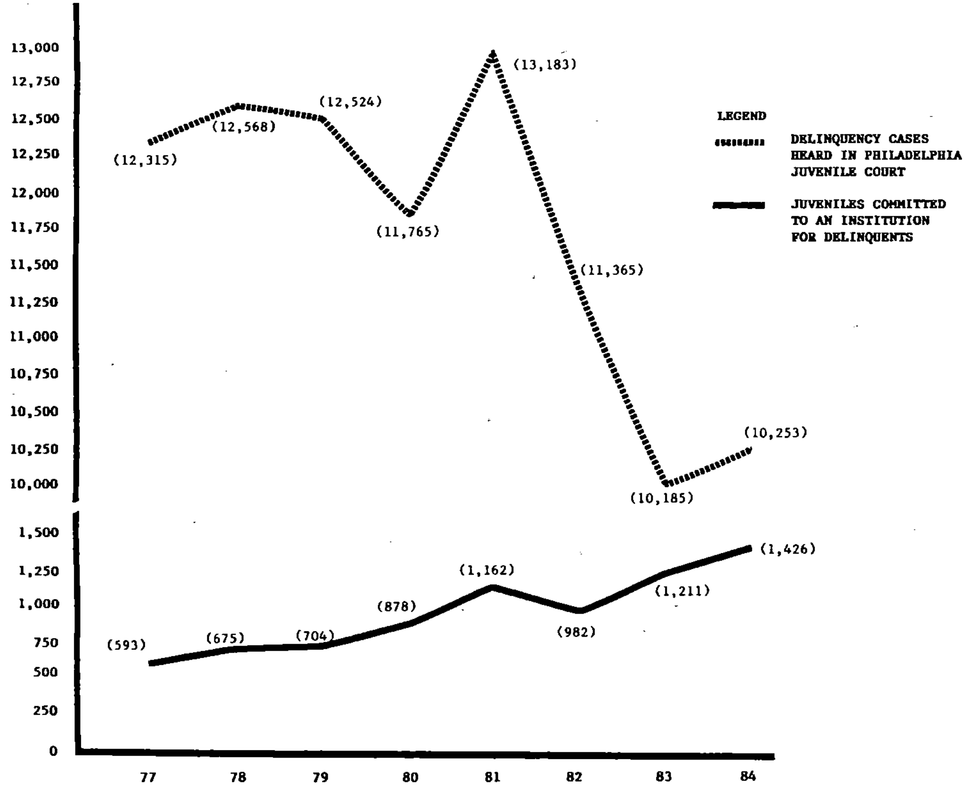

LEGEND

░░░░░░░ DELINQUENCY CASES
HEARD IN PHILADELPHIA
JUVENILE COURT

■■■■■ JUVENILES COMMITTED
TO AN INSTITUTION
FOR DELINQUENTS

(12,315)
(12,568)
(12,524)
(11,765)
(13,183)
(11,365)
(10,185)
(10,253)

(593)
(675)
(704)
(878)
(1,162)
(982)
(1,211)
(1,426)

13,000
12,750
12,500
12,250
12,000
11,750
11,500
11,250
11,000
10,750
10,500
10,250
10,000
1,500
1,250
1,000
750
500
250
0

77   78   79   80   81   82   83   84

point. There are many who believe that, if Sam Ferrainola did not exist, the Schools would not have survived 1976. But for all the director's skills, success required more: the history of juvenile corrections does not lack for programs which have failed despite the best efforts of talented and dedicated leaders and staff.

Success requires *both* a sound program model and strong implementation. The genius of Sam Ferrainola lies in his designing and implementing an effective model. In its basic values, philosophy, and norms Glen Mills culture is without precedent in the field of corrections. Itself the Schools' major therapeutic element, the culture also provides the context within which formal academic, vocational and athletic programs can be effective.

The model is replicable. The lessons Glen Mills offers about this and other issues of importance to the field form the subject matter of the final chapter.

5

Lessons from Glen Mills: New Possibilities for Juvenile Corrections

Many juvenile correctional facilities have ceased making serious attempts to improve the effectiveness of their programs or to measure their results.

Greenwood and Zimring, 1985: v

When a juvenile is adjudicated delinquent and the court assumes its role *in loco parentis*, it accepts the responsibility to provide the care the child requires. At the minimum, this includes a clean and safe living environment, educational opportunities appropriate to the child's academic level, nutritious food, good medical and dental care, organized recreational activities, and a social climate that encourages responsible behavior.

In considering the available options, an appropriate standard might be: If my child were adjudicated delinquent, is this an option I would want for him or her? Is this a placement which would help *my* child to straighten out his or her life? Of the thousands of juveniles committed annually to correctional institutions, very few are placed in settings which the professionals in the field would welcome for their own children. Too often the state acts like an irresponsible parent, placing its charges in settings that provide few of the requisites for growth and then failing to monitor program results or to hold caregivers accountable for achieving reasonable levels of success. Juvenile courts have abdicated their responsibility to the extent that few even monitor recidivism, and therefore have no basis for deciding what a "reasonable level of success" might be.

The state has a clear obligation and self-interest in supporting the development of effective programs. Every effort must be made to learn as much as possible from existing programs so that ineffective approaches can be discarded and those which hold promise further developed.

Progress toward effective corrections is possible through the careful documentation of programs that achieve notable success. Particular attention is due to those which break new ground. Glen Mills' model is divergent from standard correctional practice in virtually every important dimension: its view of delinquents; performance monitoring and accountability for staff and students; organizational structure; emphasis upon continued improvement; staff selection process; combined emphasis upon high quality facilities along with careful cost control; encouragement of staff initiative and innovation; and of course the constant attention to staff and student norms. The remainder of this chapter discusses the meaning of Glen Mills' experiment for the field of juvenile corrections.

One caveat applies to everything that follows: the lessons of Glen Mills may not apply to programs serving different types of offender populations. In particular, delinquents who evidence significant emotional disturbance have very different treatment needs than Glen Mills' students. However, the Schools' admissions criteria probably exclude less than 10 percent of all adjudicated delinquents—Glen Mills experience is broadly relevant.

Glen Mills' experience suggests four major conclusions of importance to the field. First, it contributes to a mounting body of evidence that the factors associated with program effectiveness have not been measured or even identified in most evaluation research. The widely held belief that evaluation research demonstrates that "nothing works" is, therefore, inaccurate. Second, contrary to the prevailing assumptions of recent decades, large institutions need not be inhumane "schools of crime" where juveniles become confirmed in an antisocial life-style. When properly administered, such institutions can play a positive role as a correctional option and are the placement of choice for many delinquents. Third: locks, bars, and other physical restraints are unnecessary to the achievement of security objectives in private correctional facilities for male delinquents. Finally, Glen Mills has demonstrated that delinquents have enormous potential for growth which can be realized in an appropriate environment.

The next four sections discuss these conclusions, followed by a potpourri of reflections based upon more than a decade of discussions with justice system officials who have come to the Schools to observe its program firsthand. The chapter closes with some speculations regarding replication of the Glen Mills model and the importance of learning history's lessons.

EVALUATING THE EVALUATION LITERATURE: WHAT MAKES A PROGRAM EFFECTIVE?

The successes achieved at Glen Mills assume special significance against the backdrop of other justice system developments prior to and contemporaneous with the Schools' renaissance. During the 1950s and 1960s there had been a continual, profound shift away from rehabilitative ideology (Bayer, 1981). Evaluations of correctional programs were consistently discouraging. As Mr. Ferrainola took the reins at Glen Mills, publication of the review by Lipton, Martinson, and Wilks (1975) of hundreds of evaluations of correctional programs seemed to confirm what many had suspected: nothing works. An earlier review by Bailey (1966) had reached essentially the same conclusion, though being less comprehensive in scope it had attracted less attention.

The paper by Lipton et al., sparked one of the most furious debates in the history of penology. The issue was considered of such overriding importance that the National Academy of Sciences established a Panel on Research on Rehabilitative Techniques to examine the troubling finding that rehabilitative efforts have no appreciable effect on recidivism. The conclusion of this blue-ribbon Panel was that " . . . Martinson and his associates were essentially correct. There is no body of evidence for any treatment or intervention with criminal offenders that can be relied upon to produce a decrease in recidivism" (Panel, 1979: 31).

Criticism for the failure of rehabilitation had been leveled at large institutions since the 1960s. They were regarded as inherently dehumanizing facilities where minor delinquents became hardened and hardened delinquents irredeemable; schools for crime where young people became socialized into adult criminal careers and stigmatized to a degree that made recidivism all but inevitable.

Massachusetts stunned the nation when it closed its institutions in 1972. And while other jurisdictions' reactions were less draconian than Massachusetts's, many turned to small community-based programs as an alternative for youths who in previous years would have been sent to institutions.

There was common sense justification for such a policy. Community programs would afford greater opportunities for individual attention. By providing treatment within the community, linkages crucial to post-release adjustment could be maintained. The entire correctional enterprise would be more normalized, and offenders would not be forced into the delinquent subcultures that dominated the large institutions and confirmed their identity as outcasts. At a minimum, the community programs would be more humane and less expensive. There seemed reason to hope that they would also be more effective in helping juveniles to turn away from criminal involvement.

On the whole, evaluations of community-based programs were discouraging regarding the hoped for impact upon recidivism. One evaluation of the initiative to deinstitutionalize status offenders showed that these efforts had produced a small but statistically significant *increase* in recidivism (Kobrin and Klein, 1982). The National Center for the Assessment of the Juvenile Justice System, following review of more than 70 empirical studies of deinstitutionalization, concluded that it had generally had no effect upon recidivism (Schneider, 1985). Lerman's (1975) analysis of data from the California Youth Authority's Community Treatment Project led him to conclude that the project had not achieved a significant improvement in recidivism. Rigorous evaluation of deinstitutionalization in Massachusetts (Coates et al., 1978) confirmed that the reforms yielded no reduction in recidivism. A "matched samples" study of 64 institutionalized juveniles and 63 community placements in Georgia found better short-term educational adjustment among the institutionalized group, but no significant differences in subsequent recidivism (Webb and Scanlon, 1981). Finally, evaluations of the UDIS program in Illinois found a lower recidivism rate for those who were removed from the community. Though aspects of this result have been challenged (McCleary et al., 1978), the UDIS evaluation represents yet one more failure to demonstrate a favorable impact of community corrections upon recidivism.

The findings were not necessarily discouraging to supporters of the deinstitutionalization movement. Indeed, the point is often made that, since the move toward community-based programs has not generally led to an *increase* in recidivism, the policy can be pronounced sound on the basis of humanitarian and cost-effectiveness considerations. Others interpret the findings as evidence that the trend toward community corrections is misguided. There is reason to question whether community-based programs are the least harmful alternatives for many delinquents (Murray and Cox, 1979).

The technicians have presented their findings; it is up to the politicians to decide whether the community corrections glass is half full or half empty. But with regard to the development of more effective correctional programs, the stark conclusion is that evaluations of community corrections appear to suggest yet again that "nothing works" to reduce recidivism.

Numerous commentators have pointed out that surrender to despair is premature, that "the evidence is nowhere near compelling enough to warrant scuttling the entire (rehabilitation) concept" (Greenwood and Zimring, 1985: 32). First, it may be that evaluators have been focusing upon the wrong variables in their studies of correctional programs. Most assume that treatment method is the primary determinant of outcomes. This assumption is dubious at best, a point made most strongly by Greenwood and Zimring (1985). Evaluation results to date do not indicate that rehabilitation does not work, but rather that treatment method is not a dominant variable: "the 'nothing works' conclusion is based upon an inappropriate interpretation of data. . . . Because some individual experimental programs have resulted in lower recidivism rates, even though most of the other programs in the treatment category to which they were assigned do not, other variables than those now used may be important determinants (of program effectiveness)" (p. ix). A similar point was made in an earlier Rand study (Mann, 1976) which noted that significant differences between program models should not be expected, since the variations among programs implementing the same model are often as great as the differences between programs using distinct models.

A second criticism of the evaluation literature is that studies routinely fail to consider the strength of program implementation, or even whether program specification and implementation correspond with one another (Rezmovic,

1979). Careful attention to the strength of implementation may reveal poorly designed activities conducted by staff who are untrained, unmotivated, and unpersuaded regarding the efficacy of their work (Quay, 1977). This was a prime concern of the Panel on Research on Rehabilitative Techniques (1979) which noted that "many of the interventions tested seem to have been so weak in proportion to the problem involved that it would scarcely have been credible had any effect been found" (p. 32). It may be that what is lacking is not effective program models but effective implementation of existing approaches.

A third criticism of the evaluation literature is that it provides little basis for deciding whether a program is effective or not, and too little guidance as to what levels of performance should realistically be expected. Imagine an administrator who has taken the trouble to collect some very basic information about his program. Armed with a description of the juveniles served and their post-release experience with respect to arrest, conviction, and reincarceration within two years after discharge, the administrator approaches the evaluation literature to find out how effective his program is relative to others serving the same types of students. When next seen, his eyes will be glazed and his countenance depressed. He will have found articles on arcane methodological issues, treatises extolling the virtues of experimental designs, comparisons of incompletely specified program models, and shelves full of the inevitable swordplay among methodologists critiquing each other's interpretations of research data. But he will have found precious little that is relevant to the most basic question of all: How well is my program performing? It is as though sports fans, in their endless squabbling over which team is the greatest and what the decision criteria should be, neglected to keep score when the games were played.

The conclusion of the evaluators that "nothing works" is not a cause for despair, because the evaluations are seriously flawed. "Nothing works" is as valid an assessment of the evaluations as of the programs which were their focus.

Leaving aside the inadequacies for the evaluation literature, it remains true that many programs are ineffective or worse. However, the landscape is not uniformly bleak. While no treatment models have been consistently found effective, various individual programs *do* achieve unusually positive results. Lipton et al., (1975) cited studies of an Outward Bound School, a program of individual psychotherapy within the Boy's Industrial School in Ohio, a program providing sociopsychologically oriented counseling, and vocationally oriented training among apparent exceptions to their "nothing works" conclusion.

Martinson's original article attracted wide attention. Subsequent studies, which reach quite different conclusions, have had less impact. Most recently, an extensive literature review focusing upon the period 1981–87 found strong evidence for the effectiveness of some programs. The authors (Gendreau and Ross, 1987) pronounced the "nothing works" conclusion "ridiculous." They point out that Martinson himself took a giant step back, recanting that dismal conclusion in a later article (Martinson, 1979), which Gendreau and Ross characterize as "probably the most infrequently read article in the criminal justice debate on rehabilitation" (p. 350).

Some programs *are* more effective than others. What makes the difference? Evaluations have demonstrated convincingly that "treatment method" is not the answer; except possibly as one factor interacting with others. Perhaps other factors could be identified through the study of programs which seem effective. This was the approach taken in two Rand studies (Mann, 1976; Greenwood and Zimring, 1985) which made major strides toward identifying program variables related to effectiveness. The Rand research provides a foundation and direction that holds promise of genuine improvement in correctional programs.

Dale Mann (1976) directed a study of four treatment interventions with serious juvenile offenders based on clinical psychology/psychiatry, sociology/social work, schooling, and career education. Study teams reviewed the research and practice literature for each type of intervention, and prepared case studies of treatment sites. Though no intervention stood out as clearly more effective than the others, each model achieved at least limited success with some juveniles. The striking and unexpected finding was that the characteristics of effective programs were quite consistent across treatment models. Successful programs:

1. Maximized client choice, including in some cases discretion about which program to enter and how long to stay.
2. Maximized involvement and ownership of clients in the program.
3. Incorporated elements of learning theory, including:
   a. Clear tasks, where clients have a precise understanding of program requirements.
   b. Positive behavior models: "Programs that sought to instill responsible, fair, consistent, and thoughtful behavior in juveniles often succeeded by having a staff that acted in this way, with which the juveniles could identify."
   c. Opportunities for early and frequent successes, to help clients build confidence in themselves and their own efficacy.
   d. Significant rewards contingent on relevant tasks and realistic levels of achievement.
   e. Training conducted in situations as similar as possible to the real-world.
4. Availability of many different forms of treatment, reflecting the diversity of students' needs.
5. Performance consciousness coupled with an eclectic, problem-solving, trial-and-error attitude toward program development.
6. Valuing the client: "Vengeance is not compatible with treating youth adjudicated for a serious offense as a valuable person, yet in the absence for the latter attitude, rehabilitation may be impossible."

Mann's work is highly significant in directing attention away from the formal "treatment" approach as the dominant variable in program effectiveness, and in identifying factors for further scrutiny.

The Greenwood and Zimring (1985) study focused upon programs for chronic juvenile offenders. Like Mann, the authors conclude that treatment method is not the primary variable in program effectiveness. The features identified as essential to program effectiveness are quite similar to those suggested by Mann. Effective programs:

1. Provide opportunities to overcome adversity and experience success.
2. Facilitate bonds of affection and respect between students and staff.
3. Promote involvement in conventional family and community activities.
4. Provide frequent, timely, and accurate feedback for both positive and negative behavior.
5. Reduce or eliminate negative role models and peer support for negative attitudes or behavior.
6. Require students to recognize thought processes that rationalize negative behavior.
7. Create opportunities for students to discuss family matters and early experiences in a nonjudgmental atmosphere (N.B. This is not an emphasis of Glen Mills' program).
8. Adapt program components to the needs and capabilities of participating students.
9. Emphasize management style and attitudes. Key features are leadership and support by top administrators; high expectations for student performance; schoolwide recognitions of success; frequent monitoring of student progress, maintenance of an orderly and quiet but not oppressive learning environment; collaborative planning and collegial relationships among staff; and minimized turnover among the most competent staff.

In examining two exemplary programs, the authors note that each was founded by "dynamic individuals who were discontented with the programs offered by public agencies. The programs aim at changing behavior, not simply at custody or academic and vocational training. Line level staff and middle management are held closely accountable for their actions and results. None of these programs will tolerate incompetent or inattentive staff. The morale of the staff appears to be quite high and there is a shared sense of purpose, allegiance to the program, and belief that they are having an effect. Program components are in a constant state of evolution in the search for more effective or efficient approaches" (p. xi).

Apart from the exception noted above, all of the elements identified by Rand as characteristic of effective programs (or, more accurately, "promising" programs: the authors stress the usual lament regarding inadequate evaluation data) are integral to Glen Mills' model. The Schools' experience suggests that other features may be important as well:

- Valuing of the student. Glen Mills' attitude toward its students goes beyond Mann's statement and is quite explicit: students are not "bad." They are neither less deserving of respect nor more deserving of punishment than any other member of the Glen Mills community. This attitude is an essential element of the normative culture.
- Student responsibility to the community. Students learn that their appearance and

behavior reflects upon their upon their unit and the Schools; they are expected to dress and act appropriately. Students support their peers' accomplishments and confront any negative behavior.

- Emphasis upon current and future behavior. Glen Mills regards an emphasis upon early childhood experience as neither necessary nor helpful. In most cases the potential benefits are more than outweighed by the risk that students will regard themselves as handicapped, use past deprivations to justify irresponsible behavior, or seek to gain approval through "insight" in lieu of behavioral change.
- Low staff to student ratio. The staffing for each cottage of 50 boys includes a team leader, two senior counselors, and eight or nine counselors—less than one staff member for each four students. The ratio of all staff (including support staff and part-timers) to students is slightly more than 6 to 10. A larger staff complement is undesirable. A ratio above .7 is regarded as detrimental to program objectives in that it reduces the money available for equipment and other resources without yielding any commensurate benefit to students, and works against high levels of staff involvement, initiative, and responsibility.
- Respect. All members of the Glen Mills community are expected to treat one another and visitors with respect at all times. Like "valuing," respect is an essential element of the culture.
- Strong emphasis upon teamwork and mutual support among all staff. Undercutting or back-stabbing are absolute taboos.
- Fiscal consciousness. Staff are kept aware of the Schools' financial circumstances and priorities. Cost-effective operations are regarded as a shared responsibility benefitting the entire community.
- Quality environment. Food, clothing, equipment, furniture, landscaping, etc., are all of top quality. This policy plays an important part in building pride and self-esteem among both students and staff.

Sustained improvement in correctional practice is unlikely to occur until a great deal more effort is devoted to systematic analysis of factors associated with effectiveness. Research to date suggests that organizational factors such as core values, positive staff norms, and performance monitoring systems are of primary importance. It is likely that program effectiveness is determined more by factors such as staff pride, teamwork, respect, and initiative than by professional degrees and treatment approach.

The field has much to learn from programs which have succeeded in establishing organizational climates conducive to success. It has been recognized for some time that an institution's formal organization and programs affect the nature of the inmate subculture in correctional institutions (McEwen, 1978; Feld, 1977). Glen Mills' contribution has been to demonstrate the importance of the informal organization, to show how organizational, programmatic, and cultural factors can be engineered to create an organization where the informal staff culture supports institutional goals, and the "inmate subculture" is manipulated to serve institutional purposes. The end result is a unified normative culture conducive to habilitation and very powerful in its effects.

Each year thousands of new staff begin work in juvenile correctional programs. Many of them are dedicated, sincere, and caring people who want to do a good job. Too often they fall victim to the cynicism of negative institutional cultures which stifle innovation, tolerate conflicts among staff, and accept failure as the norm. Even the most promising employees are no match for such a work climate. At best, they become disillusioned and burn out. At worst, they find themselves transformed into brutal caricatures of their former selves (Haney, Banks, and Zimbardo, 1973).

The lesson of Glen Mills is that positive institutional cultures are equally powerful in their effects. Few staff come to the Schools with experience in the human services; virtually none have worked with delinquents. But the pride, enthusiasm, and dedication of Glen Mills' staff prove infectious. Within weeks those who are unsuited to Glen Mills' program are weeded out. The others find themselves an integral part of a proud team, developing skills heretofore unrecognized. Staff, like students, bring enormous undeveloped potential; the Schools' culture is designed to nurture it.

Glen Mills has demonstrated that organizational cultures are not immutable. Norms must not be left to evolve by chance, but must be shaped to insure that organizational objectives are served. In illustrating how this can be achieved, the Schools have made a vital contribution to the understanding of institutional effectiveness.

THE ROLE OF THE LARGE RESIDENTIAL INSTITUTION

During the past quarter century large juvenile correctional institutions have come under heavy criticism, most of it well deserved. Informal but powerful staff and student subcultures in such facilities seemed to represent insurmountable obstacles to humane and effective treatment. Many large institutions were little more than expensive facilities for the warehousing, and sometimes brutalization, of juveniles. Society's return on investment came in the form of astronomical recidivism and ruined lives.

Frustration finally breeded strong action in 1972. After failing in his efforts to establish therapeutic communities within Massachusetts's institutions, Jerome Miller ordered them closed (Ohlin et al., 1977).

Various professional groups soon weighed in with their own condemnations of large institutions, as summarized in a 1979 publication by the Office of Juvenile Justice and Delinquency Prevention:

National legislation and authoritative bodies in the field of juvenile justice . . . designate a level of 20 residents or less as optimal in terms of cost efficiency and program effectiveness for several reasons: First, . . . the National Council on Crime and Delinquency states that a capacity of from 15 to 20 boys and girls is the smallest unit practicable for satisfactory staff and program. Second, the 1974 Juvenile Justice and Delinquency Act is clear in its intent to limit new construction and renovation to community-based facilities for under 20 persons . . . underscoring congressional intent to discourage the development of larger juvenile residential facilities. A third major factor is the overwhelming support for small facilities by authoritative bodies in the area of juvenile justice and delinquency prevention. (Brown and McMillen, 1979: 48)

The authors go on to cite the National Council on Crime and Delinquency, the National Advisory Commission on Juvenile Justice Standards and Goals, and the American Bar Association's Juvenile Justice Standards Project as groups who have cautioned against institutions housing more than 20 residents.

Pessimism regarding large institutions is fed by high reported levels of recidivism and incidents of suicide, degradation, and abuse. Specific criticisms are summarized by Brown and McMillen (1979). Drawing upon work by Sarri (1974), Reuterman et al. (1971), the National Advisory Committee on Criminal Justice Standards and Goals (1976), and others, the authors claim that increased facility size is associated with:

- bureaucratization
- reduced service delivery
- reduced supervision and individualized attention
- a decline in the ratio of professional staff to youth
- increased operating costs
- socially and emotionally destructive subcultures
- emphasis upon control rather than program services
- dehumanization
- lack of safety, normalcy and fairness

The authors' appeal for the restriction of facility size to 20 or less includes the following composite of text from the U.S. Department of Justice (1972) and various individual authors:

Larger facilities require regimentation and routinization for staff to maintain control, conflicting with the goal of individualization. Smaller groups reduce custody problems. . . . Larger facilities convey an atmosphere of anonymity to the resident and tend to engulf him in feelings of powerlessness, meaninglessness, isolation and self-estrangement . . . [they] reinforce the image of rejection of the individual by society, . . . [and] develop their own in-house programs rather than utilizing available community resources, thus reducing the potential for reintegration into the community. . . . Larger facilities reduce communication between staff and residents as well as between staff members themselves. . . . [They] exhibit an increased reliance upon "hardware" for security . . . rather than program and staffing. (Brown and McMillen, 1979: 49–50)

They conclude that "It is clear, then, that large residential facilities are detrimental to effective program operation."

Bertrand Russell once commented upon the carefully reasoned argument advanced by a colleague that everything in it was excellent except for the con-clusion. The same might be said of Brown and McMillen's work. Having documented the range of indictments that have deservedly been leveled against large institutions, they reach a conclusion which implies that these problems are inescapable, that large institutions are inherently ineffective. It is a view shared by many in the field.

Glen Mills has demonstrated that it is wrong.

Brown and McMillen's list of particulars is nearly 100 percent inaccurate with respect to Glen Mills. Bureaucracy, for example, is nearly nonexistent. There is an absolute minimum of administrative staff: the Group Living Department, with more than 100 staff, is run by a director with one administrative assistant. There are no memoranda except for an occasional announcement posted on a bulletin board, less than a dozen per year. Every issue of significance is discussed face-to-face by the parties involved, and the Schools' system of meetings insures that information is rapidly and accurately disseminated. Authority and respon-sibility are clearly defined, never diffused. No one—staff or student—is ever "treated like a number."

During more than a decade of interviewing Glen Mills' students, staff, visitors, and even critics, the authors have never heard anyone describe the Schools as "dehumanizing" or in terms even remotely carrying that connotation. To the contrary, those who observe the program without understanding the normative culture model sometimes mistakenly believe that the positive psychological and physical environment amounts to coddling. Terms like "hell hole," applied to some institutions, have not been used in connection with Glen Mills since at least 1976, though "country club" is not unknown.

Probably the most serious charge against large institutions is their tendency to nurture delinquent subcultures, sustaining antisocial peer pressures which undercut the best rehabilitative efforts of professional staff. Ohlin (1958) has described how cottage staff in many institutions unwittingly strengthen the delinquent subculture within their units:

Faced with the necessity of maintaining order and discipline within the cottage without anyone outside knowing of trouble, many houseparents resolve the dilemma by forming friendships with the natural leaders among their charges. Through conferring special privileges and rewards on these persons the houseparent secures their help in controlling the activities of his other charges. . . . Thus the most rebellious and hostile young persons become dominant and exact conformity from their more tractable peers. (Ohlin, 1958: 66)

Where power is wielded by the most aggressive and manipulative students, the delinquent behavior of the strong is reinforced and the victimization of weaker students assured.

Glen Mills' most significant achievement is the eradication of delinquent subcultures. Once established, the positive normative culture is as formidable a force as its delinquent counterpart. However, each new admission brings with him the potential for reintroduction of "street" norms. The battle against the delinquent subculture is continual or it is lost.

"Control" is not a concern at Glen Mills. The focus is upon behavioral change. In order to gain the acceptance of his peers and staff a Glen Mills student must behave like a gentleman and show respect to others. The Schools' results demonstrate the power of acceptance and status as incentives to regulate this behavior.

Positive techniques of behavioral change are central to the model, but they are not accompanied by coercive forms of behavioral control—locks, fences, sedative drugs, physical restraints, security guards, isolation units, etc.

The Schools carefully assess each student's level of academic, vocational, and social functioning. Individualized goals are set. Progress toward those goals is recognized and rewarded at every level of ability. At Glen Mills it is the willingness to try, the commitment to improvement (however gradual) that is rewarded, not merely major achievements. The effect is to involve and empower. Helplessness and depression are alien to Glen Mills. Suicide, the most terrible consequence of powerlessness and isolation, is unknown.

It is difficult to specify optimal levels of staff/student ratios. The topic is usually addressed in general terms—the underlying assumption that a ratio which is too low is a very bad thing. True, but a ratio which is too high carries its own dangers—diffusion of responsibility, stifling of staff involvement and initiative, low productivity, and a waste of financial resources which might be better utilized for equipment and facilities. Glen Mills' ratio, which fluctuates in the range from .6 to .7, is low compared to most programs. There is no reason to believe that it is "too" low. Contrary to the nearly universal assumption that, cost aside, it is scarcely possible to have too many staff, Glen Mills suggests the intriguing possibility that utilization of staff and the staff normative culture are more critical factors than absolute numbers. Overstaffing may be as detrimental to sound program operations as understaffing.

These examples indicate that Glen Mills does not suffer from the weaknesses common to large institutions. But the Schools' history suggests far more. First, growth in program size does not necessarily result in reduced effectiveness: bigger can be better. Second, the trend away from large residential facilities is misguided. Properly administered, large institutions may be the placement of choice for many juveniles.

The increase in Glen Mills' population from 30 to more than 600 was accompanied by a steady increase in program effectiveness. The increase in population brought economies of scale and the higher revenues necessary to support diversification of programs. A student entering Glen Mills in 1988 could be confident that one of the five academic programs would be appropriate to his needs. He could select from among more than a dozen vocational training programs, or try out for one of twenty athletic teams. An institution with 20 students, or even 200 students, could not support nearly so broad a range of quality programs. An effective institution must offer its students the opportunity to experiment by trying their hand at new activities, to develop their skills and interests, to discover and realize their potential. The ability to do so increases directly with enrollment.

An equally important by-product of expansion was the strengthening of the normative culture. The norms of a student body numbering 500 are far less vulnerable to the "street" norms which accompany new admissions than those of a student body numbering 50. When an institution is small, the admission of even one strong negative leader can threaten the culture. If there are too few strong, positive leaders a delinquent subgroup may form around the negative leader; at one point in Glen Mills' history a negative Bulls Club emerged and survived until the expulsion of its leaders. As Glen Mills grew, its culture became even stronger. The incidence of theft, vandalism, assault, and other negative behaviors declined as enrollment increased (see Exhibits 4.13–4.17).

Most importantly, as Glen Mills grew its students suffered none of the depersonalization, regimentation, and bureaucratization predicated by critics. The validation each student experiences in his GGI group and living unit remains the same regardless of the overall institutional enrollment.

Large institutions of Glen Mills' caliber have an important role to play in juvenile corrections. They are clearly not a panacea: the program model is inappropriate for the emotionally disturbed; it is possible (though by no means certain) that juveniles whose families are willing to participate in on-going family therapy may benefit more from community-based placements as might those with strong positive ties (e.g., employment, school, church) to their communities. But for many delinquents an institution such as Glen Mills is the placement of choice.

Advocates of smaller, community-based programs stress the importance of normalization—delinquents who are "sent away" from their families and community become stigmatized, confirmed in a delinquent identity, cut off from familiar sources of support, rejected by the very community where they will one day be expected to function as a law-abiding citizen and sent to an environment so dissimilar that the prospects for successful reintegration are reduced. This argument is valid in many cases and especially appealing when considered in the context of the dismal performance of many large institutions. But it is far less compelling when the institutional options include a facility where enrollment is experienced as a privilege rather than a punishment; an institutional environment where delinquent pressures and threats to self-esteem have been systematically extinguished; where there are an array of academic, vocational, and athletic opportunities appropriate to every level of functioning; where positive effort is encouraged rather than ridiculed by peers; where a new student finds himself in the company of hundreds of former delinquents acting like gentlemen, with pride.

The ability to control the student's total living environment is a critical factor which works to the advantage of large institutions. A new student experiences a far more genuine welcome at Glen Mills than he will receive in most communities; the latter usually have decidedly mixed feelings about accepting a house full of delinquents as neighbors. Most community folk suspect that delinquents are a bit "off" psychologically, and certainly not up to snuff morally. The local school system and teachers rarely seek out delinquents, either. Local service providers, employers, teachers, etc., will all relate to the student on the basis of their own views regarding delinquency: some will feel he should be treated just like everyone else, some that he requires a stern, no-nonsense task master, some that special allowances must be made for him in view of his victimization by parents/racism/poverty/"the system"/etc. When frustration sets in—community schools, vocational training, etc., are, of course, designed for "normal" kids, not delinquents—the student can always count upon delinquent peers for acceptance. They will take him just as he is. In fact, they will insist he stay just as he is.

Advocates of community programs may feel that this picture is overdrawn—it is possible to work in partnership with the community, local schools, etc., to help them avoid the type of handling most detrimental to delinquents. In general, though, part of the rationale for community-based programs is that delinquents are best served when they are subject to all the normal problems and pressures of community living, and provided with professional assistance in learning to cope with them so that they will be better able to do so post-discharge. But most will never succeed unless they construct a new self-concept, a sense of their own potential, a realization that the future can be very different than they had supposed.

In a study of self-concept Markus and Oyserman (1987) found striking differences between delinquents and nondelinquents. The authors studied individuals' fears of who they might become if their life course goes badly ("feared possible selves"—e.g., a destitute skid-row wino) and their hopes for the future ("hoped-for possible selves"—e.g., a financially secure, respected professional). The delinquents had much more intensely negative "feared possible selves," which were not balanced by positive, "hoped-for possible selves." The authors note that a successful transition to adulthood requires the construction of a compelling set of positive possible selves that can serve as a guide; that when these are unavailable the "feared selves" dominate the self-concept and control decisions and behavior in ways that tend to bring about the feared possible self.

The construction of a set of positive "possible selves" may in many cases be best achieved outside the community. Like a medical patient who must spend time in a sterile operating room before he can again function in an environment which is not germ-free, many delinquents are best served by temporary placement in an environment where contaminants such as negative peer pressures and inconsistent adult handling have been removed and the medicines of respect; varied, appropriate programs; and recognition are readily available. Large institutions are best able to provide such environments.

SECURITY WITHOUT LOCKS AND BARS

Security and order are primary concerns in all correctional institutions. Runaways must be prevented. Control must be firmly established so that stronger, more violent residents do not prey upon others. An orderly atmosphere is necessary to the functioning of rehabilitation or training programs. Stress and tensions would overwhelm students and staff alike if there were no way to cope with the potential for violence which is always present in facilities which admit serious violent offenders.

For some institutions security hardware is necessary. But in private facilities serving populations similar to Glen Mills', and for whom expulsion is an available option, physical security is not only unnecessary, but an obstacle to program effectiveness.

Glen Mills has demonstrated that security and order can be achieved without locks, bars, or other physical restraints. Security is provided by the Schools' powerful normative culture with its emphasis upon respect, confrontation, and the maintenance of a high quality living environment.

The normative culture does not seek security by maintaining the upper hand in a sort of institutional arms race, but by removing the root causes of disorder and violence. Violence can be caused by psychopathology, but Glen Mills does not admit students who are emotionally disturbed. Violence can be a reaction to fear, but students rarely experience fear where any attempt at physical or psychological intimidation is effectively confronted by staff and student leaders alike. Violence can be a reaction to demeaning treatment, but the Schools' normative culture holds that there are no circumstances which justify "taking the dignity" of another person. Violence, in delinquent subcultures, can be a tool used to achieve peer group status, but at Glen Mills there is no surer route to diminished status. Violence can be a response to the frustrations of daily living, but frustrations rarely build when physical living conditions are excellent, performance objectives (e.g., academic, vocational) are appropriate, and genuine effort is recognized and rewarded.

Most large institutions rely upon walls, fences, and security staff to minimize runaways. In contrast, Glen Mills prevents runaways by offering its students an environment preferable to any of the available alternatives. The crucial difference between the Schools and most other institutions is that *Glen Mills strives to reduce the incentive, not the opportunity to escape.*

As a private institution Glen Mills, unlike some public correctional facilities, is able to expel students. This sanction has seldom been invoked in recent years. Typically 2 to 4 percent of students are returned to court for "failure to adjust" to Glen Mills' program. However, the power to expel is a significant safety valve enabling the Schools to operate without a single "secure" cell.

Ultimately, security at Glen Mills is provided by the staff and students working together to maintain positive norms. Those who benefit the most are the students themselves. Student leaders understand this and make certain that the message gets through to new students. For example, when a student embarrassed his cottage by his behavior at a football game, he received feedback from his unit's Bulls during the evening Townhouse meeting: "This ain't no lock-up. Nobody treats you like an animal here, so if you act like one it's on you. But if you want to stay in this cottage you better learn to act a lot different than you did today." Where high status students deliver such messages, there is no need for security staff.

Glen Mills' administrators believe that physical restraints are not merely unnecessary, but detrimental to security. The director, whose first official act was to order the removal of locks and bars, refused to consider establishing any secure units even when chaos prevailed during the early years of his adminis-tration. He felt that the use of even a single lock-up would be incompatible with the most basic values and principles he sought to establish. There is no dignity in an isolation cell. Use of physical restraints may control acting out behavior in the short run, but reinforces it in the long term by creating an environment where staff and students regard one another with suspicion; where control is the dominant concern and is achieved by recourse to raw power and threats of punishment; where manipulativeness is respected as a legitimate re-sponse to authority; where genuine cooperation with adults leads to reduced peer group status. Intimidation and manipulation, the cornerstones of the de-linquent subculture, are reinforced. Respect may be feigned, but genuine respect is rare when one party is holding a club.

There is no need for physical security hardware in an institution for psycho-logically normal delinquents. The belief that locks and bars provide "security" is very widespread, but it is as misguided as it is prevalent. Locks and bars are far more often associated with tension and anxiety, the antithesis of security. A secure environment is one where fear has no place, because the entire com-munity—staff and students alike—is committed to respecting all of its members.

In short, use of lock-ups and physical restraints represents a major obsta-cle to habilitation. Lock-ups make it difficult, perhaps impossible, to rid the normative culture of delinquent peer group pressures. Habilitation is diffi-cult, perhaps impossible, where the culture supports or even tolerates delin-quent peer pressures.

Behavioral control can be achieved with or without locks and bars. Only in their absence can positive behavioral change occur.

DELINQUENTS' POTENTIAL FOR GROWTH AND ACHIEVEMENT

The common assumption that many delinquents are either "bad," "sick," or both suggests that their potential for positive achievement is limited, at least in the near term. Glen Mills does not accept this view. The belief that its "socialized" delinquents are normal adolescents with great potential is basic to the Schools' program.

New students arrive with significant deficits, particularly in education and work habits. But most—particularly those with gang backgrounds—show unusual strengths as well, including a well-developed ability to "read" people and social situations ("street smarts") and loyalty to peers. These qualities enable them to adjust well to Glen Mills' group-based program model.

Glen Mills' program and staff performance standards reflect the view that delinquents possess greater unrealized potential for growth than any other group of adolescents. The expectation is that a sound program, ably implemented, will produce clear, positive change during a student's stay.

The results were documented in Chapter 4. The behavior of students on campus, both in terms of "manners" and the responsibility students show toward each other and the community, must be judged remarkable in relation to the typical high school. Violence and "conning," the twin staples of life on the streets, are rarely exhibited and always confronted. Achievement in academic, vocational, and athletic areas is as extraordinary as the change in social behavior.

Glen Mills has demonstrated that the delinquents it serves have *far* greater potential for growth and achievement than is commonly supposed.

It is simply not possible to overemphasize the significance of the latter point. Too often, mediocre programs succeed in blaming the students for their lack of progress. The claim of those who consider delinquents "bad" is that most are uneducable losers—lazy, manipulative, unmotivated, hostile, and just plain dumb—it is unrealistic to expect much of such unpromising material. Those in the helping professions, who view delinquents as "sick" victims of emotional disturbance, point to traumatic developmental experiences, personality disorders, or other individual characteristics as the reasons for failure. This formula for blaming the victim has the added advantage of allowing program staff to feel kindly, tolerant, and nonjudgmental. By failing to insist upon meaningful progress, courts acquiesce in these fictions.

Glen Mills has proven that responsibility for failure belongs with the *program*, not with the student. With student populations similar to Glen Mills', program characteristics are of overwhelmingly greater importance than the personalities, developmental histories, etc., of students. It is possible to create an open environment where growth in academic, vocational, athletic, and social skills is dramatic; where students and staff respect and support one another; where aggression and fear have no place. To continue to tolerate anything less is an unconscionable abdication of society's responsibility *in loco parentis*.

Ever since the ascendancy of rehabilitation as a major goal of juvenile corrections, the field has been stuck on the horns of a dilemma: should we provide treatment because delinquents are sick, punishment because they are bad, or both (Empey, 1972)? Glen Mills' most significant contribution to juvenile corrections has been to resolve this dilemma once and for all. We should do neither.

CONVERSATIONS AT GLEN MILLS

Thanks to Glen Mills, some things can be claimed with certainty. It is certain that most delinquents possess great potential; that large institutions can play a powerful, positive role in habilitation of delinquents; that private institutions for serious offenders can maintain a very high level of order and security without abuse or security hardware. The Schools' history also sheds light on other issues that warrant discussion. As Glen Mills' reputation has spread, the Schools have attracted visitors from throughout the United States and abroad. The explorations of issues that follow are based upon conversations with academicians, judges, probation officers, politicians, reporters, and others who have visited the Schools in recent years, and with Glen Mills' staff and students.

The Role of Individual Counseling

Glen Mills employs no trained social workers or counselors. The role of individual counseling at the Schools is not to help the student to explore and resolve developmental problems he may have experienced, but rather to ensure that he derives the maximum benefit from GGI and other programs.

The Schools' administrators feel that "therapeutic" counseling for their students is, at best, unnecessary since Glen Mills does not admit students with significant psychopathology. At worst, the counseling process could be counterproductive if it conflicted with the imperatives of the normative culture. The culture is designed to reinforce positive behavior. Emphasis is on the present and the future. To the extent that counseling focuses upon past, negative life experiences, some feel, it accentuates the wrong feelings, to disempowering effect.

A student in counseling might come to believe that he suffered from developmental deficits that justify irresponsible behavior. Or having established a nurturing relationship with his counselor, he might be less responsive to peer pressures, or more interested in pleasing (or manipulating) the therapist than in meeting the expectations of his cottage staff and peers. "I'm working on it with my therapist" can be a convenient excuse to dodge accountability to others. Finally, the Schools' managers note that there is no evidence of the effectiveness of counseling with delinquents. Nor should it be expected, since delinquents rarely voluntarily seek treatment or consider themselves in need of it.

Counseling in correctional institutions has sometimes led to divisions and resentments among staff. Therapists tend to believe that the "real" treatment is provided in their offices, where therapy goals are established, personal problems discussed, and progress monitored. They may devalue the contributions of paraprofessional cottage staff, feeling that staff have at most a secondary impact upon the "patient's" progress—unless, through clumsy handling, they impede the therapy. Most Glen Mills administrators believe that the risks of introducing individual therapy into the Schools' program far outweigh any possible benefits.

Not surprisingly, many treatment professionals dissent from this view. Within Glen Mills' community itself there are advocates of at least a limited role for the trained counselor. They note that there are doubtless some students who, although not "emotionally disturbed," might freely seek and benefit from skilled counseling. Indeed, therapists agree that the less "crazy" the client the better the chances for a favorable outcome, where counseling is voluntarily sought. While it is true that inexperienced or incompetent therapists can create far more problems than they solve, both for the client and for the program, this does not justify excluding those who are committed and skilled.

Finally, though the evidence is strong that reliance upon the counselor as the primary change agent in delinquency programs is a prescription for failure (Teuber and Powers, 1953; McCord, 1978), this does *not* imply that counseling can play no productive role. It may be that counseling in institutions has been ineffective for precisely the same reason that so many other types of programs fail—because the organizational culture does not support them. At Glen Mills, where the "right" norms have been established, a well-designed counseling program might be effective.

Perhaps some difficulties could be overcome by standing the traditional approach on its head, and making the counselor a resource person to cottage staff (thereby explicitly acknowledging that the "real" treatment occurs during social interactions on campus) who might seek advice, refer students to discuss specific problems, or involve the counselor in joint sessions with their students when the staff felt it necessary. Individual counseling would need to be, at most, an adjunct to GGI involvement. There are a variety of models that could be tried.

It may be, as Glen Mills' administrators believe, that the normative culture program model and "therapeutic" counseling are fundamentally incompatible. But the issue must still be regarded as open.

Contracts with Correctional Programs

When jurisdictions consider using a correctional program as a treatment resource, they are often concerned to know the staff to student ratio, number of certified teachers, percent of staff who hold professional degrees, etc. These are among the least important characteristics of a correctional program, from which very little of real significance can be inferred. They are the wrong questions.

What are the "right" questions? If the professionals in the field were paying $30,000 of their own money to support their own child's institutionalization they would demand a strong academic program with report cards showing objective measures of progress, good and plentiful food, top quality medical care, a clean and safe environment, evening and weekend programming. Jurisdictions should be specific about the services to be provided, and monitor the quality of those services. Furthermore, programs should be required to establish measurable treatment objectives and evaluate their effectiveness in achieving them.

Glen Mills commits itself to provide several dozen specific services, great and small, in addition to those mentioned above. Examples include:

Every new student will be

—given a complete medical examination within three days of admittance
—given a complete dental checkup and provided with a plan for all services, including cosmetic, within 14 days of admittance
—administered academic classroom diagnostic tests within seven days of admission
—given the opportunity to select clothing from a variety of colors and styles within 24 hours of admission
—oriented by his staff and peers and introduced to all members of his living unit on the day of his arrival.

Every student will

—have the right to uncensored correspondence with courts, family, and friends
—receive $1.25 spending money each Monday
—have free access to telephones 12–1 P.M., 3–5 P.M., and 6–8 P.M. daily
—be provided with transportation costs for all home visits
—be provided with clean linens at least once per week
—have the opportunity to eat four meals per day: unlimited quantity of top quality food
—receive an education appropriate to his academic level.

Glen Mills will

—provide a representative for court hearings involving its students (upon request)
—provide monthly progress reports, quarterly comprehensive, and six-month reviews to court systems or appropriate social services
—underwrite the cost of two probation officer visits per year to its campus
—provide transcripts, letters of recommendation, and other pertinent data to assist students in college placement.

Last, but certainly not least, Glen Mills evaluates the effectiveness of its programs and provides a description of the evaluations and their results to interested parties.

Normative Cultures in Corporations

In recent years the culture of corporations has received increased attention. Questions of the relationship of culture to organizational effectiveness, and strategies for managing corporate cultures are explored at conferences and in the research literature (Frost et al., 1985). The Glen Mills story is highly relevant to this dialogue.

In the corporate context the normative culture is often described in the context of the "informal" or "shadow" organization (Allen and Pilnick, 1973), in contrast with the visible, formal organization described by the corporation's organization chart and employee handbook. The normative culture plays a powerful role influencing workers' behavior; its impact upon corporate effectiveness matches or exceeds that of the formal organization. Overall effectiveness is directly related to the degree to which the goals of the informal organization support those of the formal organization.

As at Glen Mills, successful companies systematically shape and strengthen their cultures to harness the power of the informal system. Indeed, Peters and Waterman, after studying 43 companies they considered to be among the most excellent in the nation, claim that

> without exception, the dominance and coherence of culture proved to be an essential quality of the excellent companies. Moreover, the stronger the culture . . . the less need was there for policy manuals, organization charts, or detailed procedures and rules. In these companies, people way down the line know what they are supposed to do in most situations because the handful of guiding values is crystal clear. . . . Poorer-performing companies often have strong cultures too, but dysfunctional ones. They are usually focused on internal politics. . . . The excellent companies are marked by cultures so strong that you either buy into their norms or get out. (Peters and Waterman, 1982: 75–77)

The role and importance of corporate culture has long been recognized; articles have found their way into practitioner publications and even the popular press (e.g., Childress, 1984; Kilmann, 1985).

Attempts to mold corporate cultures outnumber success stories, probably by a wide margin. The description by Reynolds (1987) of a failed attempt to impose a culture upon a small Silicon Valley microcomputer firm ("Falcon Computer"; 250 employees) provides an excellent case study. The process involved a series of closed, top management "culture meetings," which yielded a "Falcon Values" document describing the desired culture. Unfortunately, the "Falcon Values" were clearly at wide variance with the actual values and behaviors of the managers who promulgated them. The document itself was ridiculed by incredulous staff. According to Reynolds, "The obvious disparity between the official and actual values sanctioned a culture of hypocrisy" which soon undermined employee morale and productivity.

The debacle at Falcon Computer is instructive because it confirms that successful and presumably intelligent executives can be sufficiently naive as to suppose that shaping a corporate culture is a matter of listing the relevant values, attitudes, and behaviors and then urging staff to adopt them. Glen Mills' experience indicates that a good bit more is required.

Glen Mills' normative change strategy was modeled upon a process initially developed by Drs. Robert Allen and Saul Pilnick. The general strategy (Allen and Pilnick, 1973; Pilnick, 1975) involves being clear about objectives, identifying existing norms which are positive or negative in relation to the objectives, and developing strategies to reinforce the former and change the latter.

The process of establishing Glen Mills' culture was described in detail in

Chapter 1. It is worth reiterating here that Glen Mills' process, though guided by a general theory of normative systems change, also involved large doses of instinct, opportunism, and ad hoc tactical management. Normative cultures are complex and, once established, highly resistant to change. The change process involves numerous intangibles, most importantly the strength of top management commitment. While the process ingredients have been described by Pilnick and others, combining them in the optimal sequence and proportions is as much an art form as a science. There can be no cookbook.

It must also be noted that Glen Mills' situation differs in some important respects from that of most corporations. First, the Schools' highly developed confrontation process, an important tool in establishing and maintaining norms, is far more appropriate to a correctional setting than to a corporation. Second, there are no unions at Glen Mills. To the extent that unions introduce an adversarial dimension to staff-management relations, some important norms (e.g., teamwork) will be more difficult to establish. Finally, the process of normative change at Glen Mills was more complex and extended because it involved not only staff but students. The latter, in most institutions, are at least suspicious of and usually hostile to administration initiatives. Falcon Computer had only its staff to consider, the computers' norms were fine.

These differences notwithstanding, Glen Mills' experience suggests principles of normative change which may be useful to corporate change agents. Some may not be applicable to a given corporate setting. None will be of use in a firm where the norm is to jump from a proposal to a list of reasons why "it wouldn't work here." But at a minimum, they suggest the range of ingredients in an effective change process and indicate why simplistic approaches like Falcon's have little prospect of success.

The following principles are drawn from Glen Mills' experience with the process originally described by Allen and Pilnick.

1. The elements of the desired culture (i.e., corporate values, beliefs, and norms) should be clearly specified, linked to corporate goals, and communicated to staff.
2. Top management must be fully committed, intellectually and behaviorally, to the values and norms of the culture. Modeling of desired behaviors by all managers is crucial. Employees take their cues from what managers do, not what they say.
3. Involve staff in designing and implementing norms change strategies (e.g., through quality circles). Be certain that staff understand how a positive normative culture benefits them.
4. Identify high status members of work groups and make concerted effort to gain their support for the desired culture. For example, these individuals are prime candidates for a quality circle.
5. Establishment and maintenance of normative cultures does not occur in a vacuum. Structures, procedures, and ceremonies which reinforce the culture are essential. (At Glen Mills the Bulls Club, the confrontation process, the Big Brother program, and the various awards ceremonies are examples.) Develop mechanisms to identify, recognize, and reward staff who actively support positive norms.

6. Supervisory staff must discuss desired norms with their subordinates and consistently confront negative behavior. Every failure to do so conveys the impression that the behavior is acceptable, thereby making it more difficult to change. Confrontations should be respectful and always focused on specific behavior.

7. Identify negative norms which are inconsistent with the desired culture. Select one that is relatively easy to change (e.g., not too well established; not important to high status employees; easily monitored) and mount a focused campaign to change it. Use the experience as a learning process, and to build commitment to the change process.

8. Establish systems to monitor key norms. Disseminate indications of progress, or lack thereof to all employees.

9. It is especially important that negative individuals whose behavior conflicts with significant norms *not* be promoted into supervisory or management positions. Though this may require sacrificing some degree of technical expertise, the alternative of undermining the culture by rewarding negative behavior is in the long run a far greater peril.

10. Develop explicit criteria for hiring and promotion, linked to the desired culture. The single most important question in considering a new applicant or a candidate for promotion is "How well does he or she 'fit' the culture?" With rare exceptions (e.g., an individual in a highly specialized role involving minimal interaction with other staff and no supervisory responsibilities) this issue is as important as task competency in evaluating candidates.

11. Arrange for new employees to be trained and oriented by positive employees who model the desired norms. The normative culture should be explicitly discussed during the orientation. Avoid assignment of a new employee to a work group with negative norms.

12. Make every effort to "convert" negative staff to the desired culture. If these efforts are unsuccessful, terminate the individual(s) or assign them to roles which minimize their interaction and influence with other staff. Do not promote them.

Under the best of circumstances normative change is difficult, requiring continual effort over a long period of time. The establishment of Glen Mills' normative culture required nearly five years. Special circumstances (e.g., union restrictions on assignment of personnel; an "untouchable" but incompetent individual in a key management role) may make the process even more difficult. Furthermore, the most positive culture is not a panacea guaranteeing a successful future; all companies face critical problems (e.g., market conditions) having little or nothing to do with their culture.

Why bother, then? Because *all* companies have norms and informal organizations affecting their performance. The informal organization is a potent force for good or ill, and in the absence of a focused effort to shape key norms it is likely to be "for ill," or at best benign. It is certain that no firm can achieve its potential without a normative culture supportive of its goals. The culture is to an organization like a mighty warrior to an army. When going into battle, it is better to have him fighting by your side than against you, or asleep.

Guarding Against Abuse of the Normative Culture

The understanding of normative cultures and how to shape group norms is an extremely powerful, potentially dangerous tool. Some visitors to Glen Mills express serious concerns about the potential for abuse of the powers to control behavior inherent in the normative culture model. Glen Mills represents a subculture where behavior is very tightly controlled. Concerns extend beyond the issue of preventing physical abuse (see Chapter 2). They reflect both the degree of control and its subtlety: the control process is as powerful but far less obvious than that of most other "managed" environments, for example, the military.

The potential for misuse of the power to design and create a subculture "to specifications" is great. In the laboratory, Stanley Milgram (1963) has demonstrated that interpersonal conditions can be created which induce perfectly normal, respectable individuals to turn a deaf ear to screams and inflict extreme pain upon others even when they themselves are in no way threatened with harm.

When the elements of threat and group pressures are introduced, there appear to be no limits to the terrible results achievable through control of group norms. The mass suicides at Jonestown are the most infamous example of the power of normative cultures in some cults. Though cult members are not representative of the broader society, there is no reason to believe that more conventional individuals are less vulnerable to group pressures.

The history of the twentieth century suggests that no race, no people is exempt from the power of social forces to convert otherwise humane and peace-loving individuals into murderous thugs. Even those with long and well-deserved reputations for gentleness (e.g., Cambodians), when subjected to social pressures engineered by a clever, malevolent leader, can be induced to torture, maim, and kill their brethren.

In its potential for good or evil, the technology for manipulating norms and cultures is the social equivalent of nuclear power.

Protections against misuse of this power are of the utmost importance. At Glen Mills, these take the form of a celebration of individuality within explicit boundaries, an inviolable core value of respect for the dignity of every person, constant program monitoring to insure that abuse does not occur and that the actual program operation corresponds in all respects to the intended ("on paper") program operation, and an openness to observation by outsiders that may be unprecedented in the history of institutional corrections.

In most managed societies individual differences are deemphasized. Regimentation is the norm. Glen Mills encourages diversity through a vast array of program options, and celebrates individual effort and achievement. Program plans, rewards, and sanctions are all individualized and highly specific to the needs of the student.

There are two boundaries limiting individuality, both explicit. First, since all students must live in a group, individuality is not tolerated where it interferes with the students' rights to a clean, orderly, secure living environment (e.g., no loud radios) and effective programs (e.g., no talking in classrooms without raising hand). Second, dress and appearance must not reflect "street" styles. The latter prohibition, including many norms proposed by the Bulls Club, is intended to strongly differentiate Glen Mills' culture from the delinquent subculture and to discourage students' identification with street gangs.

The absolute prohibition against treating others disrespectfully is a strong protection against the coercion characteristic of repressive cults or controlled societies. The humiliation heaped upon the victims of China's Cultural Revolution, for example, would be impossible at the Schools; as would the milder forms of degradation suffered by those in the wider society who publicly espouse unpopular views or causes.

Basic to Glen Mills' model is the principle that the "informal" organization (reflecting the actual values, behaviors, and expectations of staff) must be constantly monitored to ensure that it contributes to the goals of the "formal" organization. The informal organization must never be in conflict with institutional values. Furthermore, all program effects bearing upon students' well-being (e.g., medical, educational, behavioral, recidivism) are monitored to alert management to any troubling trends. These policies help ensure that no renegade individual or group will use their position in ways that are harmful to the Schools or its students.

Finally, Glen Mills welcomes literally dozens of "outsiders" each month to its campus. These visitors span the full spectrum of critics, cynics, and admirers; justice system professionals and laymen. Visitors are invited to tour the Schools and speak with whomever they choose among the ranks of students and staff. Most freely discuss their reactions with Glen Mills' managers. This extraordinary openness is further protection against the insular, defensive management styles associated with abusive institutions.

Can Corrections Professionals be Entrusted with the Administration of Large Institutions?

During the 1950s and 1960s, as more and more major universities hired presidents from fields other than education, it was said that "Higher education is too important to be left to the educators." Colleges and universities had become major businesses whose survival required that top administrators possess business development, management, financial planning, fundraising, and public relations skills. There was little in the backgrounds of most academicians to qualify them for the top jobs.

In a similar vein, it could be argued that corrections is too important to be left to corrections professionals. In the case of Glen Mills, Sam Ferrainola brought to the Schools a theory of delinquency and a program concept informed by more than a decade of work in the field. These were important assets. But the translation of the concept into practice—the implementation of the nor-mative culture—drew primarily upon his prior experiences as a business owner and as an organizational consultant, not his background in juvenile corrections. Core skills included organizational design, finance, business planning and admin-istration, personnel management and training, management information systems development, legal, political, and social systems expertise. Each of these was critically important at some point in the development of the Schools' program. Had the new director's work experience been limited to corrections, the insti-tution's one-hundred fiftieth year (1976) may well have been its last.

The need for skills in business and finance is probably less acute in the public sector, which operates most large institutions. However, even in the public sector it is by no means clear that experience "in the trenches," without ex-tensive training or experience in management and organizational dynamics, is adequate preparation for the administration of a major institution. Program effectiveness requires *both* sound design *and* strong implementation. Failures of correctional programs for delinquents may be due as much to poor implemen-tation by unskilled administrators as to weakness in concept.

Community Reintegration

Immersion in Glen Mills' normative culture leads to a rapid and dramatic change in students' behavior. Within days of arrival the new student begins to behave like a gentleman: he greets others, establishes eye contact, dresses neatly, takes care of property, and shows respect and consideration for others. At first, of course, the behavior is only a front—a sort of play acting until he learns the lay of the land. Antisocial attitudes have not changed. The extent to which the positive, prosocial values and beliefs of Glen Mills' culture later become internalized is an open question, and doubtless varies from student to student. What is clear is that, for most students, the behavior itself remains consistent during their stay at Glen Mills.

However promising the student's campus behavior, the more important test of an institution's effectiveness is the young man's conduct in the community following discharge. Will his positive behavior persist without GGI? Daily Town-house meetings? The Bulls Club? A "big brother"? Will he continue to strive to improve when the equation governing peer group status is altered? When there are fewer opportunities for recognition and awards?

In returning to the community after discharge, the student leaves behind the most managed, consistently prosocial environment he will ever experience. In its place are the different and often conflicting expectations of the student, employee, family, and street cultures. He is no longer a Glen Mills student entitled, unconditionally, to respectful treatment. Many (including teachers and police) remember him as a bad kid, or at least a troublemaker. Responsible parents in the community do not encourage their children to associate with him. During the first crucial months after discharge a student who returns to his former community may have to choose between the negative influence of his former gang or social isolation, until he can begin to live down his reputation and build more positive peer friendships.

The readjustment problem was described by one (black) student who reported that, upon return to his neighborhood: "I could feel just by the way they (his friends) looked at me they saw I was a different person, and didn't like it. They started calling me 'whitey'! I kept to myself a lot. If it weren't for my girlfriend, I couldn't have stood it."

These are very real concerns for the large majority of students. Five out of six return to the same neighborhoods where they had earlier become delinquent (Grissom, 1984). Eighty-one percent say they associate with some or most of the same peers they had known prior to Glen Mills. In short, they are exposed to the same physical environment and peer pressures which in most cases figured prominently in their delinquency. Can the positive effects of Glen Mills' program survive so radical a transition?

One school of thought holds that the very success of Glen Mills in demonstrating the power of the normative culture suggests that positive effects will be short-lived. If social forces exert so powerful an influence in creating delinquents, and then converting the delinquents to gentlemen, surely the return to delinquency will occur swiftly upon the student's discharge to an environment where delinquency is commonplace, former (delinquent) friends are eager to welcome him back to the fold and prosocial behavior is often unrecognized and unrewarded.

Ironically, some feel that the very excellence of Glen Mills' physical environment may be an obstacle to community readjustment. Glen Mills' managers believe that the quality of the Schools environment will engender pride and self-esteem, and help induce its graduates to strive for a better quality of life after discharge. But, some visitors wonder whether memories of "the good life" at Glen Mills may serve to exacerbate feelings of frustration with current deprivations. If there are no legitimate avenues to restore the standard of living he had come to expect at the Schools, the young man may be all the more receptive to opportunities for criminal involvement.

This concern may reflect a misunderstanding of strain theory or the crucial distinction between blocked opportunities and levels of aspiration. Review of empirical studies (Johnson et al., 1979) indicates that perceptions of blocked opportunities are associated with delinquency, but that only insignificant or *negative* associations between aspiration and delinquency have been found. That is, while no studies have demonstrated that high aspirations are associated with delinquent behavior, some have found that *low* aspirations are associated with delinquency. Glen Mills teaches its students to overcome obstacles, take life one step at a time, and strive for the best. The important point is that the impact of Glen Mills is to reduce perceptions of blocked opportunities and increase aspiration levels. Consequently, strain theory and related research would suggest that former students would be less, not more, delinquency prone for having experienced a first class living environment.

Aftercare services might help the student to readjust to the community. However, it is not clear what these services should be or who should provide them. Following a review of dozens of studies, Genevie, Margolies, and Muhlin conclude that

juveniles who are released with no supervision . . . (experienced) higher rates of recidivism than juveniles receiving any form of supervision after release. However, the data yield no clear-cut direction for the form such supervision should take. (Genevie et al., 1986: 55)

In view of its complications for later recidivism, the development of effective aftercare programs is a high priority concern.

One solution to the problems posed by the transition from institution to community may be intensive reintegration programming. Reintegration, the process of cultivating community support for the offender, is considered by some to be critically important to minimizing recidivism. The various approaches to reintegration include (Altschuler, 1984):

- Preparation of students for progressively increased involvement in the community.
- Facilitation of student-community interaction.
- Development of understandings and commitments between the student and existing community support systems (family, peers, schools, employers, churches).
- Establishment of new resources and supports where necessary.
- Monitoring of the ability of the students and community to deal with each other productively.

The approach stresses involvement with community support systems. Glen Mills has resisted extension of its efforts beyond its own student body for three reasons. First, Glen Mills finds dubious the implicit assumption that the Schools can significantly impact upon the performance of community support systems. Second, though reintegration sounds good "on paper," it is difficult to document the active ingredients of a successful program. Reintegration programming is by no means a new idea, and there have been some notable failures of apparently well-designed programs.

Post-institutional adjustment in the community was to be facilitated by a program of Mobilization for Youth in New York called the Reintegration Project (RP). Designed to ease transition, to reintroduce the youth into getting together with his family, get into school, or (if over 16 years of age) get and hold a job, and dissuade youth from reuniting with delinquent or criminal associates, the RP used small case load family counseling and active client advocacy. . . . It did not succeed . . . and a comparison of RP with the control cases fails to demonstrate any reduction in recidivism. (Kasselbaum, 1974: 130–31)

Glen Mills' third reservation is the belief that responsibility for reintegration more appropriately belongs to the aftercare service agencies. All students have at least one, and some have as many as four, probation officers, counselors, and social workers to assist them after discharge.

Glen Mills chooses to focus its attention upon the students. Preparing a student for discharge is the responsibility of his counselor, and preparations begin early. After six weeks at Glen Mills students from the surrounding counties become eligible for weekend passes home every second week. The student's experiences at home are discussed with his counselor and peers so that any problematic situations can be resolved prior to discharge. Apart from these discussions, prerelease activities include planning discussions with the student's family and probation officer, securing enrollment in a school or training program if appropriate, or assistance with job hunting.

The student who has completed Glen Mills' program has learned how to accept confrontation and resolve disputes without using his fists. He has experienced success in academics and/or vocational training. Appropriate "middle class" academic, workplace, and social behavior is part of his repertoire. He may have a GED or a vocational certificate. Educational trips, in many cases to Florida (a few have gone to Europe!), have exposed him to a world very different from his home community. He has come to value himself and others in a new way. Most importantly, he has experienced acceptance and respect from prosocial, achievement-oriented staff and peers. He has learned to feel that he belongs in such company, and enjoys it. He has seen that "right living" can bring very rich rewards. He feels pride in his new persona.

He has developed life skills which will help him to sustain educational, vocational, and personal growth begun at the Schools. He is better equipped to resist the allure of the delinquent subculture.

The progressive improvement in Glen Mills' recidivism data beginning with the establishment of its normative culture in 1980, and continuing as the culture strengthened, is evidence that the Glen Mills experience helps students to turn away from delinquency. During the five-year period 1980–84 recidivism among program completers improved by 34 percent and 28 percent for rearrest and reincarceration, respectively. Further major improvement through strengthening of the normative culture is unlikely. The culture has now been stable, with only relatively minor fine-tuning for several years. It is likely that the Schools' recidivism rates will also remain stable in the near future.

The next substantial improvement will come from a breakthrough with regard to the community reintegration problem. There are two options which hold promise—the establishment of community-based half-way houses and a significant extension of the students' length of stay at the Schools.

The community-based option would permit an extension of the normative culture into the community, permitting a more gradual and controlled reentry process for students who had completed their time on the main campus. In addition to peer support, the student would benefit from normatively positive apprenticeship or tutoring programs. Glen Mills' ability to establish positive, powerful normative cultures is critical to success. Community work programs, for example, have generally failed to reduce delinquency (Johnson et al., 1979) despite sound theoretical grounds for expecting positive results. It has been suggested that the reason for many failures is the characteristics of the work site psychosocial environment and reward structure (Hawkins and Lishner, 1981; Beville, 1981). In his discussion of relevant research, Anderson points to

serious doubt about the assumption that unemployment is a major cause of recidivism ... the need for inmate improvement is not simply in the provision of skills, but in attitudes toward the working situation. ... The principal problems of ex-offenders identified by employers were absenteeism, alcohol and drugs. Lack of skill was cited in only 3 [out of 33] instances. The principal reason for termination was absenteeism. (Anderson, 1981: 14)

A strong normative culture in the work setting would likely yield much better results.

Alternatively, the Schools might extend their program so that students stay a minimum of 18 months, with most remaining for two years or more. If this were done, it would be possible to ensure that virtually every student was either in college, in an advanced vocational program, or employable in a skilled trade upon discharge. He would hold one of the two "tickets" (i.e., education, meaningful employment) which provide entree into mainstream middle-class society. Furthermore, he would return to the community at an age, 19 or 20, when many adolescent gangs begin to break up, reducing the potential for further criminal involvement.

There are obstacles to each approach. It would not be feasible to establish halfway houses in all jurisdictions serviced by Glen Mills. Also, the inability of other community-based programs to reduce recidivism, and some notable failures of the halfway house model itself (Vasoli and Fahey, 1970), raise doubts about the fundamental assumptions of this approach. There are also problems associated with an extended length of stay. Few adolescent boys relish the prospect of a two or three year commitment to a single sex institution. The counties may balk at the substantial additional expense of an extended program.

Only this is certain: a significant portion of the benefit of the Glen Mills experience is lost when a student leaves the Schools and returns to his neighborhood. The problem of community reintegration represents the most significant challenge facing Glen Mills.

IMPROVING JUVENILE CORRECTIONS: REPLICATION OF THE GLEN MILLS MODEL

In the mid 1970s, faced with the disappointing findings of evaluations of juvenile correctional programs, policymakers and practitioners chose from among four options: continue with business as usual, give up, try harder, or try something different.

A common response to program evaluations—proceed with business as usual or with only token changes—is dictated by inertia. Many in the justice system, child welfare agencies, political leaders, and program staff have a vested interest in the status quo. As has been said, nothing is more difficult than to initiate a new order of things.

There is rarely a shortage of rationalizations for changing nothing:

1. Can anyone be certain that a different approach would be any more effective? Why risk making matters worse?

2. Perhaps the evaluations are faulty—it seems that each one touches off a flurry of critiques of its methodology and conclusions. When those who are schooled in the arcane disciplines of research design and statistics so often disagree with one another, what hope has the layperson of making an informed decision based upon the studies?

3. Finally, perhaps the true message of the evaluations is not that "nothing works," but that *everything* works. A potpourri of approaches are equally and commendably effective. After all, given the often severely deprived and traumatic life histories of many institutionalized delinquents, compounded by the likelihood of post-discharge return to the same depressed environment, it is a wonder that recidivism rates are not even higher. Under these unpromising circumstances, helping even one out of three delinquents to "go straight" is a magnificent achievement.

To some, these considerations suggest that there is no need to do anything different.

Those who would give up concluded that current programs are ineffective and attempts at rehabilitation wasteful because it is simply not possible to help most delinquents. The best that could be hoped for was to keep them off the streets, and perhaps "teach them a lesson" through spartan living conditions and harsh discipline. Juvenile corrections should serve as a shot across the bow, a warning of things to come if the offender does not straighten out his life.

Unfortunately, the evidence is that such an approach confirms negative self-images and nurtures the delinquent subcultures which play so large a role in antisocial behavior. The lessons learned are not those that are intended. Delinquents in these settings seldom learn to respect themselves and treat others with dignity, to accept responsibility for their behavior, or to recognize their potential and experience the satisfactions of meaningful achievement. Rather, they absorb the values and attitudes of their peers, learn to manipulate authority figures and otherwise improve delinquent skills, and become tough enough to victimize others or at least escape victimization and resolve not to get caught next time.

The try harder option was favored by those who believe that current programs are well designed, but underfunded or poorly implemented. Custody and rehabilitation were judged legitimate goals: programs should confine and "treat" individuals to help them overcome the psychological conflicts or weakness of character which led to their delinquency. The offender needs to be fixed and a large complement of highly trained professional staff from the "helping professions" were required to do the job right. The usual prescription for improving programs is to hire more and better qualified staff, particularly social workers, psychologists, and counselors. This view may be quite accurate when applied to programs for delinquents who suffer from some form of mental illness. But it can be an expensive formula for failure when applied to youths who are not psychologically disturbed, and its failure is assured in the absence of a supportive peer culture. In such a milieu the price of genuine program involvement is alienation from one's peer group, and few adolescents are willing or able to pay it. The rejection experienced by those who do may, in psychological terms, outweigh any benefits.

Sam Ferrainola, believing that giving up was unwarranted and putting more effort into the failed "custody-clinical" model unconscionable, was determined to try something different. Other innovators developed community corrections and programs stressing physical activity/wilderness experiences. All have their advocates and detractors. Some settings and program types are no doubt better suited than others to the needs of an individual offender, though it is not yet clear what the decision criteria should be. It is clear that giving up is unjustified, and that a shift away from the traditional "custody-clinical" model is emphatically warranted.

The path toward more effective corrections is marked by an understanding of the strengths and weaknesses of traditional approaches and the contributions of successful innovations. Glen Mills' establishment of a truly habilitative normative culture represents a major achievement with the potential to move the field forward. Its impact depends upon the replicability of the normative culture model.

The main characteristics of Glen Mills normative culture and the process through which norms are established have been described in earlier chapters. The following discussion examines some central issues in replication: the integration and interdependence of organizational components; the qualities to be sought in the executive director; performance excellence norms; opposition of external systems; and the importance of program evaluation.

An Integrated System

From an organizational perspective, Glen Mills' most significant achievement has been the integration of a variety of organizational elements into a framework which shapes, strengthens, and harnesses the power of the normative culture. Program components are interdependent among themselves and with the values and norms of the culture. *Replication can not be achieved by focusing upon individual elements in isolation.* In particular, the model cannot be duplicated merely by grafting GGI and management by objectives onto a custody-clinical treatment approach.

A culture that promotes the goals of the organization can be neither established or maintained solely by exhorting staff to behave in certain ways. The process through which Glen Mills' culture was established has been described earlier. The culture is maintained via a supporting framework which includes Glen Mills' ecology, routines, symbols, transactions with outside systems and, most importantly, program structures which provide for staff and student reinforcement of positive norms.

Glen Mills' *ecology*, the quality of its physical plant, is important for several reasons. First, it communicates to students a core message of the culture: You are valued. It is quite clear to students that they are the primary beneficiaries of Glen Mills' "why not the best?" philosophy. The experience of being valued is a powerful antidote to frustration and anger, major obstacles to habilitation which are spawned by the needless deprivations of most correctional programs. The value of students is further reinforced by the principle that the quality of students' living conditions is never sacrificed to improve that of staff. At Glen Mills a separate dining facility for staff would be as unthinkable as a separate dining room for parents in a home.

Second, the quality of the environment serves to support an important norm: Around here, we take care of Schools property. Students are more likely to conform to this expectation and to confront those who violate it, when they experience the benefits of a first-class environment.

Third, students feel proud to be part of a first-class organization. Pride is an important element of Glen Mills culture—pride in self, pride in community. The quality of the Schools' environment is a constant reminder of what can be achieved when individuals commit themselves to gradual, steady improvement. There are few more important learnings for those who will begin their adult lives in America's inner cities.

Most importantly, the quality of the Schools' environment provides an important "win" for students who work to maintain it. They have a direct stake in positive behavior; a self-interest in preserving a system that invests in student clothing, housing, and travel rather than locks and bars.

In short, the power of Glen Mills' normative culture would be seriously diminished if the quality of its environment were eroded. Replication requires a commitment to excellence of facilities as well as programs. In practical terms, it requires the ability to "make do" with available resources without surrendering the commitment to continually improve.

Routines and traditions also play an important role. Annual festivals (e.g., homecoming celebrations, Halloween programs, "Firecracker" Fourth of July races) build cohesion among staff and students alike as all work together to make an event successful, and then enjoy the fruits of their labor. By designing its own float, skit or program each cottage unit offers something to the community. The richness and history of these traditions conveys to staff, who can recall earlier years, a sense of the continuity and stability of the culture whose values are reflected in the rituals.

Awards ceremonies, whether for vocational, athletic, or educational achievement, transmit the culture by honoring those in whom Glen Mills' values are most fully reflected. It is, of course, crucial that the "right" people receive rewards. When a hard-working student functioning at the fifth grade level is honored with induction into Academic Hall, while those who are far more advanced academically but less motivated are denied admission, the normative culture grows stronger. When staff awards are bestowed upon those who have contributed most, regardless of length of service, the normative culture grows stronger.

Program rituals are designed to bolster the culture. Each evening, during Townhouse, students who have violated important norms during the day stand up in front of the group and say "I want to own up and apologize to my peers and staff for. . . . " That act makes concrete the norm of personal responsibility for one's behavior and obligation to the community. There are no excuses offered. Peer feedback following the apology is sometimes gentle ("That's not like you. You just slipped up. Don't do it again"), sometimes harsh ("You've messed up your work assignments a lot, lately. Maybe you'd do better if you stayed in the cottage the next couple of weekends and practiced"), but does not "take the dignity" of the offender or humiliate him. Glen Mills' rituals transmit its culture.

Glen Mills' mascot is the bull, a symbol that conveys strength and masculinity. To Glen Mills' students, it conveys a great deal more:

The symbol of the Bull means pride, the pride that we have in our school and our Bulls Club. The Bull also means strong leaders. Whatever we do we give it our best. The Bull also is a believer, he believes that whatever he does he will come out on top. The Bull has a look of determination in his eyes, and he knows he can't be stopped. Bulls never stand alone. They are always with other Bulls helping each other out when it is needed. (By James Brown, Glen Mills Schools *Yearbook*, 1987, p. 74)

Determination. Pride. Coming out on top. Never standing alone. Glen Mills' primary symbol is a part of its culture, and vice versa.

Organizations do not exist in isolation. The nature of their transactions with the external environment shapes and is shaped by their cultures. The events described in Chapter 2 were "critical" because, in each instance, the integrity of Glen Mills' normative culture was threatened by external forces. Preservation of the culture required recognition of the threat and appropriate response. Had Glen Mills failed to engineer the passage of Act 30, the key norm of teamwork among staff would have been jeopardized. Confrontation, the foundation of the normative culture, would have been seriously weakened had the Schools let stand an unsubstantiated charge of staff abuse. Since the Schools' normative culture is not designed to accommodate students who are emotionally disturbed, loss of control over admissions would be fatal to it. Finally, nearly all the key values of Glen Mills' culture were at risk in the confrontation with the Philadelphia district attorney. Pride, respect, honor, integrity: capitulation to the D.A.'s threats would have sacrificed them all.

In one important respect these "critical incidents" were atypical: most involved a winner and a loser. Glen Mills' transactions with outside systems are guided by the same "win-win" philosophy which dominates internal affairs. It is usually possible to reach an agreement satisfactory to all parties. But in maintaining a normative culture it is necessary to make fundamental values and principles explicit, scan the environment for possible threats, and when these arise either change the external environment (e.g., work to pass Act 30) or negotiate an agreement which does minimum damage to core principles.

By far the most important factors in maintaining the culture are the organizational structures (discussed in Chapter 2) which support it. The molecular structure, management information and communication systems, confrontation process, and Bulls Club are among Glen Mills' most significant innovations. They are the vehicles through which cultural values and norms are manifested in the daily life of the Glen Mills community. They are the implementational nuts and bolts that operationalize the normative culture model, transforming it from an interesting but hypothetical possibility into an observable program with the power to change lives.

Less innovative but equally vital are the Schools performance evaluation and monitoring systems. The principle that growth is best achieved through setting concrete goals and carefully monitoring progress is central to Glen Mills' model. It applies to staff, students, and the program itself. Systems to operationalize it are essential.

Leadership: The Executive Director

An essential element of the normative change process is the modeling of desired norms by the organization's leaders. It is not possible for an arrogant leader to establish a normative culture having mutual respect as a core value or for a self-serving director to preside over a culture where loyalty is expected behavior.

The qualities Mr. Ferrainola brings to his role suggest leadership characteristics that are important to replication. In his personality, skills, and life experience Mr. Ferrainola brought a great deal more to Glen Mills than a vision of the Schools' potential. He held strong beliefs regarding delinquents and delinquency. The model could not be established by a director who believed delinquents to be "bad" or psychologically disturbed or who undervalued the importance of eradicating antisocial behavior. Mr. Ferrainola's work among Pittsburgh's street gangs exposed him to the terrible consequences of juvenile crime to the entire community. The same experiences persuaded him that delinquents, as a group, were neither psychologically nor morally inferior to the rest of society; that "they had done bad things but were not bad kids." Grounded in universal needs for safety, belonging, and status, the antisocial acts of most young offenders are a predictable result of their social/psychological environment. Change in both the boy and the environment are required, but the best way to achieve the former is by concentrating upon the latter.

The importance of the director's experience "in the trenches" deserves emphasis. Apart from shaping his views, it enabled him to model effectively the role he wanted line staff to play in the new Glen Mills. It provided credibility, an important commodity during the early years of staff discontent and resistance. It enabled him to resist the challenges of critics or well-meaning but misguided supporters who insisted that his methods could not work.

The model requires a director with a strong sense of loyalty to his staff. The son of a Sicilian laborer, Mr. Ferrainola had been taught early in life that loyalty to family was of far greater importance than wealth, education, professional achievement, or social position. The Glen Mills community is the director's extended family. No one in need is turned away from the director's door; he has an uncanny ability to sense and respond to a need without a person's even needing to ask. Furthermore, Mr. Ferrainola keeps no scorecard of favors rendered, asking only that staff contribute their best efforts on behalf of the Schools.

A steadfast, trustworthy, clear commitment to both the goals and the people of the community are essential to effective leadership. In their absence, strong teamwork norms are impossible. Where management opts for expediency over principle in its relations with staff, an everybody-for-himself norm soon emerges.

There are countless anecdotes illustrating the importance of loyalty at Glen Mills. On one occasion, an elderly staff member became disabled and could no longer work. Though the Schools had no legal obligation to him, the director assured him of free room and board and medical care at the Schools for as long as he wished to stay. Mr. Ferrainola felt that the man had been a loyal employee who needed a family to help him, but had none: "We are his only family. When a family member needs you, you don't put him out on the street." The director's feelings about loyalty are well known and pay handsome dividends to Glen Mills. On the frequent occasions when he has appealed to staff to "go the extra mile" on behalf of the Schools, he has rarely been disappointed. Staff know that he does not ask on behalf of Sam Ferrainola, but on behalf of Glen Mills. They know that the director's door is literally and figuratively always open to them without appointment, as a member of the family.

Respect is a cornerstone of the normative culture, and must be modeled by its leadership. Ridiculing, blaming, insulting, or otherwise "taking the dignity" of another person are absolute taboos. The director shows his respect for staff by giving managers wide authority to direct their programs, and by publicly and privately honoring staff. It is a rare meeting at Glen Mills where no one is commended for some achievement. The director tells visitors that Glen Mills' program strengths reflect not his own ideas but the contributions of his staff, a claim that is true. But it is the director who molded the climate in which staff potential flourishes; where failures in pursuit of excellence are never condemned and successes rarely go unacknowledged; where working to make Glen Mills a little bit better is a sure path to recognition and esteem.

Of equal importance to beliefs and personality traits are administrative skills. The director knows his own strengths. He also recognizes and cultivates other's abilities. Believing that each of his top managers is more knowledgeable than he about their areas of responsibility, he delegates virtually every day-to-day operational responsibility and very rarely intervenes in the administration of individual departments. Key administrative skills include an exceptional ability to communicate and rally staff around core values; to make hard and sometimes unpopular decisions in the best interest of the Schools; to avoid allowing his own ego needs to intrude in decision-making; to hold staff accountable while remaining their ally; to remain visible and involved without undercutting managers' authority or second-guessing their decisions. The director has the instincts of a politician and the commitment of a zealot, a well-honed ability to identify individuals' motivations, sort out competing agendas, and find "win-win" solutions which do not compromise key objectives. One visitor who spent six months observing Glen Mills' program pronounced Mr. Ferrainola's social engineering skills the element most indispensable to the Schools' functioning.

Of the director's remaining qualities several are helpful, but probably not essential, to replication of the model.

Mr. Ferrainola is an unassuming man, few who did not know him would suppose that he was the architect of one of history's most effective correctional programs. Combining the large frame of a former athlete with a warm and generous spirit, he seems at once unintimidating and unintimidatable. He claims an IQ of 100 (many who know Sam suspect this estimate is low)—ideal, he says, for relating to the full spectrum of humankind. Delinquents, judges, staff, legislators, and board members feel immediately comfortable and welcomed in his office.

When problems arise, the director betrays no anxieties or dismay. Rather, he conveys to staff strong confidence in both their willingness and ability to work together as a team to overcome the difficulties, and a conviction that the final result will be a more effective program. What others consider obstacles, he regards as opportunities to grow. Mr. Ferrainola subscribes to Nietzsche's view, "That which does not kill me makes me stronger."

The director excels in developing subordinates. He believes that ordinary individuals, exposed to the proper doses of challenge and support within an atmosphere of trust, can achieve extraordinary things. Developing subordinates, Mr. Ferrainola says, is like training mountain climbers. The joy, excitement and challenge are in the "climb": getting better, overcoming obstacles. Whether you reach the peak isn't important. This philosophy permeates Glen Mills' culture, and may explain why the Schools seem to bring out the best in staff and students alike.

The incident involving Philadelphia's threat to reduce per diem payments for students on home pass (Chapter 2) illustrates another of Mr. Ferrainola's strong qualities. He excels at brinkmanship. He is a master of all steps of the process: "reading" his adversary's motivations and intentions; clarifying his own position and objectives; developing a strategy and building support for it among board members and staff; and ensuring that the consequences to the Schools will not be disastrous if it becomes necessary to follow through with any threatened action.

The director seems very secure in himself and his achievements. He seeks no personal recognition or credit. His dress and speech are simple, not intended to impress.

The simplicity belies a surprising range of interests and aptitudes. Musical accomplishments include the composing of alma maters for his own high school and for Glen Mills; the director has been known to entertain guests with a strong singing voice that he accompanies with the banjo. Fluency in German is adequate to enable him to lecture to West German university students in their native language.

According to Machiavelli, those in positions of authority ought to " . . . read history and study the actions of eminent men, see how they acted in warfare, examine the causes of their victories and defeats in order to imitate the former and avoid the latter" (Buskirk, 1974: 42). Sam Ferrainola has taken this advice to heart. His knowledge of European and Western history is vast. He is able to relate, with ease and in great detail, the life stories of major political and military leaders. The director's respect is particularly great for those who, like Queen Elizabeth I, overcame seemingly insurmountable obstacles through cleverness and judicious exercise of power in achieving their goals.

There is an intensely private, even shy aspect of the director's personality. He rarely addresses audiences outside the Glen Mills community. He attends no conferences, delivers no speeches. Relations with staff are friendly and informal, but the focus is usually Glen Mills. Mr. Ferrainola does not socialize with staff outside of Glen Mills' functions. Except for his family, his total commitment is to Glen Mills. He believes this facilitates a team approach to management where dedication is the norm and jealousies do not intrude.

The establishment of Glen Mills' program required extraordinary leadership, because in 1975 there was no Glen Mills to serve as a model or as proof that Sam Ferrainola's grandiose visions were not those of a lunatic, but achievable: removal of locks and bars; creation of a school delinquents would be proud of, where they would choose to stay; athletic teams competing successfully against Pennsylvania's best athletes; students excelling academically and going on to college; delinquents adjudicated for serious violent offenses treating staff and each other with courtesy and respect. The new director made Don Quixote seem a pragmatist.

Sam Ferrainola's leadership style conforms closely to that which Peters and Waterman (1982) consider characteristic of excellent companies: "Leadership is . . . being visible when things go awry, and invisible when they are working well. It is building a loyal team at the top that speaks more or less with one voice. It's listening carefully much of the time, frequently speaking with encouragement, and reinforcing words with believable action. It's being tough when necessary, and it's the occasional naked use of power—or the 'subtle accumulation of nuances, a hundred things done a little better', as Henry Kissinger once put it" (p. 82).

The authors go on to describe the special strengths of the "transforming leader": he/she creates institutional purpose; arouses, engages, and satisfies the motives of followers (quoting James MacGregor Burns, "Leadership, unlike naked power wielding, is inseparable from followers' needs and goals"); stirs emotions; strengthens, inspirits and arouses confidence in his/her followers; believes in the impossible; creates environments where staff can flourish. These are, without exception, characteristics of Sam Ferrainola.

In focusing exclusively upon his positive qualities there is a danger that the director may appear superhuman and the Schools' success attributable to divine intervention. Neither is the case. Mr. Ferrainola's judgments have proven fallible. Even his strongest admirers do not consider him omniscient or a saint. In his willingness to take risks, he has made his share of mistakes.

Since 1975 Glen Mills has been the constant focus of Sam Ferrainola's life. His home is adjacent to the campus. Only his family competes for his attention, and even family activities often revolve around Schools functions.

Glen Mills unmistakably bears the mark of Sam Ferrainola. The man and the institution are integral to one another. It is inconceivable that Glen Mills could have developed in its present form without him. However, in its essential features the normative culture is replicable. Sam Ferrainola was indispensable to the first Glen Mills, but he is not essential to a second.

Performance Excellence Norms

Among the most critical organizational factors in program success are performance excellence norms, the expectation that staff will continually work to improve their performance even in areas that seem insignificant to outside observers. There is a story of a rookie playing for the New York Yankees who trotted slowly toward first base after hitting a routine infield pop up. As he headed back to the dugout after the ball was caught, he was surprised to encounter a furious Joe DiMaggio, who had stormed out to meet him: "Rookie, if you want to play for this team, you run those out!" The Yankees had become a great team by never letting down, by playing every aspect of the game as well as possible. Giving 100 percent was something that new players learned not from their coaches, but from their teammates; Yankee pride was synonymous with performance excellence in baseball.

Performance excellence does not come cheap. The attention to detail and level of effort devoted to seemingly minor issues at Glen Mills is characteristic of excellent organizations in all fields. John Wooden, winner of ten national championships during his last 12 years as basketball coach at UCLA and arguably the most effective coach who ever lived, had a legendary appetite for detail and hard work. He weighed his players every day. His lectures to players each year included the proper method for putting on their socks. Every practice drill and its result for 29 years was recorded on 3″ × 5″ cards. "Failing to prepare," he said, "is preparing to fail."

Performance excellence norms are common to effective organizations, whether they are athletic teams, businesses, armies, or social service agencies. Standards are high. At Glen Mills, it is not expected that staff will perform their roles flawlessly. It is expected, however, that every individual will do his best and strive to improve. Staff are selected for their initiative and involvement, traits nourished by the normative culture. Fear of failure, an impediment to performance excellence, is not a significant obstacle since the only failure that is punished at the Schools is failure to try.

Challenging the Status Quo

Political considerations represent the final set of factors affecting replication. The development of a successful alternative to existing programs is threatening to those who have a vested interest in the status quo. As Glen Mills' program grew, it drew attacks from district attorneys who favored more secure facilities, teachers' unions who decried the lack of certification of the Schools' counselor/ teachers, and state social workers concerned about the precedent of a successful youth services program in which their profession played no role.

As Glen Mills' program began to attract students from states outside Pennsylvania, it experienced attacks by some states' youth services agencies. In some instances state youth authority officials have a self-interest in discrediting programs which are alternatives to their own institutions. Caseworkers from states whose own institutions were overcrowded or destructive nonetheless opposed placements at Glen Mills, usually on the grounds that family contact would be too infrequent. In some cases, Glen Mills' students who were encouraged to believe that reports of abuse would hasten their discharge obliged their caseworkers with tales that were later used in attempts to discredit the Schools.

In one instance, representatives of a state youth authority interviewed all Glen Mills students from their state. Several weeks later the Schools were notified that the state was considering withdrawing the students because several had reported being abused. The director's response went directly to the state's senate: First, if the youth agency were concerned about abuse, why had he, as the only person in a position to alleviate the problem, not been notified at once? Why had the agency allowed their children to remain in an institution it believed to be abusive for several weeks without taking any action? Second, he welcomed an independent investigation of the abuse charges. (None was substantiated. The primary source turned out to be students who had not returned to Glen Mills after a home pass and justified their behavior with allegations of abuse.) Finally, he suggested that the state conduct an independent evaluation of Glen Mills along with its own institutions, apply the same criteria to each, and make its placement decisions on the basis of what is in the best interests of its children. None of the students was withdrawn.

Following this incident an investigator stressed the need to carefully examine all abuse charges in order to protect both the students *and* the institution: "If you have authority over a discharge decision, you can take any ten institution-alized kids and get at least two of them to sign a paper saying their mother is purple."

This is one of several instances where political acumen in understanding how and when to bring pressure on self-serving bureaucracies has been an important factor in the Schools' growth. Jurisdictions seeking to replicate the model should not anticipate that they will enjoy the support of the "helping" professions. Glen Mills' experience suggests that the successes of the model combined with its low cost and humane approach can translate into political leverage sufficient to overcome unprincipled attacks.

The lesson is that political support must be cultivated. Objective, independent evaluations are essential. A policy of openness must be adopted in which key political and justice system leaders are encouraged to visit the program, speak to whomever (staff and students) they choose, and arrive at their own judgments regarding the program's merit. Responsible criticism must be welcomed, but immediate and vigorous challenges must be launched against those who seek to harm the program.

Political leaders and agency officials, whose support is important to replication, are subject to strong pressures from those with a vested interest in the status quo. A great deal of money and many jobs are at stake. Sadly, the best interests of the youths seems only rarely to be an important parameter in the decision process.

The Unexamined Program Is not Worth Establishing

The Glen Mills story illustrates how a failing institution can be transformed through the establishment and management of a positive organizational culture. Among its most fundamental "lessons" is the role and importance of rigorous, continuous self-evaluation in the development of the culture.

In the belief that progress is possible only through innovation coupled with objective assessment, Sam Ferrainola has presided over an institution as open to scrutiny as any in the history of corrections. During his entire tenure he has welcomed observations and research by independent professionals, in the expectation that on-going monitoring would help his program to become stronger.

The director initiated a research program during his first year at Glen Mills, when the program was in chaos and the Schools in financial crisis. For several years the findings were discouraging, as recidivism rates climbed. During this period the director, who might have been tempted to discontinue research as an unnecessary distraction at best and an embarrassment at worst, was unwavering in his strong support for the program. At no time did he ever attempt to influence either the interpretation of the findings or the way the findings were presented to his board. In discussing negative findings with staff Mr. Ferrainola noted that they were not surprising, since "we're not a good school yet." Even the most negative findings were viewed "positively" as pointing the way to program improvements. The important question was never whether the findings were favorable, but whether they were useful in strengthening the program.

This book is the product of more than a decade of continuous research, during which time the authors have had unrestricted access to staff, students, and all school records. As any visitor to the Schools will attest, Glen Mills has nothing to hide. It does not seek to cover up its failures, because it is not ashamed of them. All failures are regrettable, but they are not an occasion for shame unless their lessons are ignored. At Glen Mills, failures and successes alike are part of the growth process, part of what makes the Schools stronger. Each contributes to a fuller understanding of the conditions that make programs more effective.

Opportunities to learn from the experiences of correctional programs must not be squandered. It is not failure that must be avoided, but meaningless failure. Failure that teaches us nothing renders meaningless the sacrifices of those who devoted their best efforts to an unsuccessful course, and condemns "those who do not learn from history" to the same fate. In the context of corrections, this means that more taxpayers' dollars will be wasted; more juvenile offenders will move on to adult criminal careers; more elderly will barricade themselves in their homes out of fear of crime; more lives will be destroyed by rape, crippling assault or murder; more families will be torn apart by the victimization of loved ones.

There is an alternative. By seeking to learn as much as possible from its own experience and making these lessons available to the field, Glen Mills has modeled a process which, were it generally adopted, would provide the basis for a continual improvement in correctional effectiveness. It is the surest formula for making society a little safer tomorrow than it is today.

CONCLUSION

The significance of Glen Mills lies in having demonstrated how various organizational, programmatic, and cultural elements can be combined to produce a humane and effective correctional environment, at less cost than that of traditional programs.

Glen Mills is a world apart. Where young men who for their entire lives have had to choose between being an intimidator or being intimidated can safely be neither. Where undeveloped potential flourishes in the rich soil of staff encouragement, competent and individualized instruction, varied programs, excellent facilities, and positive peer pressure. Where status and self-esteem can never be secured in service to Aggression and Manipulation, the twin gods of the delinquent subculture, but rather are built with every step, however modest, toward self-improvement. Where students take pride in and accept responsibility for themselves *and* the community. Where boredom yields to a full daily schedule of educational and recreational activities rather than to that staple of the institutional environment, the television set. Where staff and students regard one another as allies. Where all are entitled to the basics of respect, safety, good food, and clean living quarters, and no reward is beyond the reach of a student willing to invest whatever talents he possesses on his own and his peers' behalf.

The world of Glen Mills seems unreal. Ironically, some regard this as a serious criticism of an institution for the treatment of the social disease of delinquency, citing the difficulty of transition back to the "real world." Most would never level a similar charge against the hospital, a highly artificial, controlled, unreal environment for the treatment of physical disease. The problem of helping students make the transition to their home communities is far from solved, but there is not a shred of evidence that it is complicated by the quality of Glen Mills' environment.

Glen Mills represents both a gift and a challenge to the field of juvenile corrections. The gift is a willingness to share what has been learned. The challenge is to improve upon the results achieved by "the Glen Mills way." It is the authors' hope that some who read this book will accept both the gift and the challenge.

Appendix 1

Glen Mills Norms

There is no "official" list of Glen Mills' norms. The following is a list of norms compiled by Dr. Claus Ottmüller (1987) after six months' on-site observation at the Schools.

CAMPUS NORMS

Norms that Protect Confrontation, the Mutual Support, the Physical Integrity and the Dignity of Staff and Students

Around here:

—We confront to help, not to hurt.
—We accept confrontation, regardless if its justified or not.
—We don't fight. There is no horseplaying.
—We don't play staff on staff.
—We treat staff members with respect.
—We respect each other.
—We don't lie.
—We pay high respect to female staff.

Norms that Prohibit Deviant Activity

Around here:

—There is no borrowing and lending.
—We don't steal.

—We do not use racist slurs.

—There is no buying and selling.

—We don't commit homosexual acts.

—We don't drink alcohol.

—We don't gamble.

—We don't play cards.

—We don't destroy furniture.

Common Norms of Conduct (To Differentiate Glen Mills and "Street" Norms)

Around here:

—We don't run on campus.

—We don't go into other cottages.

—We don't go into the Administration Building without prior permission.

—We don't go over the white fence, because then we are truant.

—We keep eye to eye contact when spoken to.

—We have our shoes laced.

—We see personal hygiene as a must.

—We keep our combs in the breast pocket.

—We don't wear slippers outside the unit.

—We comb our hair.

—We don't yell on campus.

—We don't talk slang.

—We don't touch the fire equipment.

—We spit on the grass and not on the sidewalks.

—We don't wear raggy clothes.

—We walk on the sidewalks, not on the grass.

—We don't leave the unit after midnight.

—We don't throw cigarette butts on the walkways.

—We don't lean on the walls.

—We don't smoke in the nurse's office.

Norms that Forbid a Subcultural Appearance and Steal the "Identity Outfit" from the Students

Around here:

—We do not tolerate graffiti.

—We have our shirt tucked in at all times.

—We use no nick-names.
—We don't talk slang.
—We don't wear shirts with street names.
—We don't wear street insignias.
—We don't wear jewelry in the unit.
—We don't wear earrings.
—We don't pass shorts.
—We keep our shirt and jacket collars down.

UNIT NORMS

Around here:

—We don't go into other people's rooms.
—We don't smoke in the rooms.
—We don't smoke in the hallway.
—We shut the TV off before we go to bed.
—We don't listen to the radio after bed-time.
—We knock on the door before we enter the office.
—We take off our shoes when we enter the unit.
—We don't wear hats in the unit.
—We don't hang on the basketball net.
—We are on time for details.
—We have our beds made by 8:30 hrs.
—We have our details done by 8:30 hrs.
—Radio and TV sets are off during details.
—We don't smoke during details.
—We only use the telephone with permission.
—We do not eat and drink in our rooms.
—We don't write on furniture.
—We don't lie on the sofa.
—We don't smoke in the bathroom.
—We don't go through staff's door.
—We don't wear jewelry in the unit.
—We ask for cleaning equipment.
—We don't throw things around in the unit.
—We don't wear glasses without prescription.
—We don't let our dirty clothing pile up.
—We put our shoes into the shoe-shelf.

—We do not lie on bed during detail.

—We don't sleep on the bed cover at night.

—We don't change beds without consent of staff.

GROUP NORMS

Norms that Influence the Group Process

Around here:

—We give feedback to help, not to hurt.

—We don't take anybody's dignity.

—We accept confrontation.

—We don't fight in group.

—We don't support negative behavior.

—We give and accept feedback.

—We admit when we have done something wrong.

—We have no subgroups.

Rules of Order for the Group

Around here:

—There is no side lining in group.

—We don't play with our hands when we receive feedback.

—We don't throw facial expressions in the group.

—We don't laugh in group.

—We don't wear coats in group.

—We don't wear jackets in group.

—We sit up straight in group.

Arcade Norms

Around here:

—We don't go into the Bulls lounge when we are not Bulls.

—We don't stand in line for the telephone with more than two people.

—We don't talk when we are standing in line.

—We don't run down the stairway, we walk.

—We keep our pool stick on the ground when we are not playing.

Cafeteria Norms

Around here:

—We don't talk when we are standing in line.
—We don't talk from table to table in the cafeteria.
—We don't smoke in the cafeteria.
—We don't take food out of the cafeteria, we eat as much as we want there.

Norms for Home Pass

Around here:

—We don't bring drugs to Glen Mills.
—We come back from home pass on time.
—We don't come back high from home pass.

Appendix 2

Glen Mills Schools Board of Managers, 1988

BOARD OF MANAGERS

Frank Albero	Vice President, I.A. Construction Corporation
Frank Davis	Administrator, Philadelphia Family Court
Jill Duvall	Political writer and researcher
Harvey Ellis	Administrator, Public Defender Association
Randall Esterly	President, Pamico Insurance Company
Edgar T. Harvey	President of Delaware Solid Waste Association (ret.)
Mitzi Hepps	President, Brookhaven Beverage Company
Frederick Hodosh	Attorney; Vice President, American Institute for Property and Liability Underwriters (ret.)
Curtis Johnson	Owner, Eveready Building Maintenance Company
Donald Jones	Controller, Sun Oil Company (ret.)
Ruth Leach	Publisher
Fritz Lechner	Owner, Dutchman Fountain Company
M. S. Malkin	Director Space Shuttle Program, NASA Hdqrs. 1973–80 Deputy Assistant Secretary of Defense (Intelligence) 1972–73 Office of the Secretary of Defense
Ethel Maw	Professor, Department of Human Development, Bryn Mawr College (ret.)
Mario Montanaro	Insurance consultant
Jack Pearson	Owner, Pearson Sporting Goods Company
Francis Plowman	Vice President, Scott Paper Company (ret.)

Curtis Reitz	Professor, University of Pennsylvania Law School
Faye Soffen	Professor, Department of Human Development, Bryn Mawr College (ret.)
Glenn Sullivan	Vice President, State Farm Mutual Insurance Company (ret.)
Ralph Wythes	Administrator, Scott Paper Company (ret.)

Appendix 3

Sample Letters to Glen Mills

Glen Mills frequently receives congratulatory letters from justice system officials, former students, parents of students, and visitors to the campus. This sample is representative.

Upper Merion Area School District

435 CROSSFIELD ROAD   •   KING OF PRUSSIA, PENNSYLVANIA 19406   •   (215) 337-6000

July 17, 1987

Director
Glen Mills Schools
Concordville, PA 19331

Dear Sir:

On Thursday, July 16, I had the opportunity to visit Glen Mills Schools with our township Juvenile Officer, Thomas Megless, as part of the Montgomery County Day at Glen Mills. Not only was I impressed, but I was overwhelmed by what I had observed. The facilities were superb, but more importantly, the staff and students were most cordial. My concept of Glen Mills was originally a distorted point of view; what I observed during my visit certainly changed my impression of your school. One juvenile probation officer noted to me: "I'm sure you'll want all of your students referred to Glen Mills now!" Indeed, I will!

Two of my former students, Shawn Williams and Kenneth Holmes, served as our guides for the day. The transformations Officer Megless and I observed in these young men are evidence of the success of your program with the students assigned to Glen Mills. You and your staff are to be commended and congratulated for your efforts.

The visit to Glen Mills was a very pleasant experience. As our school district looks to an alternative school program, I may be in touch with you to discuss some of the techniques you use. Both Shawn and Ken spoke very positively about the behavior modification programs used at Glen Mills and I would certainly like to learn more about these techniques which appear to be so successful.

Thank you for the opportunity to learn more about Glen Mills and to observe some real success stories.

Sincerely,

Francis X. Luther
High School Principal

10923 Templeton Dr
Phila. Pa. 19154
Sept. 24, 1984

Dear Mr. Ferrainola,
    My son Michael has been a student at Glen Mills since Nov. 9, 1984. He was a student in Plaza, then he became a C.I.T. In the eleven months my son has been there, I have seen a remarkable change for the better. He seems to have more self-esteem, more control over his negative behavior & more consideration towards his family. I am writing this letter to let you know what a fantastic staff you have at the school. I don't know everyone that has come into contact with my son, but would you please give them my heartfelt thanks. Thank you

        Sincerely yours,
        Helene Wheeler

BRIAN T. MULHERN
BUILDER
WALLINGFORD, PA
565-4846

October 10, 1984

Mr. Cosimo Ferrainola
Director of Glen Mills School
Glen Mills
Concordville, PA 19331

Dear Sir:

On October 6,1984, three of my sons and myself visited your school to watch
a football game with Chester High. I have never enjoyed a competion between
two schools more!

I thought I would write to you to convey some of my thoughts about my impression
of the morning. When we arrived we were greeted very cordially by a young
man who gave us programs and directions to park our car. All of the attendants
in the parking area were helpful and very gracious.

The game was most enjoyable and I was particularly impressed with the show
of enthusiasm of the Glen Mills players and coaches. Your team morale was
very obvious and contagious. We were at the game to support Chester High,
but we couldn't help being impressed with your team.

After the game, we visited your concession stand and once again were greeted
by very helpful, cheerful, genuinely nice people. My three boys enjoyed hot
dogs and sodas, while we discussed what a nice morning we had. My most
difficult task of the day was explaining to an 11, 8 and 5 year old how Glen
Mills school is different than other high schools, because to me we had spent
the morning at what appeared to be a model for other schools to emulate.

You and your staff are to be complimented on a job well done. My congratulations
on your victory and wish your school, and all it's students, continued success.

Sincerely,

Brian T. Mulhern

BTM/cbs6

P.S. Even the officiating was good!

10/1/84

Mr. Farinola:

I was down to Glen Mills 2 weeks ago to visit my friends Mr & Mrs Hughes.

I would like to congratulate you and all the people responsible for the improvements and changes affected under your supervision.

The attitude and general good feeling one gets there is unbelievable.

What a great feeling it must be to have a part in your program.

Again my wishes for continued success and good luck in all of the phases of Glen Mills.

Sincerely

Robert J. McGuire Sr.
153 Regent St.
Wilkes-Barre, Pa
18702

Cottage Director at Glen Mills, 1963-1966

7/6/87

Director of Glen Mills School or,
To Whom it May Concern,

        I would like to comend your staff
or a excellent job they have done with
my son Mark Henry. Especially Mr Chris
Squiress who has made contact with me
and who seems to have reached my son
and put him in the right direction. It
is something that I couldn't do when he
lived with my wife and I for six months.
Mark would have a negitive attitude, be lazy,
never would listen or help around the house,
Wouldn't do his home work or even pick up
after himself and never cared about anything
or anyone except himself. He was in Boys
Village in Southern Maryland and in Montrose
in Baltimore and he never changed at
all. I don't know how your staff and
Mr Squiress did it But Mark came to
our house on a home pass for the first
time in a year and a half and his hole
attitude has changed towards everything
and everybody. He has calmed down
200% More than he has ever been
and he has lost the baby way he use to
have, he seemed to have grown up. Granted
he still has a way to go but I do want
someone to know how much I appreciate the
excellent job that has been done with my
son and hope to see even more improvements
in the future

                    Thank you Very much
                    Wayne Henry
                    2104 Dennis Rd
                    Waldorf, MD
                            20601

225

June 6th, 1986

Dear Mr. Ferraiola,

My husband and I wish to thank you
and your staff for your kindness shown
to Penn Wood High School staff, students
and parents. Our son, Mark, ran track
for Penn Wood these last three years,
and we had the pleasure of attending
many track meets held at your school.
We were always impressed with the
cleanliness, courteousness and school
spirit of Glen Mills.

Last Wednesday Mark attended
the "Athletic Director's Banquet" at
your school and enjoyed it very much.
We all appreciate the transportation
you provided to Shippensburg College
this spring, something our own
school district couldn't seem to do.

We wish you continued success in
all your endeavors at Glen Mills. You're
doing a great job!

Sincerely,
John and Carol Innis
13 Martin Dr.
Lansdowne, Pa.
19050

Bibliography

Allen, R., Pilnick, S., and Silverzweig, S. 1971. *Guided Group Interaction*. New York: National Association of Social Workers.

Allen, R. F., and Pilnick, S. 1973. "Confronting the Shadow Organization: How to Detect and Defeat Negative Norms." *Organizational Dynamics* (Spring).

Altschuler, David M. 1984. "Community Reintegration in Juvenile Offender Programming." In *Violent Juvenile Offenders: An Anthology*, ed. Robert A. Mathias, Paul De Muro, Richard S. Allinson. San Francisco, California: National Council on Crime and Delinquency.

Anderson, Dennis. 1981. "The Relationship Between Correctional Education and Parole Success." *Journal of Offender Counseling, Services and Rehabilitation:* 5 (Spring/Summer).

Ariessohn, Richard M. 1981. "Recidivism Revisited." *Juvenile and Family Court Journal* (November): 59–68.

Babst, D. V., and Hubble, M. E. 1965. *Juvenile Base Expectancies: Wisconsin School for Boys*. Madison: Wisconsin State Department of Public Welfare Research Bulletin C–7.

Bailey, W. C. 1966. "Correctional Outcome: An Evaluation of 100 Reports." *Journal of Criminal Law, Criminology and Political Science* 57:153–60.

Bandura, A. 1969. *Principles of Behavior Modification*. New York: Holt, Rinehart and Winston.

Barton, William H., and Sarri, Rosemary. 1979. "Where Are They Now? A Follow-Up Study of Youths in Juvenile Correction Programs." *Crime and Delinquency* (April): 162–76.

Bayer, Ronald. 1981. "Crime, Punishment and the Decline of Liberal Optimism." *Crime and Delinquency* 27, no. 2 (April): 169–90.

Beck, Allen J., and Shipley, Bernard E. 1987. *Recidivism of Young Parolees*. Bureau of Justice Statistics Special Report. Washington, D.C.: U.S. Department of Justice.

Beville, Sylvia L. 1981. *Improving the Quality of Youth Work: A Strategy for Delinquency Prevention*. Office of Juvenile Justice and Delinquency Prevention. Washington, D.C.: U.S. Department of Justice (May).

Blumstein, Alfred, and Larson, Richard. 1969. "Models of a Total Criminal Justice System." *Operations Research* 17, no. 2 (March): 199–232.

Bradford, L. P., Gibb, J. R., and Benne, K. eds. 1964. *T-Group Theory and Laboratory Method: Innovation in Re-education*. New York: Wiley and Sons.

Brown, James W., and McMillen, Michael J. 1979. *Residential Environments for the Juvenile Justice System*. Washington D.C.: Office of Juvenile Justice and Delinquency Prevention.

Buskirk, Richard H. 1974. *Modern Management and Machiavelli*. Boston: Wadsworth.

Childress, John. 1984/1985. "Reshaping Corporate Culture." *Chief Executive* 30 (Winter).

Citizens Crime Commission of the Delaware Valley. 1985. *Trends and Indicators in Criminal Justice*. Philadelphia.

Clark, K. B. 1959. "Color, Class, Personality and Juvenile Delinquency." *Journal of Negro Education* (Summer): 240–51.

Cloward, R. A., and Ohlin, L. E. 1960. *Delinquency and Opportunity: A Theory of Delinquent Gangs*. New York: Free Press.

Coates, Robert B., Miller, Alden D., and Ohlin, Lloyd E. 1978. *Diversity in a Youth Correctional System: Handling Delinquents in Massachusetts*. Cambridge: Ballinger.

Cohen, A. K. 1955. *Delinquent Boys: The Culture of the Gang*. New York: Free Press.

Cressey, D. R. 1955. "Changing Criminals: 'The Application of the Theory of Differential Association.' " *American Journal of Sociology* 61 (Sept).

Cullen, F., and Gendreau, P. 1988. "The Effectiveness of Correctional Rehabilitation." In *The American Prison: Issues in Research Policy*, ed. L. Goodstein and D. L. MacKensie. New York: Plenum.

Duffee, D. 1974. "Correction Officer Subculture and Organizational Change." *Journal of Research in Crime and Delinquency* 11, no. 2 (July): 155–72.

Empey, Lamar T. 1972. "Contemporary Programs for Convicted Juvenile Offenders: Problems of Theory, Practice and Research." In *Faces of Delinquency*, ed. John Reed and Fuad Baali. Englewood Cliffs, N.J.: Prentice-Hall.

Feld, Barry C. 1977. *Neutralizing Inmate Violence: Juvenile Offenders in Institutions*. Cambridge, Massachusetts: Ballinger.

Frost, Peter J., Moore, Larry F., Louis, Meryl R., Lundberb, Graig C., and Martin, Joanne. 1985. *Organizational Culture*. Beverly Hills, California: Sage Publications.

Gendreau, Paul, and Ross, Robert. 1987. "Revivification of Rehabilitation: Evidence from the 1980s." *Justice Quarterly* 4, no. 3 (September).

Genevie, Louis, Margolies, Eva, and Muhlin, Gregory. 1986. "How Effective is Correctional Intervention?" *Social Policy* (Winter): 52–57.

Gold, Martin. 1974. "A Time for Skepticism." *Crime and Delinquency* (January): 20–24.

Goodstein, Lynne, and Sontheimer, Henry. 1987. *A Study of the Impact of Ten Pennsylvania Residential Placements on Juvenile Recidivism*. Shippensburg, PA: Center for Juvenile Justice Training and Research.

Greenfeld, Lawrence A. 1985. *Examining Recidivism*. Bureau of Justice Statistics Special Report. Washington, D.C.: U.S. Department of Justice.

Greenwood, Peter W., and Turner, Susan. 1987. *The VisionQuest Program: An Evaluation*. Doc. # R–3445-OJJDP. Santa Monica, California: Rand Corporation.

Greenwood, Peter W., and Zimring, Franklin E. 1985. *One More Chance*. Santa Monica: Rand Corporation.

Greiner, Larry E. 1972. "Evolution and Revolution as Organizations Grow." *Harvard Business Review* (July–August).

Grissom, G. 1988. *Glen Mills Schools Research Project: Summary Report*. Philadelphia, PA: University City Science Center.

———. 1984. *Glen Mills Schools Research Project*. Philadelphia, PA: University City Science Center.

———. 1977. "Effects of Cottage Staff Norms and Peer Group Norms on the Attitudes Toward Aggression and Manipulation of Institutionalized Delinquent Boys." Ph.D. diss., Bryn Mawr College.

Hamparian, Donna M., Davis, Joseph M., Jacobsen, Judith M., and McGraw, Robert E. 1985. *The Young Criminal Years of the Violent Few*. Washington, D.C.: Office of Juvenile Justice and Delinquency Prevention.

Haney, Craig, Banks, Curtis, and Zimbardo, Philip. 1973. "A Study of Prisoners and Guards in a Simulated Prison" *Naval Research Reviews*. Washington, D.C.: Department of the Navy.

Haskell, M., and Yablonski, L. 1970. *Crime and Delinquency*. Rand McNally and Co.

Hawkins, J., and Lishner, D., 1981. "Youth Employment and Delinquency Prevention." Seattle, Washington: Center for Law and Justice, University of Washington.

Hirshi, T. 1969. *Causes of Delinquency*. Berkeley: University of California Press.

Johnson, Grant, Bird, Tom, and Little, Judith L. 1979. *Delinquency Prevention: Theories and Strategies*. Law Enforcement Assistance Administration. Washington, D.C.: U.S. Department of Justice.

Kasselbaum, Gene. 1974. *Delinquency and Social Policy*. Englewood Cliffs, N.J.: Prentice-Hall.

Kilmann, Ralph H. 1985. "Corporate Culture." *Psychology Today* (April).

Kobrin, Solomon, and Klein, Malcolm W. 1982. *National Evaluation of the Deinstitutionalization of Status Offender Programs*. Washington, D.C.: U.S. Department of Justice.

Lavine, Abe, and McAlpin, Deborah. 1985. "A Follow-up Study of Four Programs for Delinquent Youth in Florida." Available from Hurricane Island Outward Bound School, Tallahassee, Florida.

Legislative Commission on Expenditure Review. 1982. *Impact of Youth Rehabilitation Programs*. Albany: New York State Legislature Research Report.

Lerman, Paul. 1975. *Community Treatment and Social Control: A Critical Analysis of Juvenile Correctional Policy*. Chicago: University of Chicago Press.

Lewin, K. 1951. *Field Theory in Social Science*. New York: Harper.

Lipton, D., Martinson, R., and Wilks, J. 1975. *The Effectiveness of Correctional Treatment: A Survey of Treatment Evaluation Studies*. New York: Praeger Publishers.

MacIver, R. 1966. *The Prevention and Control of Delinquency*. Atherton Press.

Mann, Dale. 1976. *Intervening with Convicted Serious Juvenile Offenders*. Washington, D.C.: U.S. Dept. of Justice.

Markus, Hazel, and Oyserman, Daphna. 1987. "Possible Selves and Delinquency." In *ISR Newsletter* (Spring/Summer). University of Michigan: Ann Arbor, Michigan.

Marquis, K. 1981. *Quality of Prisoner Self-Reports*. Santa Monica: Rand Corp.

Martinson, R. 1979. "New Findings, New Views: A Note of Caution Regarding Sentencing Reform." *Hofstra Law Review* 7:242–58.

McCleary, R., Gorden, A. C., McDowall, D., and Maltz, M. D. 1978. *A Reanalysis of UDIS*. Chicago: University of Illinois.

McCord, J. 1978. "A Thirty-Year Follow-up of Treatment Effects." *American Psychologist* 33, no. 3: 284–89.

McCorkle, L., Elias, A., and Bixby, F. 1958. *The Highfields Story*. New York: Henry Holt and Co.

McEwen, Craig C. 1978. *Designing Correctional Organizations for Youths: Dilemmas of Subcultural Development*. Cambridge, Mass: Ballinger.

Menninger, Karl. 1973. *Whatever Became of Sin*. New York: Hawthorn Books.

Milgram, S. 1963. "Behavioral Study of Obedience." *Journal of Abnormal and Social Psychology* 67.

Miller, Dallas. 1984. *A Survey of Recidivism Research in the United States and Canada*. Publication #13709, Massachusetts Department of Correction (July).

Murray, Charles A., Thompson, Doug, and Israel, Cindy B. 1978. *UDIS: Deinstitutionalizing the Chronic Juvenile Offender*. Washington, D.C.: American Institutes for Research.

Murray, Charles A., and Cox, Louis A., Jr. 1979. *Beyond Probation: Juvenile Corrections and the Chronic Delinquent*. Beverly Hills, California: Sage.

Nachman, Sharon. 1977. *Juvenile Institutionalization and Adult Criminal Career*. Ph.D. diss., University of Wisconsin.

National Advisory Committee on Juvenile Justice Standards and Goals. 1976. *Report of the Task Force on Juvenile Justice and Delinquency Prevention*. Washington, D.C.

National Institute on Drug Abuse. 1985. *Self-Report Methods of Estimating Drug Use*. Research Monograph Series #57. Washington, D.C.: U.S. Dept. of Health and Human Services.

Neithercutt, M. C. 1978. "Effectiveness of Intervention Impacting Violent Juvenile Offenders." Washington, D.C.: U.S. Department of Justice.

Office of Juvenile Justice and Delinquency Prevention. 1981. *Violent Juvenile Offender Program. Part I*. Washington, D.C.: U.S. Government Printing Office.

Ohlin, L. 1958. "The Reduction of Role Conflict in Institutional Staff." *Children* 5, no. 2.

Ohlin, Lloyd E., Miller, Alden D., and Coates, Rubert B. 1977. *Juvenile Correctional Reform in Massachusetts*. Washington, D.C.: U.S. Department of Justice.

Ottmüler, C. 1988. *Glen Mills Schools: Ein Modell der Jugendkriminalrechtsplege in den U.S.A.* West Germany: Centaurus Publishing Co.

———. 1987. "The Glen Mills Schools: A Normative Approach to Change Delinquent Behavior Through the Peer Group." Ph.D. diss., University of Luneburg, West Germany.

Panel on Research on Rehabilitative Techniques. 1979. *The Rehabilitation of Criminal Offenders: Problems and Prospects*, eds. Lee Sechrest, Susan White, and Elizabeth Brown. Washington, D.C.: National Academy of Sciences.

Peters, Thomas J., and Waterman, Robert H. 1982. *In Search of Excellence*. New York: Warner Books.

Plinick, Saul. 1975. "Getting to Grips with the Group Sub-Culture." *Personnel Management* (July).

Pisciotta, Alexander W. 1982. "Saving the Children: The Promise and Practice of *Parens Patriae*, 1838–1898." *Crime and Delinquency* 28, no. 3 (July): 410–25.

Platt, Anthony, M. 1969. *The Child Savers*. Chicago: University of Chicago Press.

Polich. J. M. 1982. "The Validity of Self-Reports in Alcoholism Research." *Addictive Behaviors* 7: 123–32.

Polsky, Howard W. 1962. *Cottage Six*. New York: John Wiley and Sons.

Quay, Herbert C. 1977. "The Three Faces of Evaluation: What can be Expected to Work?" *Criminal Justice and Behavior* (December): 341–54.

Reuterman, Nicholas A., Hughes, Thomas R., and Love, Mary J. 1971. "Juvenile Detention Facilities: Summary Report of a National Survey." *Criminology* 9 (May).

Reynolds, Peter C. 1987. "Imposing a Corporate Culture." *Psychology Today* (March).

Rezmovic, Eva. 1979. "Methodological Considerations in Evaluating Correctional Effectiveness: Issues and Chronic Problems." In *The Rehabilitation of Criminal Offenders: Problems and Prospects*, ed. Lee Sechrest, Susan White, and Elizabeth Brown. Washington, D.C.: National Academy of Sciences.

Sarri, Rosemary. 1974. *Under Lock and Key: Juveniles in Jail and Detention*. University of Michigan: Ann Arbor, Michigan.

Schneider, Anne. 1985. *Reports of the National Juvenile Justice Assessment Centers: The Impact of Deinstitutionalization on Recidivism and Secure Confinement of Status Offenders*. Washington, D.C.: U.S. Department of Justice.

Skinner, H. A. 1984. "Assessing Alcohol Use by Patients in Treatment." In *Research Advances in Alcohol and Drug Problems*, ed. R. G. Smart, H. Cappel, F. Glazer, Y. Israel, H. Kalant, R. E. Popham, W. Schmidt, and E. M. Sellers, vol. 8, pp. 183–207. New York: Plenum.

Smith, Charles P., Alexander, Paul S., and Thalheimer, Donald J. 1980. *A National Assessment of Serious Juvenile Crime and the Juvenile Justice System: The Need for a Rational Response*, Vol. 4. Washington, D.C.: U.S. Department of Justice.

Sobell, L. C., and Sobell, M. B. 1982. "Alcoholism Treatment Outcome Evaluation Methodology." In *Prevention, Intervention and Treatment: Concerns and Models* (Alcohol and Health Monograph No. 3, pp. 293–324). Rockville, MD: National Institute on Alcohol Abuse and Alcoholism.

Southerland, Edwin H., and Cressey, Donald R. 1970. *Principles of Criminology*. Philadelphia: J. P. Lippincott.

STEP. 1984. "Telephone Survey of STEP." Tallahassee, Florida: Hurricane Island Outward Bound School.

Teuber, H. L., and Powers, E. 1953. "Evaluating Therapy in a Delinquency Prevention Program." *Proceedings of the Association for Research on Nervous and Mental Disorders* vol. 31, pp. 138–47. Baltimore: Williams and Wilkins.

Tichy, N. 1983. *Managing Strategic Change*. New York: John Wiley & Sons.

Tracy, Paul E., Wolfgang, Marvin E., and Figlio, Robert M. 1985. *Delinquency in Two Birth Cohorts: Executive Summary*. Washington, D.C.: U.S. Department of Justice.

U.S. Department of Justice, Bureau of Justice Statistics. 1986. *Children in Custody 1982/83 Census of Juvenile Detention and Correctional Facilities*, NCJ–101686. Washington, D.C.: U.S. Government Printing Office.

U.S. Department of Justice. 1972. *Planning and Design for Juvenile Justice*. Washington, D.C.: Law Enforcement Assistance Administration.

Vasoli, Robert H., and Fahey, Frank J. 1970. "Halfway House for Reformatory Releases." *Crime and Delinquency* (July).

Vinter, Robert D. 1976. *Time Out: A National Study of Juvenile Correctional Programs.* Ann Arbor: University of Michigan.

Webb, Larry, and Scanlon, John. 1981. "The Effectiveness of Institutional and Community-Based Programs for Juvenile Offenders." *Juvenile and Family Court Journal* (August): 11–16.

Weeks, H. 1958. *Youthful Offenders at Highfields.* Ann Arbor: University of Michigan Press.

Wolfgang, M. E., and Ferracuti, F. 1967. *The Subculture of Violence: Towards an Integrated Theory in Criminology.* London: Tavistock.

Name Index

Allen, R. F., 190, 191
Altschuler, David M., 197
Anderson, Dennis, 199
Ariessohn, Richard, 160

Babst, D. V., 164
Bailey, W. C., 172
Bandura, A., 109
Banks, Curtis, 178
Barcus, Herman, 79
Barton, W. H., 159
Bayer, Ronald, 172
Beck, Allen J., 160, 163, 164, 165, 166
Beecher, Tom, 6, 9, 10, 11, 26, 34, 47, 75, 89
Beville, S. L., 199
Blumstein, Alfred, 166
Braun, Joseph, 11
Bradford, L. P., 67
Brown, James, 179, 180, 203
Buskirk, Richard, 33, 207

Childress, John, 190
Clark, K. B., 108
Cloward, R. A., 107
Coates, Robert, 173
Cohen, A. K., 108

Constanzo, Sam, 11
Cox, Louis, 173
Cullen, F., 110

Davis, Frank, 90
Dubnov, Wm. L., 126, 127–28

Empey, Lamar T., 186
Erikson, Erik, 1

Fahey, Frank, 199
Feld, Barry, 177
Feracutti, F., 108
Ferrainola, Joseph, 62
Ferrainola, Gerda, 3
Ferrainola, Rita, 3
Ferrainola, Rose, 3
Ferrainola, Sam, 1, 3–13, 20–21, 24, 25, 26, 30, 31, 32, 34, 35, 37, 55, 67, 75, 79, 80, 83, 86, 89–91, 169, 172, 194–95, 201, 204–8, 210–11
Ferrainola, Tresa, 7
Ford, Henry, 39
Forjohn, Peter, 55
Frost, Peter, 190

Gendreau, P., 110, 174
Genevie, Louis, 197

Goodstein, Lynne, 160, 164, 165
Greenfeld, Lawrence A., 129, 160
Greenwood, Peter W., 160, 173, 175
Grissom, G., 196

Halverson, Jay, 22
Hamparian, Donna M., 165
Haney, Craig, 178
Hawkins, J., 199
Hubble, M. E., 164

Ipock, Garrison, 9, 10, 25, 26, 34, 75
Ireson, Randy, 73

Johnson, Grant, 196, 199

Kasselbaum, Gene, 197–98
Kilmann, Ralph, 190
Klein, Malcolm, 172
Kobrin, Solomon, 172
Krieg, Bernard, 58

Larson, Richard, 166
Lavine, Abe, 162, 163
Lerman, Paul, 172
Lewin, K., 66
Lipton, D., 172, 174
Lishner, D., 199

Machiavelli, Niccolo, 33, 35
Mann, Dale, 106, 173, 175, 176
Marcus, Hazel, 183
Margolies, Eva, 197
Marquis, K., 129
Martinson, R., 172, 175
Mason, Robert, 74
McAlpin, Deborah, 162, 163
McCleary, R., 173
McCord, J., 188
McCorkle, Lloyd, 47
McEwen, Craig, 177
McMillen, Michael, 179, 180

Menninger, Karl, 112
Milgram, Stanley, 193
Miller, Dallas, 154
Miller, Jerome, 178
Muhlin, Gregory, 197
Murray, Charles A., 163, 173

Nachman, Sharon, 164
Neithercutt, M. C., 159

Ohlin, L., 3, 107, 162, 165, 178, 180
Ottmüller, Claus, 77
Oyserman, Daphna, 183

Peters, Thomas, 190, 208
Pilnick, Saul, 3, 5, 7, 9, 10–11, 32, 34, 79, 190
Plowman, Francis, 8
Polsky, Howard, 2, 27, 66
Polich, J. M., 128
Powers, E., 188

Quay, Herbert C., 174

Rendell, Edward, 88–91
Reuterman, Nicholas, 179
Reynolds, Peter, 190
Rezmovic, Eva Lantos, 105, 106, 173
Ross, Robert, 174

Sarri, Rosemary, 159, 179
Scanlon, John, 173
Schneider, Anne, 172
Shipley, Bernard E., 160, 163, 164, 165, 166
Shuman, Arthur, 89
Skinner, H. A., 128
Smith, Charles P. Alexander, 162
Sobell, L. C., 128
Sobell, M. B., 128
Soffen, Faye, 11, 80
Sontheimer, Henry, 160, 164, 165

Teuber, H. L., 188
Tichy, Noel, 31
Tracy, Paul E., 166

Vasoli, Robert, 199
Vinter, Robert D., 159

Waterman, Robert, 190, 208
Webb, Larry, 173

Wilks, J., 172
Wolfgang, M. E., 108

Yin, Robert, 106

Zimbardo, Philip, 178
Zimring, Franklin E., 160, 173, 175

Subject Index

academic education department, 40, 71–75

academic hall, 40, 73, 74, 97, 103

academic programs, 37, 106, 131–34, 137, 169

achievement awards, 137–38, 203

admissions, 35, 37, 85, 166

admissions department, 40, 58–61

aftercare, 154, 158, 197, 198

Allegheny County Juvenile Court, 26, 35

analyses of program evaluations, 50

assault, 143, 149, 152

athletics, 35, 37, 39, 40, 55–58, 134–36, 137, 169

Battling Bulletin, 62

Battling Bulls Club, 20, 21–22, 24, 45, 51, 58, 68, 70, 76–78, 87, 96–97, 99, 100, 101, 104, 109, 138, 185, 194, 203, 204

behavior modification, 152

big brother, 19, 76, 78, 95, 102, 138

blocked opportunities, 196

board of managers, 3, 5, 6, 7, 8, 30, 40, 56, 79–81, 89, 91

Bulls Club. See Battling Bulls Club

Bureau of Justice Statistics, 165

business manager, 7, 11, 40, 45

California Youth Authority's community treatment project, 172

career counseling, 72

career development department, 61–70

chess club, 98

Chester county intermediate program, 71

Citizens Crime Commission, 167

classes, 45

classrooms, 7, 12, 194

college prep program, 72–73

college program, 73

community reintegration, 195–99. See also discharge

community relations, 58

confrontation, 16, 19, 20, 21, 22, 24, 27, 30, 34, 46, 49, 52–55, 57, 63, 65, 66, 68, 76, 77, 85, 87, 95, 96, 98, 102–3, 106, 109, 140–43, 149, 177, 184, 191, 192, 198, 202, 204

control theory, 109

cost, 137–39, 167, 177

cottage counselors, 56, 63, 103

cottage sessions, 19

counseling. *See* individual counseling

counselors: senior, 46; specialists, 45–46, 50, 69; teacher, 45, 50, 72, 73, 98

cottage staff, 68

cultural theory, 107, 108–9

curfew, 7, 12, 99

custody, 111

custody-clinical model, 201

Delaware County Community College, 73

delinquency: causation, 106–10; treatment, 47–52, 107–8, 109–10, 111–12, 184–86. *See also* humane environment

Department of Corrections, 163–64

diagnostic and evaluation (DE), 61

differential association theory, 108

directors: academic, 2, 7, 9, 43; admissions, 9, 25; clinical, 2; cottage life, 2; food service, 75; group living, 7, 9, 26, 43, 44, 47, 65, 69, 142; training, 11; vocational education and career -development, 62, 73; vocational training, 43

discharge, 27, 59, 115, 152–53, 195, 198. *See also* community reintegration

dormitories, 7, 12, 24

drug use, 78

educational awards day, 74

educational program. *See* academic program

evening activities, 5, 7, 98, 99

face-to-face interview, 125, 127, 128, 141. *See also* in-person interview

follow-up, 119, 129, 130, 131, 149–52, 153, 159

food, 4–5, 104, 189, 211

GED exam, 131, 134, 153, 198

GED program, 71–72, 74, 99

Guided Group Interaction (GGI), 9, 14, 19, 20, 27, 45, 47–50, 51, 54, 59, 60, 65, 66, 97, 100, 102, 136, 137, 141, 182, 187

groups expected response of the individual (GERI), 65

group living department, 39–41, 44, 47, 73, 75, 180

Herman Barcus Scholarship Fund, 73

heurism, 32

home passes, 50, 70, 198

home visits, 7, 15, 59, 63, 100, 101, 137, 189

homosexuality, 60

human systems institute, 9–10, 11

humane environment, 139–52, 167, 211

isolation, 15

individual counseling, 50–52, 187–88, 198

individualized education program, 71

in-person interview, 126–29, 136, 143. *See also* face-to-face interview

intake, 115

intermediate program, 71

interview method, 119–27

intramural programs, 7, 21, 39, 58, 63, 98

job description, 69

learning center program, 71, 73, 98, 103

learning theory, 152, 175

Lewinian method, 17

Lewinian force-field analysis, 66, 68–69

long term effectiveness, 152–69

marketing, 44

metropolitan achievement test (MAT), 71, 74, 96, 103, 113, 115, 131

Modern Management and Machiavelli, 33

National Academy of Sciences, 172

national training laboratory, 66

negative behavior, 143, 162, 176, 177, 182

negative bulls club, 182

NIDA, 128

norm stabilizers, 20, 45, 64

normalization, 182

normative culture, 9, 11, 15–24, 25, 27–30, 34, 40, 46, 47, 51, 52, 55, 75, 76, 78, 81, 83, 87, 88, 95, 101, 102, 106, 109, 111, 136, 138, 141, 143, 149–52, 166, 167, 178, 180–82, 184, 185, 187, 188, 189–91, 196, 198, 199, 201–4, 205, 208

norms, 30, 64–66, 68, 69, 72, 85, 97, 98, 102, 136, 139, 140, 143, 152, 169, 171, 184, 190, 191–92, 193–94, 201–4, 207, 208–9

off-campus employment, 63

open program. *See* open system

open system, 4, 8

outward bound school, 174

panel on research on rehabilitative techniques, 172, 174

part I offense, 130

peer pressure, 51, 60, 65, 69, 77, 78, 106, 108, 110, 113, 159, 183, 185, 187, 193–94, 196

Pennsylvania's Act, 30, 82, 84

Pennsylvania Department of Education, 71

Pennsylvania Department of Public Welfare, 82, 86

Pennsylvania Interscholastic Athletic Association, 55

Pennsylvania Juvenile Court Judges Commission, 164

performance evaluation system (PES), 14, 65, 69

Philadelphia's Family Court, 59, 167

planning committee, 79

Polsky's delinquent diamond, 66–68, 69–70, 78

positive behavior, 76–77, 160, 175, 176, 187

positive peer culture, 60

probation officer, 198

project help, 72, 98

psychosocial development, 56

public relations, 59

punishment, 139

Rand Corporation, 32, 173, 175

recidivism, 154–69, 170, 172–73, 197, 198, 199, 211

reintegration project, 197. *See also* community reintegration

rehabilitative ideology, 172

replication of Glen Mills model, 170–211

resource team meeting, 76, 78, 102, 104

review board, 24

scholastic aptitude test (SAT), 72

security, 184–85

self-concept, 183

self-report, 129, 131, 149, 157, 159, 166

settlement agreement, 91

short term effectiveness, 131–36, 167

Sleighton Farms, 6

social learning theory, 109

staff, 4, 5, 6, 7, 8, 9, 12, 15, 20, 22, 25, 32–33, 35, 38, 39, 45, 52, 139, 141–42, 149, 153–54, 171, 176, 177, 178, 179, 181, 190, 191–92, 198, 202, 205–6, 209; cottage, 61, 64, 66, 109; group living, 61, 63, 64

staff allocation, 44

staff recruitment, 7, 61–64, 192

staff training, 5, 7, 10, 13–18, 31–32, 37, 48–49, 84–86, 93, 192

START, 162

STEP, 127

strain theory, 196–97

structural/strain theory, 107–8

student travel, 59

student union, 7, 62

subculture theory, 108

support services department, 64, 75

t-Group model, 67
team leaders, 46, 49
teamwork, 32, 37, 41, 43, 45, 46, 56, 58, 64, 65, 70, 75, 83, 139
telephone interview, 125–28
townhouse meeting, 99–100, 112, 185, 203
tradesman hall, 40, 61, 62, 63, 73, 97
travel. *See* student travel
treatment method, 173–74, 175
Tresa Hall, 72
truancy, 59, 143, 149

Unified Delinquency Intervention Services (UDIS), 163–64, 173

vocational education and career development department, 61–70
vocational programs, 7, 12, 19, 24, 35, 37, 39, 41, 43, 61–70, 106, 136, 169
vocational assessment center, 61
vocational instructors, 63–64
vocational learning center, 62, 63

weekend programs, 7, 39
WZZE, 62